The Chef's Guide to Practical Restaurant Cookery

The Chef's Guide to Practical Restaurant Cookery

William H. Emery

 Van Nostrand Reinhold Company
New York

Printed in the United States of America

Designed by Rosa Delia Vasquez

Van Nostrand Reinhold Company Inc.
115 Fifth Avenue
New York, New York 10003

Van Nostrand Reinhold Company Limited
Molly Millars Lane
Wokingham, Berkshire RG11 2PY, England

Van Nostrand Reinhold
480 La Trobe Street
Melbourne, Victoria 3000, Australia

Macmillan of Canada
Division of Canada Publishing Corporation
164 Commander Boulevard
Agincourt, Ontario M1S 3C7, Canada

16   15   14   13   12   11   10   9   8   7   6   5   4   3   2   1

Library of Congress Cataloging in Publication Data

Emery, William H.
   The chef's guide to practical restaurant cookery / William H.
Emery.
      p.   cm.
   Includes index.
   ISBN 0-442-22173-8:
   1. Cookery. 2. Quantity cookery.   I. Title.   II. Title: Restaurant
cookery.
TX651.E48   1988   87-33955
641.5'72—dc19   CIP

Contents

Preface

One of the major problems facing young cooks and aspiring chefs today is that, while their initial training has taught them the essential fundamental kitchen skills and techniques, their ability to produce complete menus is often limited to the repertoire of menu items prepared in the kitchen where their training took place. So we find that sometimes, after four or five years' training, many young cooks are able to produce fewer than 100 complete dishes, which is very few indeed.

Generally these young people move to another establishment with a different, but equally limited, menu pattern in order to gain further experience, and study culinary reference books in an effort to learn something of the thousands of exciting dishes that are possible. Unfortunately, many of these excellent books fail to give details of quantities of ingredients required and specific instructions regarding preparation techniques often are unclear. In fact, a degree of culinary knowledge is presupposed that few cooks and chefs actually possess.

This book has been written to overcome most of these problems. It contains over 2,000 entries, from soup to dessert, with clear instructions regarding preparation and quantities required. This information is written in *précis* form and in terminology used in international kitchens. While a book of this sort will not take the place of practical experience, it does provide the essential information in a concise form and will allow the aspiring chef to produce any of these items.

You will find that the recipes are most suitable for establishments in the "good to very good" category, are entirely practical, and are geared for today's competitive market. As the title indicates, this is a culinary guide, not a textbook or a cookery book, and you will see that some of the more obvious culinary instructions are not included. For example, only rarely does a recipe mention the need to add seasoning to a dish—this is taken for granted. Neither does it explain the basic culinary processes, for a young cook with adequate training will know how to bake, boil, braise, and strain. In fact, some very simple dishes do not include a recipe at all: just instructions regarding preparation.

The recipes given should be used as a guide (as should all recipes, of course), for cooking is not an exact science. These recipes are based upon classic cuisine and therefore will be useful as a starting point. They can be modified to suit type, style, and cost pattern of a particular restaurant.

Apart from its value to cooks and chefs, I think this book will be equally useful for owners, managers, and administrators of restaurants and catering establishments who have not had kitchen training. It will assist them in understanding kitchen production problems as well as the dishes or items described. They will also be able to estimate accurately the cost and suitability of any item in relation to their menu.

I trust therefore that every reader will find in this book something interesting, instructive, or profitable. With any luck, many readers will find it will provide all these advantages.

Measure for Measure

The following is an explanation of the metric system of weights and measures with their American equivalents. There are just a few points to remember when working with metric weights and measurements.

1. Metric units replace but do not *equal* American units.

2. Metric units are rounded off to the nearest convenient figure to be practical. For example: 1 oz. equals 28.352 g. Obviously, it would be impractical to try to measure this metric quantity accurately, so 1 oz. is rounded off to 30 g in the lower weights, and then to between 25 and 30 g as the conversions enter the heavier weights. The following list shows approximate equivalents.

METRIC CONVERSIONS—MASS

½ oz.	15 g
1 oz.	30 g
2 oz.	60 g
3 oz.	90 g
4 oz.	115 g
5 oz.	140 g
6 oz.	170 g
7 oz.	200 g
8 oz.	225 g
9 oz.	250 g
10 oz.	280 g
11 oz.	310 g
12 oz.	340 g
1 lb.	450 g
1¼ lb.	575 g
1½ lb.	675 g
1¾ lb.	800 g
2 lb.	900 g

2¼ lb.	1 kg (1,000 g)
2½ lb.	1.125 kg
3 lb.	1.35 kg
4 lb.	1.80 kg
5 lb.	2.25 kg
6 lb.	2.70 kg

COMMON METRIC MEASURES

Volume	(L) liter
Mass	(g) gram and (kg) kilogram
Length	(m) meter
Temperature	(C) degrees Celsius

Metric Relationships

Volume	1,000 mL	1 (L) liter
Mass	1,000 g	1 (kg) kilogram
Length	10 mm	1 (cm) centimeter
Length	100 cm	1 (m) meter

VOLUME

1 fluid (fl.) oz.	¼ deciliter (dcL)
2 fluid (fl.) oz.	½ deciliter (dcL)
3½ fluid (fl.) oz.	1 deciliter (dcL)
5 fluid (fl.) oz.	1½ deciliter (dcL)
7 fluid (fl.) oz.	2 deciliter (dcL)
16 fluid (fl.) oz.	1 pint (U.S.), 4½ deciliters (dcL)
24 fluid (fl.) oz.	1½ pints (U.S.), 7 deciliters (dcL)
28 fluid (fl.) oz.	1¾ pints (U.S.), 8 deciliters (dcL)
32 fluid (fl.) oz.	2 pints (U.S.), 9 deciliters (dcL)
36 fluid (fl.) oz.	2¼ pints (U.S.), 10 deciliters or 1 Liter (L)
¼ teaspoon (¼ tsp.)	1 mL
½ teaspoon (½ tsp.)	2 mL
1 teaspoon (1 tsp.)	5 mL
1 tablespoon (Tbs.)	15 mL

TEMPERATURE

Fahrenheit (F)	Celsius (C)
300°	150°
325°	160°

350°	180°
375°	190°
400°	200°
425°	220°
450°	230°
500°	260°
525°	270°
550°	290°

Freezing point: Fahrenheit, 32°; Celsius, 0°
Boiling point: Fahrenheit, 212°; Celsius, 100°

Glossary

Abats—Offal or variety meats including heads, hearts, livers, feet, tongues, and kidneys.

Aiguillettes—Thin slices of meat, usually poultry, cut lengthwise from the breast.

Angelica—A plant of the Umbelliferae family. The stalks are candied and used in confections and pastries.

Aromatics—All herbs or vegetables used as flavoring.

Arrowroot—Starch from the root of the *Maranta* plant; used as a thickener.

Attereaux—Food, usually hors d'oeuvres, dipped in sauce, rolled in breadcrumbs, and served on skewers.

Bain-marie—A receptacle that is partially filled with water and used to keep sauces warm.

Bard—To cover poultry or meat with lard or bacon fat to moisten and give added flavor.

Baron—In France, the term refers to the saddle and two legs of lamb or mutton. In the United States, the term designates the hindquarters, legs, and loins of lamb.

Barquette—A boat-shaped pastry shell filled with various sweet or savory fillings.

Bâton—French for a breadstick or various preparations in the shape of little sticks.

Beurre Manié—Softened butter mixed with flour and formed into little balls; used as a thickener for sauces.

Blanch—To scald, in boiling water: a) older vegetables to rid them of any pungent flavor they may have; b) younger vegetables to set their color; c) sweetbreads and similar meats which require stiffening before further treatment. In all cases the foods are steeped in ice water after scalding and before final cooking.

Bouchée—A small pastry shell filled with creamed mixtures.

Bouquet Garni—A bundle made of parsley, thyme, and bay leaf; used as an aromatic.

Braise—To cook slowly in a covered pan with little moisture.

Brunoise—Vegetables cut into small dice.

Cassolette—Small china container, usually heatproof, used to serve individual portions.

Chiffonade—Finely shredded lettuce or sorrel leaves; used in salads or as a garnish for some soups.

Chafing Dish—A deep skillet with

a lid that sits on a stand above a burner; used to keep foods warm or to cook at the table.

Charlotte Mold—A mold used for gelatin salads, charlottes, or other desserts. It has tapered sides and decorative handles.

Clarified Butter—Butter that has been melted slowly and cooled. The milk solids sink to the bottom and are discarded. It does not burn as easily as regular butter.

Cocottes—Individual dishes resembling tiny saucepans and made of heatproof material; used for serving eggs.

Compound Butter—Butter mixed with various flavorings such as herbs, garlic, or shellfish.

Coral—The pinkish roe of the female lobster.

Croustade—A crisp container made of puff pastry or hollowed-out bread that has been brushed with beaten egg and deep-fried; filled with stews or other mixtures.

Croûtons—Small cubes of fried bread used to garnish soups and salads.

Dariole—A small, deep, cylindrical mold, slightly wider at the top than at the bottom.

Darne—A large piece cut from the center section of a fish fillet. The term is used especially in reference to salmon.

Dredge—To coat food pieces with flour or breadcrumbs so that a delicate crust is formed when fried.

Essence—A concentrated extract with the strong smell and taste of a particular food.

Etouffer—To cook under cover with very little moisture.

Fines Herbes—Mixture of chopped garlic, parsley, tarragon, and chives.

Flan Case—An open, round pastry shell of varying size, filled with sweet or savory mixtures.

Fleurons—Decorative shapes cut from thinly rolled puff pastry, brushed with egg, and baked; used as a garnish.

Fond—A basic stock or broth.

Forcemeat—Meat, fish, or poultry that has been pounded to a paste or passed through a food processor, mixed with eggs or other binder, and used as a stuffing.

Fumet—A strong, concentrated reduction of a stock.

Galette—A round, flat cake, usually made of potato or puff pastry.

Gaufrette Cutter—A cutter that shapes small, thin, fan-shaped wafers resembling a waffle.

Gild—To brush food with beaten egg or to brown a dish lightly under a broiler.

Goujon—Fillet of sole or flounder cut into strips, floured or breaded, and then panfried or deep-fried.

Lard—To insert thin strips of bacon or pork fat with special larding needles into meat or poultry.

Lardons—Thin strips of fat inserted into meat or poultry, as mentioned above.

Macédoine—Vegetables or fruits that have been diced and mixed. Fruits are then macerated in brandy. Vegetables are served with butter or a cold sauce.

Macerate—To steep fruit in liquor to flavor it.

Marmite—A tall French cooking pot used for stocks.

Mask—To cover completely, as with a sauce.

Matignon—A fondue of vegetables used as a garnish.

Mousse—A light, fluffy forcemeat or dessert preparation.

Nap—To coat or cover with sauce or aspic.

Palmiers—Pieces of puff pastry shaped like palm leaves, baked, and used as decoration.

Papillote—A heart-shaped piece of oiled parchment paper in which foods are cooked. Also paper frills used for decorating the exposed bones of chops or ham.

Parisienne Cutter—A small utensil with a semispherical bowl used to make melon or vegetable balls.

Paupiette—A suprême of chicken, fish, or meat stuffed with forcemeat, rolled, and braised.

Poêle—A skillet with tapered sides and a long handle used to sauté foods.

Poêlage—A method of cooking various meats and poultry in a covered pan on a bed of mirepoix or matignon with only butter as a moistening agent.

Purée—Foods passed through a food mill, blender, or food processor to form a thick pulp.

Rasher—One slice of bacon.

Saccharometer—Instrument for measuring the concentration of sugar solutions.

Salpicon—Meat, poultry, or fish diced into small cubes and cooked in a sauce.

Savarin Mold—A ring mold used in the preparation of a rich yeast cake called a savarin.

Suprême—French for a fillet of fish or breast of chicken or feathered game.

Sweat—To cook minced or diced vegetables in oil or butter over a low heat to soften them and extract their flavor.

Tammy—A muslin or fine cloth sieve used for straining food.

Terrine—A container, usually made of earthenware, used to cook various pâtés or mousses. Sometimes used to describe a coarse textured pâté.

Timbale—A custardlike mixture of vegetables, poultry, or fish, cooked in a tapering mold made of tin.

Truss—To skewer or tie the wings and legs of poultry before roasting.

Turban Mold—A ring mold in the shape of a turban.

Vegetable Fondue—Vegetables cooked in butter or oil until reduced to a pulp.

Zest—The colored outer skin of lemons or other citrus fruits.

Stocks, Jellies, and Basic Preparations

Beurre Manié—for thickening sauces, soups, and stews. Mix flour with creamed butter; chill or use immediately.

3 oz. (90 g) flour
4 oz. (115 g) butter

Court Bouillon, Fish—White wine and mirepoix mixture used to poach fish. Reduce the mixture of wine and mirepoix by two-thirds, add fish fumet, and strain.

To produce 5 pt. (2.2 L):
2¼ lb. (1 kg) mirepoix
48 fl. oz. (1.25 L) white wine
64 fl. oz. (2.5 L) fish fumet

Court Bouillon, Meat—Red wine and mirepoix mixture used for braising meat. Proceed as for court bouillon for fish, but use red wine instead of white wine and meat stock instead of fumet.

Duxelles—Minced mushroom mixture used to flavor sauces. Mince mushroom parings, stalks, and pieces; squeeze mushrooms in a clean towel to remove moisture. Sweat minced onions and shallots in butter and oil; add mushrooms, along with salt, pepper, chopped parsley, and a pinch of nutmeg. Stir over medium-high heat until mush-rooms are cooked and all liquid is evaporated. Cover with buttered paper and keep in a cool place.

To produce 10 oz. (280 g):
8 oz. (225 g) mushrooms
1 Tbs. (15 mL) each onions and shallots
1 Tbs. (15 mL) each butter and oil
salt and pepper
1 Tbs. (15 mL) chopped parsley
pinch of nutmeg

Essence, Chicken—Proceed as for chicken stock. Boil liquid down to produce a concentrate.

Essence, Fish—Cook heads and bones of white fish in water with lemon juice, white wine, and aromatics for 20 minutes. Strain through muslin and reduce by one-half.

To produce 2½ pt. (1 L):
4½ lb. (2 kg) fish trimmings
4½ pt. (2 L) cold water
2 Tbs. (30 mL) lemon juice
7 fl. oz. (2 dcL) white wine
3 oz. (90 g) chopped onions
8 oz. (225 g) mushroom trimmings
2 sprigs parsley

Essence, Game—Proceed as for game stock. Reduce to consistency of thick meat jelly.

Essence, Mushroom—Reduce liquid in which mushrooms have been cooked to produce a concentrate.

Essence, Truffle—Infuse truffle peelings in Madeira.

Fumet, Chicken—Chicken broth made by reducing chicken stock to a concentrated consistency.

Fumet, Fish—Fish broth made by reducing fish stock to a concentrated consistency.

Fumet, Game—Game broth made by reducing game stock to a concentrated consistency.

Fumet, Vegetable—Vegetable broth made by reducing vegetable stock to a concentrated consistency.

Jelly, Chicken—A clear chicken stock that solidifies when cold because of the gelatinous substances it contains. Jellies may be clarified to produce aspics. Brown beef bones in butter and transfer to stockpot with chicken bones and giblets. Add veal and chicken trimmings, vegetables and water, bring to a boil, and skim. Add calves' feet and bacon rinds; season. Simmer for 5 to 6 hours and strain.

To produce 5½ qt. (5 L) jelly:
4½ lb. (2 kg) beef bones
3 oz. (90 g) butter
9 qt. (8½ L) water
3¼ lb. (1½ kg) chicken bones and giblets that have been browned in the oven
3¼ lb. (1½ kg) knuckle of veal
1 lb. (500 g) chicken trimmings
2 leeks
3 stalks of celery
3 calves' feet
½ lb. (250 g) bacon rinds

2 or 3 large carrots
2 medium onions
bouquet of herbs
salt and pepper

Jelly, Fish—Proceed as for fish stock. Clarify and reduce to required consistency.

Jelly, Game—Proceed as for chicken jelly, substituting game trimmings for chicken trimmings.

Jelly, Meat—Proceed as for chicken jelly, substituting veal and beef bones for chicken bones and giblets.

Marinade, Raw—A seasoned liquid in which food is steeped to flavor and tenderize it. Chop dry ingredients, and mix with wine, vinegar, and oil. Quantities of dry ingredients may vary, to taste. However, final volume must be sufficient to cover the food item(s).

To produce 16 fl. oz. (4 dcL):
carrots
onions
shallots
celery
bay leaves
parsley
thyme
cloves
black pepper
8 fl. oz. (2 dcL) white wine
4 fl. oz. (1 dcL) wine vinegar
4 fl. oz. (1 dcL) oil

Marinade, Cooked—Proceed as for raw marinade, but lightly brown the vegetables and herbs in oil. Add white wine and vinegar. Simmer gently 25 minutes, and allow to cool before using.

Matignon—A fondue of vegetables used as a garnish. Sauté vegetables in butter. Add bay leaf, thyme, seasonings, and Madeira. Boil down until desired consistency is reached. Meat may be added to basic mixture.

To produce approximately 1¼ lb. (575 g):
18 oz. (225 g) carrots
3 oz. (90 g) celery
2 oz. (60 g) butter
1 bay leaf
pinch of thyme
salt and pepper
3½ fl. oz. (1 dcL) Madeira
8 oz. (225 g) raw ham (optional)

Meat Glaze—Used to enrich sauces, stews, and soups. Boil down rich bouillon or white consommé until it is very dark and syrupy. Pour into a pan and allow to set until very firm; cut into small squares and store.

Mirepoix—A mixture of vegetables used to enhance the flavor of various dishes. Sauté vegetables in butter with herbs and finely diced pork belly until tender.
10 oz. (285 g) carrots
8 oz. (225 g) onions
3 oz. (90 g) pork belly
2 oz. (60 g) butter
sprig of thyme
1 bay leaf

Mirepoix Bordelaise—Proceed as for mirepoix, but chop vegetables very fine. This mirepoix is used primarily in fish and shellfish dishes.
8 oz. (225 g) carrots
8 oz. (225 g) onions

parsley stalks
3 oz. (90 g) butter
pinch of thyme
1 bay leaf

Pickling Brine—Bring salted water to a boil. Add a peeled potato to test: if the potato floats, add more water until it begins to sink; if the potato sinks, add more salt. When a balance is reached and potato is floating in the brine, add saltpeter and brown sugar, allow to dissolve over a high fire, and cool.

To produce 10 qt. (9 L):
9 lb. (4 kg) coarse salt
10 qt. (8 L) water
12 oz. (340 g) sugar
16 oz. (450 g) saltpeter

Roux—A cooked mixture of butter and flour that is used as a thickening agent for many sauces. There are three main types: white, blonde, and brown. The white mixture, cooked only long enough to cook the flour but not long enough to color the roux, is used in velouté and béchamel sauces. A blonde roux, cooked until the flour is a pale golden color, is used for richer-colored sauces. A brown roux, cooked until the flour turns brown, is used for brown sauces such as demi-glace and espagnole. The roux is extended with appropriate stock (or milk/cream) until desired consistency is reached.
8 oz. (225 g) clarified butter
10 oz. (280 g) flour

Royale, Colored—Molded egg yolk-based custard colored and flavored by a purée of vegetables and cream. Used as a garnish for clear soups.

2 Tbs. (30 mL) purée and vegetable of choice
2 Tbs. (30 mL) cream
4 egg yolks

Royale, Plain—Molded and flavored egg yolk-based custard used as a garnish for clear soups. Put dried chervil into boiling consommé and leave to infuse for 10 minutes. Beat together the whole egg and the yolks. Blend eggs slowly into stock. Strain, skim, and place mixture in dariole molds and cook in a bain-marie until firm. Cool. When quite cold turn out of mold and dice neatly or cut into squares, diamonds, etc., as desired.

To produce enough royale for 54 fl. oz. (2½ L) of consommé:
½ tsp. (2 mg) dried chervil
5 fl. oz. (1½ dcL) consommé
1 whole egg
2 yolks

Stock, Brown—Also known as fonds brun or estouffade, this stock is used as a liquid in brown sauces, for braising large cuts of meat, and for meat stews. Cook and color shin of beef, shin of veal, and marrow bones in oven. Brown ham, bacon rind, carrots, and onions in butter. Place all ingredients in a stockpot and add water, salt, pepper, and nutmeg. Bring to a boil. Simmer for 6 hours, and strain.

To produce 8 qt. (7.3 L):
8 lb. (3.6 kg) shin meat and bones

4 lb. (1.8 kg) marrow bones
8 oz. (225 g) raw ham ends
8 oz. (225 g) each carrots and onions
bacon rind, as available
salt, pepper, nutmeg
280 fl. oz. (7 L) water

Stock, Chicken—Used as a flavoring in sauces and as a poaching liquid. Place bones and giblets in a stockpot and add water. Bring to a boil. Add vegetables. Boil, season, and strain.

To produce 8 qt. (7.3 L):
12½ lb. (5½ kg) poultry giblets and bones
280 fl. oz. (7 L) water
8 oz. (225 g) carrots
3 oz. (225 g) onions
5 oz. (140 g) leeks
5 oz. (140 g) celery
1 bouquet garni
salt and pepper

Stock, Game—Used as a liquid in brown game sauces or to flavor game dishes. Brown game birds and trimmings in butter in oven. Add carrots, thyme, bay leaves, sage, onions, and celery to white wine and water; simmer for 5 to 6 hours, and strain.

To produce 5½ pt. (2½ L):
4½ lb. (2 kg) game trimmings
2 oz. (60 kg) fresh pork rind
2 oz. (50 g) butter
5 oz. (140 g) carrots
5 oz. (140 g) celery
5 oz. (140 g) onions
2 bay leaves
1 sprig each of thyme and sage

9 pt. (5 L) white stock or water
2 pt. (1 L) white wine

Stock, White—Used as a liquid in white sauces, stews, and as a poaching liquid. Proceed as for chicken stock, substituting 8 lb. (3½ kg) veal shins and bones for 8 lb. (3½ kg) of chicken bones.

Soups

THICK SOUPS

Thick soups are divided into three classes: the purée soups, which have a vegetable base; the velouté soups, which are enriched with egg yolks and butter; and the cream soups, which are enriched with cream.

Purée Soups

Some vegetable purée soups, such as those made with potatoes or split peas, do not require a thickening agent in their preparation. Others, such as those made with a celery or carrot base, require a thickener to give them body. Rice or potatoes are excellent thickeners. About 3 oz. of rice or 8 oz. of potato for every 16 oz. (450 g) of vegetables will give good results. The thickening agent is cooked with the vegetable, and the mixture is then passed through a sieve. To finish all purées, you will need 2 oz. (60 g) of butter per 35 fl. oz. (2½ pt./1 L) of soup. If the purée needs to be diluted, white consommé should be used.

All recipes produce 36 fl. oz. (1 L).

Bean, Red Haricot—Simmer red beans in water with onion, clove, bouquet garni, and lightly fried diced bacon. Add boiling red wine, and cook until beans are done. Remove bouquet. Rub remainder through a sieve, and return to cooking liquid. Dilute if necessary. Season, heat, and blend in butter.

10 oz. (280 g) red haricot beans
36 fl. oz. (1 L) water
1 onion
1 clove
bouquet garni
3 oz. (90 g) bacon
5 fl. oz. (1½ dcL) red wine
2 oz. (60 g) butter

Bean, White—Proceed as for red haricot bean purée, but use white beans and white wine.

Braird—Purée carrots and potatoes. Finish with butter, and garnish with fried croûtons and blanched julienne of chervil.

equal quantities of carrot and potato purée

Brussels Sprout—Gently cook chopped brussels sprouts in butter. Moisten with good stock, and add raw diced potatoes. Simmer until tender. Rub through a sieve, and dilute if necessary. Enrich with butter.

16 oz. (450 g) brussels sprouts
2 oz. (60 g) butter
28 fl. oz. (8 dcL) stock
8 oz. (225 g) potatoes
2 oz. (60 g) butter

Carrot—Stew sliced carrots in butter with chopped onion, salt, and sugar. When soft, add stock and raw rice. Simmer, covered, until rice is cooked. Rub through a sieve, and dilute if necessary. Finish with butter.

12 oz. (340 g) carrots
3 oz. (90 g) butter
1 oz. (30 g) onion
salt and sugar, to taste
36 fl. oz. (1 L) stock
2 oz. (60 g) rice
2 oz. (60 g) butter

Cauliflower—Cook blanched cauliflower in milk with chopped onion and potatoes, and season. Rub through a sieve. Extend with chicken stock if necessary. Reheat, and finish with butter.

16 oz. (460 g) cauliflower
20 fl. oz. (6 dcL) milk
1 oz. (30 g) onion
8 oz. (225 g) potato
20 fl. oz. (6 dcL) stock
2 oz. (60 g) butter
salt, white pepper to taste

Celery—Proceed as for brussels sprouts, using similar quantities, but replacing brussels sprouts with celery.

Chestnut—Peel chestnuts, and add to chopped celery and onion and stew in butter. Add consommé or stock. Cook until ingredients are tender. Rub through a sieve, and dilute, if necessary, with milk. Finish with butter.

16 oz. (450 g) chestnuts
8 oz. (225 g) celery
2 oz. (60 g) onions
3 oz. (90 g) butter
32 fl. oz. (9 dcL) stock
2 oz. (60 g) butter

Du Comte—Purée green beans or other garden vegetable. Mix with purée of lentils to taste, and garnish with julienne of carrots and turnip.

Endives—Slice endive and stew gently in butter. Season with salt and sugar. Add diced potatoes, moisten with white consommé, and simmer for 25 minutes. Rub through a sieve, and finish with butter.

1½ lb. (675 g) endive
2 oz. (60 g) butter
12 oz. (340 g) potatoes
28 fl. oz. (8 dcL) consommé
2 oz. (60 g) butter

Lentils—Proceed as for red haricot beans, but substitute 10 oz. of lentils for the 10 oz. of red haricot beans.

Lima Beans—Gently sauté young lima beans in butter with a pinch of summer savory and salt. Moisten with stock, and simmer until tender. Rub through a seive. Reheat, and enrich with butter.

1½ lb. (675 g) lima beans
3 oz. (90 g) butter for sauté
pinch of summer savory
pinch of salt
28 fl. oz. (8 dcL) stock
2 oz. (60 g) butter

Malakoff—Purée potatoes and blend with tomato soup, using two parts potato purée by volume to one part tomato soup. Garnish with shredded, blanched spinach. Extend with chicken stock if necessary.

Mancelle—Thick soup of game mixed with purée of chestnuts and celery, garnished with julienne of game. Use equal quantities of soup and purée.

Marianne—Purée potatoes and pumpkin, and blend with cream. Garnish with julienne of lettuce and fried croûtons dipped in grated cheese.

two parts potato purée by volume
one part pumpkin purée by volume
3½ fl. oz. (1 dcL) cream per pint

Pastourelle—Cook potatoes, leeks, onions, and mushrooms. Drain and purée. Extend with scalded milk, and garnish with sliced, sautéed mushrooms.

To produce 32 fl. oz. (9 dcL):
1 lb. (450 g) potatoes
8 oz. (225 g) leeks
4 oz. (115 g) onions
3 oz. (90 g) mushrooms

Peas (Saint-Germain)—Cook shelled peas in salted water. Drain and rub through a sieve. Add purée to white consommé. Boil and finish with butter. Add a few peas as garnish.

1¼ lb. (575 g) peas
36 fl. oz. (1 L) consommé
2 oz. (60 g) butter

Peas with Mint—Proceed as for pea purée adding a small bunch of fresh mint to purée. Remove mint before serving.

Portuguese—Sauté onions in butter. Add seeded tomatoes and season. Add garlic and bouquet garni; cook for 5 minutes. Add rice and consommé. Simmer for 20 minutes. Rub through a sieve, and return to pan. Dilute if necessary. Enrich with butter. Add cooked rice as garnish.

2 oz. (60 g) onion
1 oz. (30 g) butter
16 oz. (450 g) tomatoes
salt and pepper
garlic to taste
bouquet garni
4 oz. (115 g) rice
28 fl. oz. (8 dcL) consommé
2 oz. (60 g) butter

Potato—Cook leeks lightly in butter. Add diced raw potatoes and consommé, and season. Cook quickly until the potatoes are tender. Strain, retaining liquid. Mash potatoes and leeks, and rub through a sieve. Return to cooking liquid, and add cream. Finish with butter, and garnish with chervil leaves.

12 oz. (340 g) white leeks
2 oz. (60 g) butter
12 oz. (340 g) potatoes
32 fl. oz. (9 dcL) consommé
salt and pepper
1 fl. oz. (¼ dcL) cream
2 oz. (60 g) butter

Theresa—Purée white haricot beans. Extend with chicken consommé; garnish with julienne of cooked chicken.

1 pt. (4½ dcL) purée
1 pt. (4½ dcL) consommé

Turnip—Sauté blanched, sliced turnips in butter. Add the 7 fl. oz. consommé and cook till almost tender. Add diced raw potatoes, then the 20 fl. oz. consommé. Finish cooking, rub through a sieve, and enrich with butter.

16 oz. (450 g) white turnip
2 oz. (60 g) butter
7 fl. oz. (2 dcL) consommé
8 oz. (225 g) potatoes
20 fl. oz. (6 dcL) consommé
2 oz. (60 g) butter

Watercress—Cook watercress and potatoes in stock. Rub through a sieve. Add milk, and enrich with butter. Garnish with sprigs of blanched watercress.

2 large bunches of cress
16 oz. (450 g) potatoes
16 fl. oz. (4½ dcL) stock
milk to bring volume up to 35 fl. oz. (1 L)
2 oz. (60 g) butter

Velouté Soups

These thick soups differ from the purées in that they are thickened with a velouté. They consist of a white roux diluted with veal, chicken, or fish stock, to which meat, fish, or poultry is added. The mixture is cooked, seasoned, strained, and thickened with egg yolks and cream.

All recipes produce 36 fl. oz.

2¼ pt./1L). The fundamental preparation of velouté is the same for all types. In the recipes that follow the basics will not be repeated.

Basic Preparation: 4 oz. (115 g) roux is extended with 36 fl. oz. (1 L) of appropriate stock (chicken, fish, white consommé, or dark consommé) to make a sauce. The liaison is 4 egg yolks lightly mixed with 4 fl. oz. (1 dcL) of cream and finished with 2 oz. (60 g) of butter.

Basic Fish: Simmer boned fish in the sauce. Remove the fish and pound it in a mortar to a cream. Return the mixture to the stock, and simmer gently. Press through a sieve. Adjust the consistency, and heat to boiling. Remove from heat, add liaison, and finish with butter.

Basic Poultry and Game: The poultry or game should be fresh and cooked in the sauce. Proceed as for fish. Cooked poultry or game is often used.

Basic Shellfish: Cook shellfish in butter with mirepoix. Pound the shells and flesh. Add to sauce and simmer gently. Rub through a sieve. Add liaison, and finish with compound butter flavored with the appropriate shellfish.

Basic Vegetable: Stew the vegetables in butter, add to the sauce, and simmer gently until tender. Press through a sieve. Adjust consistency, and heat to boiling. Remove from heat, add liaison, and finish with butter.

Agnès Sorel—Proceed as for the basic preparation, using chicken velouté and minced mushrooms. Add liaison as described, and garnish with julienne of chicken, ox tongue, and mushrooms.

Asparagus—Blanch asparagus tips, then gently sauté in butter. Finish as explained under basic preparation for vegetables.

1¼ lb. (575 g) asparagus tips

Cardinal—Proceed as for the basic preparation, using fish velouté. Add liaison and compound butter, and garnish with lobster meat.

1½ lb. (675 g) lobster
6 oz. (170 g) mirepoix
2 oz. (60 g) butter

Carmélite—Proceed as for the basic preparation, using fish velouté. Garnish with poached, diced fillet of sole.

10 oz. (280 g) fillet of sole
6 oz. (170 g) fillet of whiting
liaison
6 oz. (170 g) sole as garnish

Carmen—Proceed as for the basic preparation, using chicken velouté with tomatoes and rice. Garnish with diced tomato and julienne of red peppers.

12 oz. (340 g) tomatoes
4 oz. (115 g) rice
4 oz. (115 g) tomato
4 oz. (115 g) blanched red peppers

Cherville—Proceed as for the basic preparation for chicken, using chicken or game velouté. Use only cream as liaison. Garnish with minced mushrooms sautéed in butter and julienne of rabbit meat.

1½ lb. (675 g) rabbit meat
3 fl. oz. (¾ dcL) cream

Clermont—Proceed as for the basic preparation for vegetables, using chicken velouté and the standard liaison. Garnish with cooked, chopped chestnuts.

1½ lb. (675 g) white celery
3 oz. (90 g) butter
6 oz. (170 g) chestnut purée

Crayfish—Proceed as for the basic preparation, using fish velouté.

18 crayfish
6 oz. (170 g) mirepoix
3 oz. (90 g) butter
liaison and compound butter

Dieppoise—Proceed as for the basic preparation, using fish velouté. Garnish with shrimp and chopped mussels.

16 oz. (450 g) white fish
6 oz. (170 g) shrimp
12 mussels

Montespan—Proceed as for the basic preparation for vegetable velouté using white consommé. Garnish with green peas.

1¾ lb. (800 g) asparagus
3 oz. (90 g) butter

Oyster—Proceed as for the basic preparation, using fish velouté as described. Add oyster liquor and thicken with liaison.

30 poached, chopped oysters

Petit-Duc—Proceed as for the basic preparation for game, using game velouté. Finish with butter and cream. Garnish with cooked game, add commercial oyster sauce and brandy at the end.

1½ lb. (675 g) game
butter and cream
2 fl. oz. (½ dcL) oyster sauce
5 fl. oz. (1½ dcL) brandy

Saint-Hubert—Proceed as for Petit-Duc, but use only ground game. Finish with red currant jelly and brandy.

1½ lb. (675 g) game
6 oz. (170 g) red currant jelly
5 fl. oz. (1½ dcL) brandy

Shrimp—Proceed as for the basic preparation, using fish velouté.

1½ lb. (675 g) shelled shrimp
6 oz. (170 g) mirepoix
2 oz. (60 g) compound butter

Volaille à la Reine—Pound cooked chicken and rice in mortar. Add chicken consommé and heat. Mix egg yolks with cream, and add to pan (off the heat). Enrich with cream and butter, and garnish with diced breast meat.

1½ lb. (675 g) chicken
4 oz. (115 g) rice
28 fl. oz. (8 dcL) consommé
2 egg yolks
7 fl. oz. (2 dcL) cream
2 oz. (60 g) butter

Cream Soups

The main difference between velouté and cream soups is that the latter use béchamel sauce as a thickener instead of velouté. The proper consistency is obtained by diluting the mixture with milk instead of consommé, and these soups are not enriched with butter but with fresh cream. Four to 6 fl. oz. of cream (1 dcL to 1¾ dcL) per quart should be used.

All recipes produce 36 fl. oz. (2¼ pt./1 L). A true "cream" soup is always made with a béchamel sauce (a roux extended with milk). However, on occasion the soup base is extended with a velouté, in which case it is called a *potage* and should not be brought to a boil. Remember also that a cream soup should be finished with cream and a velouté-based "cream" soup should be finished with yolks.

The basic preparations are shown below and apply to all soups. The instructions will not be repeated in the recipes that follow.

Basic Chicken: Dice cooked chicken and pound in a mortar to a cream. Rub through a sieve. Add the purée to the béchamel sauce, and heat. Dilute if necessary with milk, and finish with cream.

2 lb. (900 g) chicken
28 fl. oz. (8 dcL) béchamel sauce
7 fl. oz. (2 dcL) cream

Basic Shellfish: Sauté mirepoix in butter. Add uncooked shellfish, and sauté together. Season, and moisten with white wine. Flame brandy and add to pan. Cook till tender. Pound meat and shells in mortar, and add to béchamel sauce. Rub through a sieve. Dilute if necessary with white wine. Adjust seasoning, and finish with fresh cream.

4 oz. (115 g) mirepoix
2 oz. (60 g) butter

12–16 oz. (340–450 g) shellfish,
   depending on type
2 fl. oz. (½ dcL) white wine
1 fl. oz. (¼ dcL) brandy
28 fl. oz. (8 dcL) béchamel sauce
7 fl. oz. (2 dcL) cream

Basic Vegetable: Blanch vegetables and stew in butter. Make a roux and add vegetables to it. Simmer until tender. Rub through a sieve. Dilute if necessary. Blend in fresh cream.

2½ oz. (75 g) butter for each
   16 oz. (450 g) vegetables
Roux:
   1½ oz. (45 g) butter
   2 oz. (60 g) flour
28 fl. oz. (8 dcL) milk
7 fl. oz. (2 dcL) cream

In the following recipes, the variation from the basic recipe described is only in the quantity of the main ingredient used.

Argenteuil—2¼ lb. (1 kg) white asparagus; garnish with green asparagus tips.

Artichoke—12 blanched hearts; 1½ oz. (45 g) butter; garnish with fried croûtons.

Asparagus—1½ lb. (675 g) asparagus tips; 3 oz. (90 g) butter.

Green Beans—16 oz. (450 g) blanched french beans.

Leeks—1½ lb. (675 g) white part of leeks.

CLEAR SOUPS

These soups consist of clear stocks made with meat or poultry. They can be used as a soup, as a base for other soups, or in sauces. Some soups of this type require very slight thickening. This can be done with arrowroot used in the proportion of 2 tsp. (10 mL) per 36 fl. oz. (1 L) of soup.

All recipes produce approximately 36 fl. oz. (2¼ pt./1 L).

Allemande—Slightly thicken beef consommé, and flavor with gin. Garnish with julienne of blanched red cabbage and slices of frankfurt sausage.

36 fl. oz. (1 L) consommé
2 fl. oz. (½ dcL) gin
4 oz. (115 g) red cabbage
4 oz. (115 g) frankfurt sausage

Ambassadeurs—Garnish chicken consommé with diced plain royale, diced chicken, and sautéed mushrooms. The custard used for garnishing consommé, known as *royale,* is poached, then diced and added to the soup. The quantity given in this recipe is shown as a liquid volume, which needs to be cooked.

36 fl. oz. (1 L) consommé
2 fl. oz. (½ dcL) plain royale
4 oz. (115 g) each chicken and
   mushrooms

Ambassadrice—Garnish chicken consommé with three different colored royales: chopped truffle (black), tomato (red), and green pea (green). Garnish with julienne of chicken.

36 fl. oz. (1 L) consommé
1 fl. oz. (¼ dcL) each black, red,
   and green royale
4 oz. (115 g) chicken

Aurore—Flavor chicken consommé with tomato paste. Thicken mixture. Garnish with julienne of chicken.

36 fl. oz. (1 L) consommé
1 Tbs. (15 mL) tomato paste
4 oz. (115 g) chicken

Belle Fermière—Garnish beef consommé with julienne of blanched cabbage diamonds, french beans, and cooked, broken noodles.

36 fl. oz. (1 L) consommé
3 oz. (90 g) each cabbage and
    french beans
2 oz. (60 g) noodles

Bergère—Slightly thicken beef consommé. Garnish with green asparagus tips, minced raw mushrooms, and blanched tarragon leaves.

36 fl. oz. (1 L) consommé
5 oz. (140 g) asparagus
2 oz. (60 g) mushrooms
tarragon leaves

Bouquetière—Garnish chicken consommé with french beans, asparagus tips, and green peas.

36 fl. oz. (1 L) consommé
4 oz. (115 g) beans
3 oz. (90 g) asparagus
4 oz. (115 g) peas

Bretonne—Garnish beef or chicken consommé with julienne of leeks, celery, onions, and mushrooms.

36 fl. oz. (1 L) consommé
8 oz. (225 g) assorted garnish

Brunoise—Garnish beef consommé with brunoise of assorted vegetables and rice or pearl barley.

36 fl. oz. (1 L) consommé
6 oz. (170 g) vegetable garnish
2 oz. (60 g) rice or barley

Célestine—Slightly thicken chicken consommé. Garnish with rolled plain crêpes and fines herbes.

36 fl. oz. (1 L) consommé
1" × 6" crêpe, cut into julienne
fines herbes

Cheveux d'Ange—Garnish chicken consommé with fine vermicelli, and serve grated cheese separately.

Consommé Blanc (White Consommé)—Cook beef shin, fowl carcass, carrots, turnips, leeks, celery, onions stuck with cloves, and water for 5 to 6 hours. Reduce by one-fourth. Strain.

To produce 4 qt. (3.5 L):
6¾ lb. beef shin
1½ lb. (675 g) fowl carcass
1½ lb. (675 g) carrots
8 oz. (275 g) turnips
1 lb. (450 g) leeks
1 head celery
2 large onions stuck with 4 cloves
10½ pt. (5 L) water

Consommé Clarifié (Clarified Consommé)—Finely mince lean beef. Put in pan with egg white beaten with water. Add to white consommé, bring to boil, and simmer gently for 1 hour. Strain.

To produce 4 qt.:
1½ lb. (675 g) beef
1 egg white
10½ pt. (5 L) white consommé

Consommé de Volaille, de Gibier, etc. (Chicken or Game Consommé)
—Proceed as for clarified consommé, using half the meat. Add an old fowl or game that has been browned in the oven.

Diane—Garnish game consommé with julienne of game and diced truffles, truffle peelings, or mushrooms. Finish with Madeira.

36 fl. oz. (1 L) consommé
5 oz. (140 g) meat
2 oz. (60 g) truffles or mushrooms
5 fl. oz. (1½ dcL) Madeira

Francillon—Garnish chicken consommé with small poached eggs and julienne of chicken meat.

36 fl. oz. (1 L) consommé
1 egg per portion
4 oz. (115 g) chicken meat

Italian—Garnish beef consommé with tomato (red) and spinach (green) royale and broken spaghetti. Serve grated cheese separately.

36 fl. oz. (1 L) consommé
1 oz. (30 g) each red and green
    royale
2 oz. (60 g) spaghetti

Juanita—Garnish chicken consommé with diced tomato and hard-boiled egg yolks passed through sieve.

36 fl. oz. (1 L) consommé
4 oz. (115 g) tomato
2 egg yolks

Madrilène—Flavor consommé with celery. Garnish with diced tomato and pimento if soup is to be served cold or vermicelli if soup is to be served hot.

36 fl. oz. (1 L) consommé
5 oz. (140 g) garnish

Messaline—Flavor chicken consommé with sherry, and garnish with julienne of red peppers and cooked rice.

36 fl. oz. (1 L) consommé
4 fl. oz. (1 dcL) sherry
4 oz. (115 g) red peppers
2 oz. (60 g) rice

Mimosa—Garnish chicken consommé with hard-boiled egg yolks passed through sieve.

36 fl. oz. (1 L) consommé
3 egg yolks

Niçoise—Flavor consommé with tomato. Garnish with diced tomatoes, french beans, and boiled potatoes.

36 fl. oz. (1 L) consommé
8 oz. (225 g) garnish

Orge Perlé—Garnish consommé with cooked pearl barley.

36 fl. oz. (1 L) consommé
3 oz. (90 g) barley

Parisienne—Garnish consommé with julienne of potato and leeks.

36 fl. oz. (1 L) consommé
6 oz. (170 g) potatoes
3 oz. (90 g) leeks

Parmesan—Garnish consommé with diced cheese. Sprinkle with broken crackers.

Petite Marmite—Garnish strong consommé with sliced carrots, turnips, julienne of cabbage, leek, diced beef, and chicken. Serve in marmites with melba toast.

28 fl. oz. (8 dcL) consommé
4 oz. (115 g) each carrot and
    turnip
3 oz. (90 g) each cabbage and leek
2 oz. (60 g) each beef and chicken

MISCELLANEOUS SOUPS

Bagration—Veal velouté garnished with cooked macaroni; liaison with cream only. Serve grated cheese separately.
2¼ pt. (1 L) veal velouté
6 oz. (175 g) macaroni
cheese

Borely—Make fish velouté using sole or whiting. Finish with a liaison of yolks and cream, and garnish with cooked, chopped mussels and shrimp.
2¼ pt. (1 L) fish velouté
6 oz. (170 g) shelled mussels
4 oz. (115 g) shrimp
4 yolks
2 fl. oz. (½ dcL) cream

Bretonne—Purée haricot beans. Mix with chopped onions and leeks sautéed in the first 2 oz. of butter. Extend with milk, add tomato paste, and enrich with the second 2 oz. of butter and cream.
28 fl.oz. (8 dcL) bean purée
6 oz. (170 g) onions
6 oz. (170 g) leeks
2 oz. (60 g) butter
1 oz. (30 g) tomato paste
2 oz. (60 g) butter
2 fl. oz. (½ dcL) cream

Champenoise—Purée potato. Mix with equal amount of celery purée.

Garnish with brunoise of carrots and julienne of blanched celery.
Divette—Make fish velouté. Finish with butter and cream. Garnish with cubes of poached white fish.
2¼ pt. (1 L) fish velouté
2 oz. (60 g) butter
2 fl. oz. (½ dcL) cream
8 oz. (225 g) fish

Esau—Purée red lentils. Finish with butter and cream. Garnish with cooked rice.
2¼ pt. (1 L) red lentil purée
1 oz. (30 g) butter
2 fl. oz. (½ dcL) cream
6 oz. (170 g) cooked rice

Flamande—Mix potato purée with cooked, sieved brussels sprouts. Finish with cream.
28 fl. oz. (8 dcL) potato purée
12 oz. (340 g) brussels sprouts
4 fl. oz. (1 dcL) cream

Fréneuse—Sauté blanched and diced white turnips in butter. Add consommé and cook until almost tender. Add diced raw potato and 20 fl. oz. consommé. Finish cooking and rub through a sieve. Enrich with butter.
16 oz. (450 g) white turnip
2 oz. (60 g) butter
7 fl. oz. (2 dcL) consommé
8 oz. (225 g) potato
20 fl. oz. (6 dcL) consommé
2 oz. (60 g) butter

Garbure—Purée assorted vegetables. Finish with butter and cream. Serve with fried croûtons.
36 fl. oz. (1 L) assorted vegetable
    purée

2 oz. (60 g) butter
2 fl. oz. (½ dcL) cream

Georgette—Make velouté of carrots. Add purée of tomatoes, thicken with arrowroot, and finish with butter.
  32 fl. oz. (9 dcL) velouté of
    carrots
  4 fl. oz. (1 dcL) purée
  2 oz. (60 g) butter

Indian—Make chicken velouté. Add shredded coconut, flavor with curry, finish with cream, and garnish with cooked rice.
  36 fl. oz. (1 L) chicken velouté
  2 oz. (60 g) coconut
  curry to taste
  4 fl. oz. (1 dcL) cream
  4 oz. (115 g) cooked rice

Marcilly—Make chicken velouté. Add purée of green peas. Finish with cream. Garnish with minced chicken and diced, blanched red peppers.
  32 fl. oz. (9 dcL) chicken velouté
  4 fl. oz. (1 dcL) two-thirds green
    pea purée
  4 fl. oz. (1 dcL) cream
  5 oz. (140 g) chicken
  3 oz. (90 g) peppers

Nivernaise—Mix carrot purée with purée of turnip and potato. Finish with cream, and garnish with brunoise of vegetables.
  three parts carrot purée
  one part fréneuse
  2 fl. oz. (½ dcL) cream
  5 oz. (140 g) vegetables

Princesse—Mix chicken purée with asparagus cream. Finish with cream. Garnish with julienne of chicken, asparagus tips, and chervil.
  equal amounts of chicken purée
    and cream soup
  4 fl. oz. (1 dcL) cream
  4 oz. (115 g) chicken
  4 oz. (115 g) asparagus
  pinch of chervil

Solferino—Mix potato purée with cream of tomato soup. Finish with butter. Garnish with cooked carrot and potato balls cut with a parisienne cutter.
  equal amounts of potato purée
    and soup
  2 oz. (60 g) butter
  garnish

Tourangelle—Mix purée of white haricot beans with purée of green beans. Finish with butter and cream. Garnish with dice of french beans.
  16 fl. oz. (4½ dcL) each green
    bean and white haricot purée
  2 oz. (60 g) butter
  1 fl. oz. (¼ dcL) cream

Washington—Make cream of sweet corn. Extend to correct consistency. Garnish with cooked corn kernels, and add whiskey and port just before serving.
  36 fl. oz. (1 L) cream of corn
  4 oz. (115 g) corn kernels
  2 fl. oz. (½ dcL) each whiskey
    and port

Sauces

BASIC SAUCES

All recipes produce approximately 16 fl. oz. (1 pt./4½ dcL).

Béchamel—Stir boiling milk into the pale roux. Add chopped onion, thyme, bay leaf, and nutmeg. Simmer for 1 hour; strain.

16 fl. oz. (4½ dcL) milk
2 oz. (60 g) roux
1 oz. (30 g) onion
sprig of thyme
1 bay leaf
pinch of nutmeg

Brown Sauce, or Espagnole—Extend roux with 18 fl. oz. light brown stock. Brown mirepoix and drain off fat. Add white wine to pan, together with thyme and bay leaf. Add to sauce, and cook gently for 2 hours. Strain, and refrigerate for 24 hours. Reheat, adding 2 fl. oz. stock mixed with tomato purée. Simmer for 1 hour. Remove scum and grease, and strain through muslin.

2 oz. (60 g) basic roux
18 fl. oz. (5 dcL) stock
3 oz. (90 g) mirepoix
5 fl. oz. (1½ dcL) white wine
2 fl. oz. (½ dcL) stock
½ tsp. (2 mg) thyme
3 bay leaves
3½ fl. oz. (1 dcL) tomato purée

Hollandaise—For vegetables, eggs, and fish. Mix wine vinegar and water. Reduce by one-half and cool. Add salt and pepper. Add egg yolks, and whip to creamy consistency in a double boiler. Add melted butter gradually, beating all the time. Add a little water and lemon juice to get correct consistency. Strain, and keep warm in bain-marie.

2 fl. oz. (½ dcL) wine vinegar
1 fl. oz. (¼ dcL) water
salt and pepper
5 egg yolks
16 oz. (450 g) butter
1 oz. (¼ dcL) water
lemon juice to taste

Suprême, or White Poultry—For eggs, poultry, and variety meats. Reduce appropriate velouté and mushroom stock by one-half. Remove from heat and strain. Add cream, then butter.

18 fl. oz. (5 dcL) velouté
3½ fl. oz. (1 dcL) mushroom
   stock
2 oz. (60 g) butter
9 fl. oz. (2½ dcL) cream

Velouté—Use appropriate stock (veal, chicken, or fish.) Blend with pale roux, and cook slowly for 1½ hours.

18 fl. oz. (5 dcL) stock
1 oz. (30 g) each butter and flour

COMPOUND SAUCES

All recipes produce approximately 36 fl. oz. (2¼ pt./1 L).

Admiral—For fish. Mince shallots, and stew in butter. Drain, and add white wine sauce no. 2, then grated rind of 1 lemon. Enrich with anchovy butter, and garnish with capers.

2 oz. (60 g) shallots
1 oz. (30 g) butter
36 fl. oz. (1 L) white wine
    sauce no. 2
1 lemon
2 oz. (60 g) anchovy butter
capers to taste

Albert—For smoked fish and meats. Mix sauce bâtarde with grated horseradish. Season with English mustard, tarragon vinegar, and sugar to taste.

Albuféra—For meats and poultry. Mix suprême sauce with meat glaze and enrich with pimento butter.

28 fl. oz. (8 dcL) suprême sauce
5 fl. oz. (1½ dcL) glaze
1½ oz. (45 g) butter

Allemande—For chicken, eggs, vegetables, and variety meats. Mix egg yolks with light veal stock. Add velouté and blend. Cook over brisk heat, and reduce by one-half so that the sauce coats the back of a spoon. Add butter and strain. Finish with either lemon juice or nutmeg, depending on the item the sauce will accompany.

4 egg yolks
28 fl. oz. (8 dcL) veal stock
35 fl. oz. (1 L) velouté
4 oz. (115 g) butter
lemon juice or nutmeg

Ambassadrice—For chicken and eggs. Mix suprême sauce with chicken purée. Enrich with cream.

28 fl. oz. (8 dcL) suprême sauce
10 oz. (280 g) chicken purée
5 fl. oz. (1½ dcL) cream

Anchovy—For fish. Enrich normande sauce with anchovy butter; add chopped anchovies.

36 fl. oz. (1 L) sauce normande
3 oz. (90 g) anchovy butter
anchovies to taste

Ancienne—For fish and eggs. Hollandaise sauce with chopped gherkins and minced raw mushrooms.

Andalouse—For fish and eggs. Mix mayonnaise with tomato purée. Garnish with finely diced red and green peppers.

36 fl. oz. (1 L) mayonnaise
2 fl. oz. (½ dcL) tomato purée
6 oz. (170 g) red and green peppers

Arlésienne—For grills and eggs. Mix béarnaise sauce with tomato purée. Add diced seeded tomatoes and anchovy fillets.

36 fl. oz. (1 L) béarnaise sauce
3½ fl. oz. (1 dcL) tomato purée

4 tomatoes
6 anchovy fillets

Aurore—For meat. Lightly flavor suprême sauce with tomato purée.

Aurore—For fish. Lightly flavor fish velouté with tomato purée. Enrich with butter.

Banquière—For meats, poultry, eggs, and variety meats. Mix suprême sauce with tomato purée and demi-glace. Flavor with Madeira, and enrich with butter.

Bâtarde—For boiled fish and vegetables. Extend white roux with water. Enrich with egg yolks and butter. Strain through a fine sieve. Add lemon juice at the end.
   6 oz. (170 g) roux
   28 fl. oz. (8 dcL) water
   4 egg yolks
   1 lb. (450 g) butter
   lemon juice to taste

Béarnaise—For grilled or sautéed meats and fish. Chop shallots, tarragon, chervil, thyme, and bay leaf. Moisten with white wine and vinegar. Add salt and coarsely ground pepper. Reduce by two-thirds, and cool. Add egg yolks mixed with water, and cook over low heat. When sauce thickens, add butter, piece by piece, beating all the time. Strain through a tammy. Add lemon juice and cayenne to sharpen, and finish with chopped tarragon and chervil.
   6 oz. (170 g) shallots
   6 Tbs. (90 g) tarragon
   3 Tbs. (45 g) chervil
   sprig of thyme
   ½ bay leaf
   16 fl. oz. (4½ dcL) white wine

16 fl. oz. (4½ dcL) vinegar
salt and pepper
16 egg yolks
lemon juice and cayenne as
   needed
4 fl. oz. (1 dcL) water
1 lb. (450 g) butter
tarragon and chervil as needed

Beauharnais—For grilled or sautéed meats and fish. Make a béarnaise sauce, omitting the tarragon and chervil. Enrich with tarragon butter.

Bercy—For fish. Toss chopped shallots lightly in melted butter. Moisten with fish fumet and white wine. Reduce by one-half. Mix with fish velouté and chopped parsley. Enrich with butter.
   2 oz. (60 g) shallots
   1 oz. (30 g) butter
   10 fl. oz. (3 dcL) each fish fumet
      and white wine
   21 fl. oz. (6 dcL) fish velouté
   parsley
   6 oz. (170 g) butter

Bercy—For grilled meats. Lightly cook chopped shallots in butter. Moisten with white wine. Reduce by one-half. Add demi-glace and parsley. Enrich with butter.
   2 oz. (60 g) shallots
   1 oz. (30 g) butter
   20 fl. oz. (6 dcL) white wine
   20 fl. oz. (6 dcL) demi-glace
   parsley
   6 oz. (170 g) butter

Beurre Noir—For both fish and meats. Cook butter to a deep brown over brisk heat.

Bigarade—For roast or pot-roast

duck. Mix duck gravy with veal stock and Madeira. Reduce by one-third. Thicken with arrowroot. Add lemon and orange juices and blanched zest of orange cut in fine julienne. Finish with orange Curaçao.

    12 fl. oz. (3½ dcL) duck gravy
    28 fl. oz. (8 dcL) veal stock
    12 fl. oz. (3 dcL) Madeira
    arrowroot as needed
    juice of 3 lemons
    juice of 5 oranges
    zest of 2 oranges
    3½ fl. oz. (1 dcL) Curaçao

Bohemian—Mix cold béchamel sauce with egg yolks, salt, and white pepper. Add tarragon vinegar and beat until vinegar is absorbed. Gradually trickle oil into mixture, beating all the time, until all ingredients are completely blended.

    3½ fl. oz. (1 dcL) cold béchamel
        sauce
    3 egg yolks
    salt and pepper to taste
    2 Tbs. (30 mL) tarragon vinegar
    32 fl. oz. (9 dcL) oil

Bonnefoy—For grilled meats and fish. Proceed as for bordelaise sauce, but substitute white wine for red wine.

Bordelaise—For grilled meats. Mix chopped shallots, coarsely ground black pepper, thyme, bay leaf, and red wine. Reduce by one-half. Mix with demi-glace, and strain. Enrich with butter.

    4 oz. (115 g) chopped shallots
    pepper, thyme, and bay leaf to
        taste

    28 fl. oz. (8 dcL) red Bordeaux
        wine
    21 fl. oz. (6 dcL) demi-glace
    3 oz. (90 g) butter

Bourguignonne—For meats, eggs, and poultry. Sweat chopped onions in butter. Add red wine, salt and pepper, and bouquet garni. Reduce by one-fourth. Add espagnole sauce, and reduce again by one-fourth. Strain, and thicken if necessary with beurre manié.

    4 oz. (115 g) onions
    1 oz. (30 g) butter
    28 fl. oz. (8 dcL) red wine
    salt and pepper
    bouquet garni
    28 fl. oz. (8 dcL) espagnole sauce
    6 oz. (170 g) beurre manié

Bretonne—For meats. Sweat chopped onions in 2 oz. butter. Moisten with white wine. Reduce by one-fourth. Add fresh tomatoes, tomato purée, demi-glace, and minced garlic. Strain, enrich with 4 oz. butter, and add chopped parsley.

    8 oz. (225 g) onions
    2 oz. (60 g) butter
    10 fl. oz. (3 dcL) white wine
    10 oz. (280 g) tomatoes
    2 oz. (60 g) tomato purée
    28 fl. oz. (8 dcL) demi-glace
    2 cloves garlic
    4 oz. (115 g) butter

Cambridge—For cold meats. Pound hard-boiled egg yolks, anchovy fillets, capers, chervil, tarragon, chives, mustard, vinegar, and cayenne pepper in mortar. Add oil in a slow stream until correct consistency is reached. Pass through a sieve, and finish with chopped parsley.

24 egg yolks
10 anchovy fillets
remaining ingredients to taste
oil as needed

Caper—For roast or boiled mutton. Proceed as for bâtarde sauce, without adding a liaison. Flavor with lemon juice. Garnish with capers.

36 fl. oz. (1 L) bâtarde sauce
6 oz. (170 g) capers

Caper—For boiled fish. Mix hollandaise sauce and anchovy essence to taste.

Cardinal—For fish. Reduce béchamel sauce and fish fumet by one-half. Add cream, and simmer for 1 minute. Add lobster butter (and lobster coral, if available).

21 fl. oz. (6 dcL) béchamel sauce
14 fl. oz. (4 dcL) fish fumet
10 fl. oz. (3 dcL) cream
7 oz. (200 g) lobster butter

Caviar—For fish. Add caviar to hollandaise sauce just before serving. Serve lukewarm.

Celery—For boiled and braised poultry. Cook white parts of celery in consommé with aromatics. Drain, reserving liquid. Pound the celery, and pass through a sieve. Extend purée with cream sauce and concentrated cooking liquid.

3 lb. (1.35 kg) celery
20 fl. oz. (6 dcL) consommé
1 onion stuck with 2 cloves
bouquet garni
30 fl. oz. (8½ dcL) cream sauce

Chantilly—For asparagus and boiled vegetables. Add a little lemon juice to mayonnaise. Add stiffly beaten cream in desired proportion.

Charcutière—For grilled or sautéed pork. Cook onions until soft in butter. Add demi-glace, and strain. Finish with chopped gherkins.

8 oz. (225 g) onions
2 oz. (60 g) butter
28 fl. oz. (8 dcL) demi-glace
5 oz. (140 g) gherkins

Chasseur—For small cuts of meat and sautéed poultry. Sauté mushrooms in 2 oz. butter with chopped shallots. Add white wine, and reduce by one-third. Mix with demi-glace and tomato sauce. Bring to a boil. Enrich with 3 oz. butter, and add chopped herbs.

8 oz. (225 g) mushrooms
2 oz. (60 g) butter
2 oz. (60 g) shallots
7 fl. oz. (2 dcL) white wine
16 fl. oz. (4½ dcL) demi-glace
10 fl. oz. (3 dcL) tomato sauce
3 oz. (90 g) butter
2 Tbs. (30 g) each tarragon, chervil, and parsley

Chateaubriand—For grilled meats. Boil minced shallots in white wine. Reduce by one-half. Add demi-glace, and reduce again by one-third. Remove from heat. Beat in butter, and add chopped tarragon, cayenne pepper, and lemon juice. Do not strain.

2 oz. (60 g) shallots
16 fl. oz. (4½ dcL) white wine
21 fl. oz. (6 dcL) demi-glace
1 lb. (450 g) butter

4 Tbs. (60 g) tarragon
cayenne pepper and lemon juice
    to taste

Chaud-froid—For meats and game. Boil demi-glace and brown stock together. Add meat jelly or aspic gradually. Reduce to correct consistency. Add Madeira, and strain. Stir until quite cold.
24 fl. oz. (7 dcL) demi-glace
16 fl. oz. (4 dcL) brown stock
28 fl. oz. (8 dcL) meat jelly
2 fl. oz. (½ dcL) Madeira

Chaud-froid—For chicken. Proceed as above but substitute chicken stock for brown stock. Flavor with wine or truffle essence.

Chivry—For eggs and poultry. Reduce chopped shallots and white wine by one-third. Add chopped herbs. Extend with chicken velouté and white stock. Reduce again by one-third. Add printanière butter, and strain.
1½ oz. (45 g) shallots
10 fl. oz. (3 dcL) white wine
3 Tbs. (45 g) each chopped tarragon and chervil
20 fl. oz. (6 dcL) chicken velouté
10 fl. oz. (3 dcL) white stock
3 oz. (90 g) printanière butter

Chivry—For fish. Proceed as for Chivry sauce for eggs and poultry, using fish velouté and fumet instead of chicken velouté and white stock.

Choron—For grilled and sautéed meats. Flavor béarnaise sauce with tomato paste.

Colbert—For meat and poultry. Beat meat or poultry glaze with but-

ter. Flavor with lemon juice, chopped tarragon, and parsley.
28 fl. oz. (8 dcL) glaze
7 oz. (200 g) butter
lemon juice and herbs to taste

Comtesse—For grilled fish. Beat fish velouté with anchovy butter, and flavor with lemon juice to taste.

Cream—For vegetables, fish, eggs, and poultry. Reduce béchamel sauce and cream by one-third. Cool slightly. Add butter and a little more cream if necessary.
28 fl. oz. (8 dcL) béchamel sauce
12 fl. oz. (3½ dcL) cream
6 oz. (170 g) butter
extra cream as needed

Curry—Sprinkle curry powder over chopped onions and stew in butter. Add seeded, chopped tomatoes and minced garlic, parsley, and thyme. Add meat velouté and cook 30 minutes, stirring frequently. Reduce by one-third, then add cream. Strain through a tammy. Reheat and sprinkle with lemon juice.
1 Tbs. (15 mL) curry powder, or as needed
1 lb. (450 g) onions
3 oz. (90 g) butter
4 large tomatoes
4 cloves garlic
sprig parsley
sprig thyme
36 fl. oz. (1 L) meat velouté
12 fl. oz. (3½ dcL) cream
lemon juice to taste

Cussy—For poultry. Mix demi-glace with poultry glaze flavored with Madeira.

24 fl. oz. (7 dcL) demi-glace
10 fl. oz. (3 dcL) poultry glaze
2 fl. oz. (½ dcL) Madeira

Demi-glace—Mix espagnole sauce and good brown stock. Reduce by two-thirds, and add Madeira.
18 fl. oz. (5 dcL) espagnole sauce
28 fl. oz. (8 dcL) brown stock
2 fl. oz. (½ dcL) Madeira

Diable—For grilled chicken. Cook white wine and vinegar with minced shallots and herbs. Reduce by one-half. Stir in demi-glace; beat and strain. Add chopped parsley and cayenne to taste, and enrich with butter.
16 fl. oz. (4½ dcL) white wine
2 fl. oz. (½ dcL) vinegar
2 oz. (60 g) shallots
sprig of thyme
2 bay leaves
24 fl. oz. (7 dcL) demi-glace
parsley and cayenne to taste
5 oz. (140 g) butter

Dieppoise—For fish. Blend fish velouté with shrimp butter.
32 fl. oz. (9 dcL) fish velouté
5 oz. (140 g) shrimp butter

Diplomat—For fish. Beat normande sauce with lobster butter. Add brandy, and flavor with cayenne pepper. Chopped lobster meat can be added.
28 fl. oz. (8 dcL) normande sauce
4 oz. (115 g) lobster butter
2 fl. oz. (½ dcL) brandy
cayenne pepper to taste

Ecossaise—For eggs, poultry, and white variety meats. Add a brunoise of celery and carrots cooked in butter to the cream sauce. Garnish with diamonds of french beans.
28 fl. oz. (8 dcL) cream sauce
12 oz. (340 g) assorted vegetables

Ecossaise—For fish. Garnish a thin béchamel sauce with hard-boiled egg whites cut in julienne and sieved egg yolks.

Fennel—For fish. Garnish bâtarde sauce with cooked, finely diced fennel.
28 fl. oz. (8 dcL) bâtarde sauce
12 oz. (340 g) fennel

Fines Herbes—For small cuts of meat. Add lemon juice and chopped herbs to strained demi-glace.
lemon juice to sharpen
4 Tbs. (60 g) each tarragon, chervil, and parsley
35 fl. oz. (1 L) demi-glace

Fines Herbes—For fish. Proceed as for fines herbes sauce for meat, but substitute fish velouté for demi-glace.

Forestière—For meats. Flavor demi-glace with sherry, and add sliced, sautéed mushrooms.

Foyot—For grilled meats. Add meat glaze to béarnaise sauce.
28 fl. oz. (8 dcL) béarnaise sauce
7 fl. oz. (2 dcL) meat glaze

Gasconne—For eggs, fish, and vegetables. Mix herbs with white wine. Reduce by two-thirds, and strain. Add veal velouté. Enrich with anchovy butter.
1 Tbs. (15 g) each tarragon, chervil, and parsley
5 fl. oz. (1½ dcL) white wine

28 fl. oz. (8 dcL) veal velouté
4 oz. (115 g) anchovy butter

Gloucester—Served cold with poached fish. Mix mayonnaise with sour cream, Worcestershire sauce, and English mustard.
  28 fl. oz. (8 dcL) mayonnaise
  10 fl. oz. (3 dcL) sour cream
  dash of Worcestershire sauce
  English mustard to taste

Godard—For sweetbreads and poultry. Mix white wine with chopped ham and mirepoix; reduce by one-half. Add demi-glace and mushroom essence. Reduce by one-fourth, and strain.
  21 fl. oz. (6 dcL) white wine
  4 oz. (115 g) ham
  4 oz. (115 g) mirepoix
  21 fl. oz. (6 dcL) demi-glace
  8 fl. oz. (2¾ dcL) mushroom
      essence

Gooseberry—For salmon and mackerel. Mix purée of green gooseberries with sugar. Strain.

Gribiche—Serve cold with fish and shellfish. Pound hard-boiled egg yolks to a paste, and mix with mustard, oil, and vinegar. Add seasonings, chopped gherkins, capers, parsley, chervil, and tarragon. Finish with hard-boiled egg whites cut into fine julienne.
  20 eggs
  1 Tbs. (15 mL) french mustard
  16 fl. oz. (4½ dcL) oil
  7 fl. oz. (2 dcL) wine vinegar
  8 oz. (225 g) gherkins
  2 Tbs. (30 g) capers
  parsley, chervil, and tarragon to
      taste

Hash—For minced meats and leftovers. Sauté onions in butter, add shallots, and finish cooking. Add vinegar, and reduce by one-half. Add demi-glace and tomato purée; simmer. Finish with chopped ham, dry duxelles, capers, gherkins, and parsley.
  2 oz. (60 g) onions
  2 oz. (60 g) butter
  1 oz. (30 g) shallots
  12 fl. oz. (3½ dcL) vinegar
  21 fl. oz. (6 dcL) demi-glace
  12 fl. oz. (4 dcL) tomato purée
  2 oz. (60 g) ham
  2 oz. (60 g) duxelles
  2 oz. (60 g) each capers and
      gherkins
  chopped parsley to taste

Hash—For fish. Proceed as above, substituting fish velouté and anchovy sauce for ham and dry duxelles.

Henry IV—For small cuts of meat. Mix Béarnaise sauce with liquid meat glaze.
  28 fl. oz. (8 dcL) béarnaise sauce
  7 fl. oz. (2 dcL) meat glaze

Hungarian—For small cuts of meat, eggs, fish, and variety meats. Sweat chopped onions in 1½ oz. butter, and sprinkle with paprika. Moisten with white wine, and add bouquet garni. Reduce by one-half. Stir in meat or fish velouté, and simmer for 10 minutes. Strain, and enrich with 6 oz. butter.
  3 oz. (90 g) onions
  1½ oz. (90 g) butter
  ½ tsp. (2 g) paprika
  14 fl. oz. (4 dcL) white wine
  bouquet garni

28 fl. oz. (8 dcL) fish or meat velouté
6 oz. (170 g) butter

Italian—Mix espagnole sauce
with chervil, parsley, and tarragon.
Add diced cooked ham.
32 fl. oz. (9 dcL) espagnole sauce
1 Tbs. (15 mL) each chervil, parsley, and tarragon
3 oz. (90 g) ham

Ivory—For eggs, sweetbreads,
and poultry. Add suprême sauce to
pale meat glaze.
28 fl. oz. (8 dcL) suprême sauce
7 fl. oz. (2 dcL) meat glaze

Joinville—For fish. Add oyster
sauce to shrimp sauce, and enrich
with shrimp butter.
7 fl. oz. (2 dcL) oyster sauce
28 fl. oz. (8 dcL) shrimp sauce
4 oz. (115 g) shrimp butter

Jus Lié (Thickened Gravy)—Dilute roasting juices with clear veal
stock or water, and boil together
until amalgamated. Add a little
thickener, such as arrowroot.
Laguipière—For fish. Mix bâtarde sauce with fish glaze, and enrich with butter.
28 fl. oz. (8 dcL) bâtarde sauce
7 fl. oz. (2 dcL) fish glaze
3 oz. (90 g) butter

Lobster—For shellfish or grilled
fish. Mix diplomate sauce with a little anchovy essence and cayenne.
Add lobster meat if desired.
Lombard—For eggs, fish, and
vegetables. Mix hollandaise sauce

with chopped, lightly sautéed mushrooms and chopped parsley.
28 fl. oz. (8 dcL) hollandaise
sauce
10 oz. (280 g) mushrooms
parsley

Lyonnaise—For leftover meats.
Sweat onions in butter. Moisten
with white wine and vinegar, and
reduce by one-half. Add demi-
glace, and cook for 2 minutes. Add
tomato paste and strain.
6 oz. (170 g) onions
2 oz. (60 g) butter
7 fl. oz. (2 dcL) each white wine
and vinegar
28 fl. oz. (8 dcL) demi-glace
2 Tbs. (30 g) tomato paste

Madeira—For small cuts of meat.
Add Madeira wine to concentrated
demi-glace.
7 fl. oz. (2 dcL) Madeira
28 fl. oz. (8 dcL) demi-glace

Maintenon—Mix béchamel sauce
with Soubise sauce, and reduce by
one-half. Thicken with egg yolks,
and add minced mushrooms sautéed
in butter.
20 fl. oz. (6 dcL) béchamel sauce
10 fl. oz. (3 dcL) Soubise sauce
5 egg yolks
4 Tbs. (60 g) minced mushrooms
1 oz. (30 g) butter

Maltese—For boiled vegetables.
Flavor hollandaise sauce with the
juice and grated rind of tangerines;
add Curaçao.
28 fl. oz. (8 dcL) hollandaise
sauce
5 fl. oz. (1½ dcL) tangerine juice

3 Tbs. (45 g) tangerine zest
3½ fl. oz. (1 dcL) Curaçao

Marengo—For meat and game. Flavor chasseur sauce with minced garlic and mushrooms lightly sautéed in butter.
28 fl. oz. (8 dcL) chasseur sauce
4 Tbs. (60 g) garlic
3 oz. (90 g) butter
8 oz. (225 g) mushrooms

Marinière—For fish and vol-au-vents. Mix Bercy sauce with mussel cooking liquid. Thicken with egg yolks, and garnish with poached chopped mussels.
21 fl. oz. (6 dcL) Bercy sauce
7 fl. oz. (2 dcL) mussel cooking liquid
5 egg yolks
24 chopped mussels

Marquise—For fish. Add caviar to hollandaise sauce before serving. Serve lukewarm.
Matelote—Soften vegetable mirepoix in butter. Add red wine, minced garlic, and chopped mushrooms. Boil down by one-third. Thicken with beurre manié.
4 oz. (115 g) vegetable mirepoix
1 oz. (30 g) butter
24 fl. oz. (7 dcL) red wine
2 cloves garlic
4 oz. (115 g) mushrooms
2 oz. (60 g) beurre manié

Mornay—For eggs and chicken. Reduce béchamel sauce and chicken stock by one-third. Add grated Gruyère and Parmesan cheese; blend. Enrich with butter, and strain.

28 fl. oz. (8 dcL) béchamel sauce
14 fl. oz. (4 dcL) chicken stock
6 oz. (170 g) mixed cheeses
6 oz. (170 g) butter

Mornay—For fish. Proceed as above, using fish fumet instead of stock.
Mousseline—For fish, boiled vegetables, and eggs. Blend hollandaise sauce with whipped cream just before serving.
21 fl. oz. (6 dcL) hollandaise sauce
10 fl. oz. (3 dcL) cream

Mustard—For grilled or boiled fish. Mix hollandaise sauce with mustard to taste.
Nantua—For shellfish, fish, and eggs. Sauté mirepoix of vegetables in crayfish butter. Moisten with white wine and Cognac. Add chopped fresh tomatoes and tomato purée. Reduce by one-half. Add fish velouté and cayenne pepper.
8 oz. (225 g) mirepoix
3 oz. (90 g) crayfish butter
16 fl. oz. (4½ dcL) white wine
5 fl. oz. (1½ dcL) Cognac
8 oz. (225 g) tomatoes
1 Tbs. (15 mL) tomato purée
21 fl. oz. (6 dcL) fish velouté
cayenne pepper to taste

Nantua—For shellfish, fish, and eggs. Mix béchamel sauce and crayfish cooking liquid, and reduce by one-half. Add cream and crayfish butter. Finish with Cognac and cayenne pepper; strain.
21 fl. oz. (6 dcL) each béchamel sauce and crayfish cooking liquid

7 fl. oz. (2 dcL) cream
5 oz. (140 g) crayfish butter
2½ fl. oz. (1 dcL) Cognac
cayenne pepper to taste

Noisette—For fish. Mix hollandaise sauce with noisette butter.

Normande—For fish. Reduce fish velouté, fish fumet, and mushroom cooking liquid by one-third. Add egg yolks mixed with cream, finish with butter, and strain through a tammy.

21 fl. oz. (6 dcL) fish velouté
10 fl. oz. (3 dcL) fish fumet
10 fl. oz. (3 dcL) mushroom cooking liquid
6 egg yolks with 3½ fl. oz.
    (1 dcL) cream
5 oz. (140 g) butter

Oyster—For fish. Mix béchamel sauce with the juice of the oysters, and garnish with chopped, poached oysters.

32 fl. oz. (9 dcL) béchamel sauce
juice of 24 oysters
oysters for garnish

Parisienne—For meats and game. Sweat shallots in butter. Moisten with white wine, add meat glaze, and reduce by half. Add demi-glace. Cook for 2 minutes. Spike with lemon juice. Strain.

6 oz. (170 g) shallots
2 oz. (60 g) butter
5 fl. oz. (1½ dcL) white wine
5 fl. oz. (1½ dcL) meat glaze
28 fl. oz. (8 dcL) demi-glace
lemon juice as needed

Parsley—For boiled poultry, rabbit, or fish. Add chopped parsley to veal or fish velouté.

Pau—For grilled meats and poultry. Proceed as for béarnaise sauce, replacing tarragon with freshly chopped mint.

Pepper—For meat. Sauté mirepoix of vegetables in oil with parsley stalks, thyme, and bay leaf. Moisten with vinegar and white wine, and reduce by one-third. Add espagnole sauce, and cook for 30 minutes. Add crushed peppercorns, and pass through a sieve.

6 oz. (170 g) mirepoix
2 fl. oz. (½ dcL) oil
herbs to taste
3½ fl. oz. (1 dcL) vinegar
7 fl. oz. (2 dcL) white wine
28 fl. oz. (8 dcL) espagnole sauce
1½ Tbs. (22 g) peppercorns

Périgourdine—A variation of perigueux. Truffles are cut in thick slices.

Périgueux—For small cuts of meat, fowl, game, and vols-au-vent. Demi-glace and truffle essence (truffle peelings infused in Madeira and strained) are reduced by one-third. Strain. Away from heat, add finely diced truffles. Do not reboil after truffles are added.

To produce 1½ pt. (7 dcL) :
28 fl. oz. (8 dcL) demi-glace
5 fl. oz. (1½ dcL) truffle essence
4 Tbs. (50 mL) truffles

Piquant—For small cuts of meat and leftovers. Mix diable sauce with chopped parsley, chopped gherkins, and crushed peppercorns to taste.

Portuguese—For eggs, fish, meat, and poultry. Cook minced onions in oil. Add roughly chopped tomatoes and crushed garlic; season. Cook for 25 minutes. Stir in brown stock, and reduce by one-third. Add chopped parsley and freshly ground pepper.

8 oz. (225 g) onions
2 fl. oz. (½ dcL) oil
1½ lb. (675 g) tomatoes
4 cloves garlic, or as needed
salt and pepper
28 fl. oz. (8 dcL) brown stock
parsley and freshly ground pepper to taste

Port Wine—For game birds, particularly duck. Mix demi-glace with port wine before serving.

Poulette—For vegetables and variety meats. Add lemon juice, chopped parsley, and mushroom essence to allemande sauce.

Printanière—For eggs and boiled poultry. Add printanière butter to allemande sauce.

28 fl. oz. (8 dcL) allemande sauce
6 oz. (170 g) printanière butter

Provençale—For eggs, fish, small meats, and fowl. Cook chopped onions in oil. Add peeled, seeded tomatoes and crushed garlic. Moisten with white wine, and reduce by one-third. Add light veal stock; cook for 15 minutes. Add chopped parsley.

8 oz. (225 g) onions
2 fl. oz. (½ dcL) oil
1 lb. (450 g) tomatoes
garlic as needed
16 fl. oz. (4½ dcL) white wine
21 fl. oz. (6 dcL) veal stock
parsley to taste

Raifort—Serve cold with cold meats and smoked fish. Mix horse-radish cream with lemon juice, salt, pepper, and a touch of wine vinegar.

Ravigote—For poultry and variety meats. Mix white wine and tarragon vinegar with chopped shallots, thyme, and bay leaves; reduce by one-half. Add chicken or veal velouté and mushroom essence (the concentrated liquid in which mushrooms have been cooked). Reduce by one-fourth. Finish with butter and cream. Add a little cayenne pepper at end. Strain, and add chopped chives and chervil.

5 fl. oz. (1½ dcL) each white wine and tarragon vinegar
4 oz. (115 g) shallots
herbs to taste
28 fl. oz. (8 dcL) chicken or veal velouté
5 fl. oz. (1½ dcL) mushroom essence
6 oz. (170 g) butter
7 fl. oz. (2 dcL) cream
dash of cayenne pepper
chives and chervil to taste

Red Wine—For fish. Reduce chopped shallots in red wine by one-third. Add fish fumet and reduce again by one-third. Beat in beurre manié to desired consistency. Season with cayenne and anchovy essence.

4 oz. (115 g) shallots
28 fl. oz. (8 dcL) red wine
28 fl. oz. (8 dcL) fish fumet
4–6 oz. (150–170 g) beurre manié
cayenne and anchovy essence to taste

Réforme—Cut all ingredients julienne style. Add to pepper sauce.

4 gherkins
whites of 4 hard-boiled eggs
8 mushrooms, sautéed
3 oz. (90 g) pickled tongue or lean
   ham
32 fl. oz. (9 dcL) pepper sauce

Rémoulade no. 1—Serve cold
with fish and eggs. Mix mayonnaise
with anchovy essence, mustard,
chopped gherkins, capers, chervil,
and parsley.

Rémoulade no. 2—Serve with fish
and eggs. Season finely chopped
hard-boiled eggs with oil, vinegar,
salt, chopped gherkins, capers,
chervil, and parsley.

Robert—For grilled pork. Cook
minced onions in butter. Moisten
with white wine; reduce by one-
third. Add demi-glace, and finish
with mustard.
   6 oz. (170 g) onions
   2 oz. (60 g) butter
   12 fl. oz. (3½ dcL) white wine
   28 fl. oz. (8 dcL) demi-glace
   1 Tbs. (15 mL) mustard

Saint-Malo—For grilled fish.
Sauté chopped onions in 2 oz. butter, and moisten with white wine.
Add thyme, parsley, and bay leaf.
Reduce by one-half. Add fish velouté and espagnole sauce, and extend with fish fumet; reduce by one-
third. Strain, and finish with prepared mustard, Worcestershire
sauce, and 3 oz. butter.
   6 oz. (170 g) onions
   2 oz. (60 g) butter
   12 fl. oz. (3½ dcL) white wine
   herbs to taste
   16 fl. oz. (4½ dcL) each fish ve-
      louté and espagnole sauce

7 fl. oz. (2 dcL) fish fumet
1 Tbs. (15 mL) each mustard and
   Worcestershire sauce
3 oz. (90 g) butter

Shrimp—For fish. Add shrimp
butter to normande sauce or a good
fish velouté.
   5 oz. (140 g) shrimp butter
   28 fl. oz. (8 dcL) normande sauce

Swedish—Serve cold with cold
pork. Mix mayonnaise with apple
purée and grated horseradish to
taste.

Tarragon—For grilled meats.
Thicken gravy, and add chopped
tarragon.

Tartare—For beef. Mix mayonnaise with yolks of hard-boiled
eggs. Add chopped chive, and
minced gherkins.
   28 fl. oz. (8 dcL) mayonnaise
   6 hard-boiled egg yolks
   chives and gherkins to taste

Valois—For chicken. Add meat
glaze to béarnaise sauce.
   4 fl. oz. (1 dcL) meat glaze
   32 fl. oz. (9 dcL) béarnaise sauce

Venetian—Add chopped shallots,
tarragon, and chervil to white wine
vinegar. Reduce by three-quarters.
Strain. Add to white wine sauce.
Beat all together and add herb butter. Garnish with chopped chervil
and tarragon.
   2 oz. (60 g) chopped shallots
   1 Tbs. (15 mL) each tarragon and
      chervil
   7 fl. oz. (2 dcL) white wine vine-
      gar

32 fl. oz. (9 dcL) white wine
    sauce
3 oz. (90 g) herb butter
chervil and tarragon for garnish
    as desired

Véron—For fish. Mix 3 parts
béarnaise sauce to 1 part normande
sauce.

Villeroi—To coat foods to be
fried *à la Villeroi*. Extend allemande sauce with light stock and
mushroom essence. Reduce over
medium fire until mixture will coat
the back of a spoon. Strain, and finish with truffle essence and onion or
tomato purée, depending upon use.
Refrigerate.
28 fl. oz. (8 dcL) allemande sauce
7 fl. oz. (2 dcL) stock
3½ fl. oz. (1 dcL) mushroom es-
    sence
truffle essence and tomato or
    onion purée to taste

Villeroi—For fish. Proceed as
above, but use an allemande sauce
based upon fish stock.

White Onion Sauce, or Soubise—
For boiled fish, boiled mutton, and
variety meats. Sweat chopped onions in butter; drain. Add béchamel
sauce; season and strain.
2¼ lb. (1 kg) onions
5 oz. (140 g) butter
28 fl. oz. (8 dcL) béchamel sauce

White Wine no. 1—For fish to be
glazed. Mix fish velouté and fish
fumet made with white wine; reduce by one-half. Add egg yolks,
and enrich with butter.
14 fl. oz. (4 dcL) each fish velouté
    and fish fumet
8 egg yolks
12 oz. (340 g) butter

White Wine no. 2—For fish. Reduce fish fumet made with white
wine by one-half. Cool. Add egg
yolks, and whisk over low heat.
24 fl. oz. (76 dcL) fish fumet
8 egg yolks

White Wine no. 3—For fish. Mix
hollandaise sauce and concentrated
fish fumet.
14 fl. oz. (4 dcL) hollandaise
    sauce
4 fl. oz. (1 dcL) fish fumet

Zingara—Mix demi-glace with tomato purée; season with cayenne
pepper and flavor with Madeira.
Garnish with julienne of lean ham,
pickled ox tongue, and mushrooms.
Cook gently, keeping warm but
never boiling.
32 fl. oz. (9 dcL) demi-glace
3½ fl. oz. (1 dcL) tomato purée
cayenne to taste
3½ fl. oz. (1 dcL) Madeira
4 Tbs. (60 mL) each ham, pickled
    ox tongue, and mushrooms

Compound Butters

After these compound butters have been prepared, they should be shaped into a baton while still cool, wrapped in foil, and refrigerated until needed. All recipes produce approximately 8 oz. (225 g).

Almond—Used as an addition to some soups and white sauces, and as a garnish in cold hors d'oeuvre. Pound blanched and peeled sweet almonds in a mortar with a little water, add salted butter, rub through a sieve, and chill.

   3 oz. (90 g) almonds
   1 Tbs. (15 mL) water
   5 oz. (140 g) butter

Anchovy—For grilled meats or fish. Pound anchovies in a mortar with butter. Sieve and chill.

   3 oz. (90 g) anchovies
   6 oz. (170 g) butter

Bercy—For grilled meat or fish. Reduce white wine with chopped shallots by one-half. Add chopped parsley, lemon juice, and pepper. Cream together with salted butter.

   7 fl. oz. (2 dcL) white wine
   1 oz. (30 g) shallots
   chopped parsley
   lemon juice and pepper to taste
   7 oz. (200 g) butter

Caviar—For grilled fish. Pound caviar in a mortar. Put caviar in a fine cloth, and twist firmly to remove oily fluid or brine. Mix with softened, salted butter. Rub through a sieve, and chill.

   4 oz. (115 g) caviar
   6 oz. (170 g) butter

Chivry—For white sauces and cold hors d'oeuvres. Finely chop parsley, tarragon, chervil, chives, and shallots; mix with softened, salted butter.

   1 Tbs. (15 g) each parsley, tarragon, chervil, chives, and shallots
   8 oz. (225 g) butter

Colbert—For fish *à la Colbert* and some grilled meats. Add meat glaze and chopped tarragon to maître d'hôtel butter.

   1 fl. oz. (¼ dcL) meat glaze
   1 Tbs. (15 mL) tarragon
   8 oz. (225 g) maître d'hôtel butter

Crayfish—For sauces, thick shellfish soup, forcemeat, and Nantua sauce. Pound trimmings and shells cooked à la mirepoix in a mortar. Add an equal amount of butter, and blend. Put mixture in a double boiler and allow it to melt gradually. Pour mixture through a tammy into bowl of iced water. Twist tammy to squeeze out all the butter. Collect solidified pieces from the water, and dry them on towel.

Garlic—For sauces and cold hors d'oeuvres. Peel, blanch, and drain garlic. Pound in a mortar with salted butter, and rub through a sieve.

  12 cloves garlic
  8 oz. (225 g) butter

Hazelnut—Proceed as for almond butter, but brown the nuts in butter first.

Herring—For grilled fish. Cream together herring paste with unsalted butter.

  2 oz. (60 g) herring paste
  7 oz. (200 g) butter

Horseradish—For grilled meats and oily fish such as mackerel, trout, and salmon. Pound grated horseradish with butter, rub through a sieve, and chill.

  3 oz. (90 g) grated horseradish
  7 oz. (200 g) butter

Laitances—For fish sauces and cold hors d'oeuvres. Poach, cool, and drain roe. Pound in a mortar with salted butter. Chill.

  4 oz. (115 g) soft roe
  7 oz. (200 g) butter

Lobster—Proceed as for crayfish butter, using lobster meat trimmings and coral instead of crayfish.

Maître d'Hôtel—For grilled meats, fish, or boiled vegetables.

Can be served melted in a sauceboat.

  7 oz. (200 g) salted butter
  2 Tbs. (30 g) chopped parsley
  salt and pepper
  lemon juice to taste

Marchand de Vin—For grilled rump steak *à la marchand de vin*. Gently stew red wine and minced shallots; reduce by one-half. Add crushed peppercorns, meat glaze, chopped parsley, and lemon juice. Cool, cream with softened salted butter. Chill.

  7 fl. oz. (2 dcL) red wine
  2 shallots
  3 peppercorns
  1 fl. oz. (¼ dcL) meat glaze
  1 Tbs. (15 g) parsley
  1 tsp. (5 ml) lemon juice
  6 oz. (170 g) butter

Meunière—For fish cooked *à la meunière* and with certain vegetables. Heat butter in pan till it acquires a light golden color. Add a dash of salt, pepper, and lemon juice.

Montpellier—For dressing cold fish dishes, spreading on croûtons, and decorating cold dishes. When used as a spread, the raw yolks and oil are omitted. Blanch parsley, chervil, cress, tarragon, chives, and minced shallots. Drain, and chill in iced water. Press to extract moisture. Pound in a mortar with gherkins, squeezed capers, anchovies, and a minced clove of garlic. Mix to a smooth paste. Add butter, hardboiled yolks, and raw yolks; mix until smooth. Add oil, little by little. Run through a sieve, and chill. This recipe produces about 2¼ lb. (1 kg) of Montpellier butter; smaller quantities are hardly worth making.

¾ oz. (20 g) each parsley, chervil, cress, tarragon, and chives
1½ oz. (45 g) shallots
3 gherkins
1 Tbs. (15 g) capers
4 anchovies
1 clove garlic
1¾ lb. (750 g) butter
3 cooked egg yolks
2 raw egg yolks
5 fl. oz. (2½ dcL) oil

Mustard—Blend French mustard with salted butter to taste.

Noir—For fish and boiled vegetables. Cook butter in pan till dark brown, add chopped capers and tarragon vinegar.

7 oz. (200 g) butter
1½ oz. (45 g) capers
1½ Tbs. (22 mL) tarragon vinegar

Noisette—Proceed as for meunière butter, omitting lemon juice.

Paprika no. 1—For canapés and cold hors d'oeuvres. Cream together salted butter and paprika; chill.

7 oz. (200 g) butter
2 Tbs. (30 g) paprika

Paprika no. 2—Same use as above. Cook together butter, paprika, and grated onion; strain through muslin. When cold, cream with more salted butter.

2 oz. (60 g) butter
2 Tbs. (30 g) paprika
1 oz. (30 g) onion
6 oz. (170 g) butter

Parsley—Proceed as for maître d'hôtel butter.

Pimento—For grilled fish and hors d'oeuvres. Blanch pimentos; pound with salted butter.

3 oz. (90 g) pimentos
6 oz. (170 g) butter

Pistachio—Proceed as for almond butter, substituting pistachios for almonds.

Printanière—For thickening soups. Cook very young vegetables such as french beans, peas, and carrots. Pass through a sieve, blend with salted butter. Sieve again, and chill. Use equal quantities of sieved vegetables and butter.

Ravigote—Another name of Chivry butter.

Shellfish—For grilled fish. Pound carcasses of shellfish in a mortar to a powder; add butter. Melt mixture slowly in a pan set in a bain-marie. Strain through muslin into iced water.

1 lb. (450 g) shellfish carcasses
6 oz. (170 g) butter

Shrimp—For soups, sauces, and cold hors d'oeuvres. Pound cooked, shelled shrimp with salted butter. Sieve and chill.

4 oz. (115 g) shrimp
4 oz. (115 g) butter

Snail—For filling snail shells cooked *à la Bourguignonne*. Pound chopped shallots, minced garlic, chopped parsley, and black pepper with salted butter.

1 oz. (30 g) shallots
1 clove garlic

parsley and pepper to taste
8 oz. (225 g) butter

Tarragon—For sauces and cold hors d'oeuvres. Blanch, pound in a mortar, and seive the tarragon leaves. Blend with salted butter. Rub the mixture through a sieve again, and chill.

3 Tbs. (45 g) chopped tarragon
    leaves
8 oz. (225 g) butter

Tomato—For fish and sautéed veal, and for thickening soups. Mix enough commercial tomato purée with butter to obtain a satisfactory flavor.

Truffle—For grilled meats and fish. Cook truffles in butter over gentle flame. Pound and rub through a sieve. Blend with three times their weight of butter. Sieve and chill.

Forcemeats and Stuffings

Anchovy Stuffing—Make a white roux with butter and flour; extend with milk. Remove from stove when cooked and very thick. Add eggs, yolks, and finely chopped fillets of desalted anchovies and rub through a sieve. Reheat sauce and cook for 2 minutes. Sieve again.

To produce 12 fl. oz. (3½ dcL):
1 oz. (30 g) butter
2 oz. (60 g) flour
6 fl. oz. (1¾ dcL) milk
2 eggs
4 egg yolks
8 anchovy fillets

Chicken Forcemeat—Pound all ingredients except eggs and brandy in a mortar or process in a food processor. Add eggs and brandy; season.

To produce 4 lb. (1.8 kg):
16 oz. (450 g) chicken or other
    poultry
8 oz. (225 g) lean veal
8 oz. (225 g) pork
16 oz. (450 g) fresh bacon
4 eggs
10 fl. oz. (3 dcL) brandy
salt and pepper

Chicken Liver Stuffing—Pound chicken livers, and sauté in butter

with chopped shallots. Add blanched, chopped spinach, anchovy fillets, butter, and eggs; season. Add nutmeg and basil. Rub through a sieve, and mix well.

To produce 1½ lb. (675 g):
10 oz. (280 g) chicken livers
2 shallots
butter as needed to sauté
8 oz. (225 g) spinach
2 desalted anchovies
4 oz. (115 g) butter
2 eggs
salt and pepper to taste
nutmeg and basil to taste

Chicken Stuffing—Mix cold, diced chicken with chopped lettuce lightly cooked in butter. Season as for Chicken Liver Stuffing.

8 oz. (225 g) chicken
lettuce as desired

Cream Forcemeat—Cream stuffing made with veal, game, or chicken. Pound the meat in a mortar or process it in a food processor. Season, and add egg whites a little at a time. Mix and continue processing. Rub mixture through a sieve, and mix again thoroughly. Keep very cool for 2 hours. Add cream a little at a time, stirring

well. Use for forcemeat balls, quenelles, mousses, and mousselines.

To produce 4½ lb. (2 kg):
2¼ lb. (1 kg) meat
salt and pepper to taste
4 egg whites
55 fl. oz. (1½ L) thick cream

Duxelles, Wet—Used to stuff vegetables. Reduce white wine and dry
duxelles; add demi-glace mixed
with tomato purée, breadcrumbs,
and chopped parsley.

To produce 8 oz. (225 g):
2 fl. oz. (½ dcL) white wine
6 oz. (170 g) dry duxelles
3 fl. oz. (1 dcL) demi-glace
1 Tbs. (15 mL) tomato purée
2 oz. (60 g) white breadcrumbs
1 Tbs. (15 mL) parsley

Fish Forcemeat—Steep breadcrumbs in a little milk and squeeze
dry. Cook minced onions and shallots in butter until soft. Cool onion
mixture and add it to the bread. Mix
in chopped mushrooms, chopped
parlsey, and minced garlic. Beat in
eggs, and season with nutmeg, salt,
and pepper.

To produce 16 oz. (450 g):
8 oz. (225 g) breadcrumbs
1 oz. (30 g) each onions and
    shallots
2 oz. (60 g) mushrooms
2 Tbs. (30 mL) parsley
1 clove garlic
4 eggs
nutmeg to taste
salt and pepper to taste

Fish Stuffing—Fry diced bacon
with finely chopped celery and on-

ions until the bacon is crisp. Add
butter; stir in diced stale bread.
Season with salt and pepper; add
poultry seasoning. Moisten lightly
with fish stock.

To produce 16 oz. (450 g):
3 slices bacon
4 oz. (115 g) each onions and
    celery
1½ oz. (45 g) butter
8 oz. (225 g) stale bread
salt and pepper to taste
½ tsp. (2½ g) poultry seasoning
fish stock as needed

Game Forcemeat—Proceed as for
chicken forcemeat, substituting
game for chicken.

Mousseline Forcemeat—Pound
the fish or meat in a mortar or process in a food processor. Add nutmeg, and add egg whites a little at a
time. Mix well. Pass through a
sieve. Stir over ice until smooth and
velvety. Chill for 1 hour. Add
cream a little at a time; mix very
gently with spatula. Use for light
quenelles and mousses.

To produce 5 lb. (2.25 kg):
2¼ lb. (1 kg) white fish, chicken,
    or veal
nutmeg to taste
4 egg whites
45 fl. oz. (1½ L) cream

Panada—A mixture used for
binding meat and fish forcemeats.
Place breadcrumbs in boiling milk,
and season. When breadcrumbs
have absorbed all the milk, place
pan over high heat; stir until mixture thickens. Chill before using.

To produce 2¼ lb. (1 kg):
1 lb. (450 g) breadcrumbs

1¼ pt. (6 dcL) milk
salt to taste

Panada, Frangipane—Used for chicken and fish forcemeat. Mix flour, egg yolks, salt, pepper, nutmeg, and melted butter in saucepan. Add boiling milk, and return to a boil over medium heat. Reduce heat, and continue to cook for 5 minutes, whisking constantly. Cool; chill before using.
 To produce 2 lb. (900 g):
 8 oz. (225 g) flour
 8 egg yolks
 salt, pepper, and nutmeg to taste
 6 oz. (170 g) butter
 1¼ pt. (6 dcL) milk

Panada, Rice—Moisten rice with white consommé. Add butter, and cook mixture for 45 minutes. Stir until the mixture becomes a smooth paste.
 To produce 2 lb. (900 g):
 8 oz. (225 g) rice
 24 fl. oz. (7 dcL) white consommé
 1½ oz. (45 g) butter

Provençale Stuffing—Used for fish. Cook finely chopped onions in oil until tender. Add minced garlic and chopped raw mushrooms. Brown the vegetables. Add fresh breadcrumbs, chopped chives, and chopped parsley; season with salt, pepper, and nutmeg.

To produce 3 lb. (1.35 kg):
8 oz. (225 g) onions
4 Tbs. (60 mL) oil
1 clove garlic
20 oz. (600 g) mushrooms
2¼ lb. (1 kg) breadcrumbs
1 Tbs. (15 g) each chives and
 parsley

Shellfish Forcemeat—Proceed as for mousseline forcemeat, substituting shellfish for fish or meat.

Veal and Pork Forcemeat—Pound all ingredients except eggs, brandy, and seasonings in a mortar or process in a food processor. Add eggs and brandy; season to taste.
 To produce 2¼ lb. (1 kg):
 11 oz. (300 g) round of veal
 9 oz. (250 g) lean pork
 9 oz. (250 g) fresh fat bacon
 2 eggs
 6 Tbs. (1 dcL) brandy
 salt and pepper to taste

Veal and Spinach Stuffing—Mix fine dice of cooked veal, spinach, cream cheese (pressed dry), grated Parmesan. Add eggs, salt, and pepper.
 To produce 1½ lb. (675 g):
 8 oz. (225 g) veal
 8 oz. (225 g) spinach
 2 eggs
 4 oz. (115 g) cream cheese
 3 oz. (90 g) Parmesan cheese
 salt and pepper to taste

Eggs

SCRAMBLED EGGS

All recipes are for 8 eggs.

Basic Preparation: Melt 2 oz.
(60 g) of the butter in a small frying
pan. Break the eggs into a bowl and
beat together lightly. Add cold
water and seasoning. Add eggs to
the butter in the pan. Cook over
low heat until the eggs are set. Remove the pan from the stove. Cut
the remaining ounce of butter into
small pieces and add to the eggs;
blend and serve. Two tablespoons
of fresh cream may be substituted
for the final addition of butter.

   3 oz. (90 g) butter
   2 Tbs. (30 mL) cold water
   salt and pepper to taste

Amiral—Surround eggs with lobster sauce that has been slightly
thinned with cream. Garnish with
diced lobster, and sprinkle with
chopped parsley.

   4 fl. oz. (1 dcL) lobster sauce
   1 fl. oz. (¼ dcL) cream
   8 oz. (225 g) lobster meat
   parsley as needed

Anchovy—Finely chop the rinsed
anchovies and mix them into the
eggs just as they begin to set. Garnish with two thin strips of anchovy
laid across each other. Place four
halves of pitted olive in the angles,
and add chopped parsley in the
center.

   6 anchovy fillets
   2 thin strips anchovy
   8 black olives
   parsley as needed

Antoine—Chop fried lean bacon.
Add to eggs with tarragon and capers.

   4 oz. (115 g) bacon
   tarragon to taste
   2 Tbs. (30 mL) chopped capers

Bordelaise—Mix diced, sautéed
mushrooms with beaten eggs.
Cover each portion with a thread of
bordelaise sauce, and garnish with
small triangles of fried bread.

   4 oz. (115 g) mushrooms
   2 fl. oz. (½ dcL) bordelaise sauce
   fried bread triangles

Cambridge—Mix sautéed, diced
mushrooms and green peppers with
diced lobster meat. Add mixture to
beaten eggs. Surround each portion
with a thread of cream sauce.

4 oz. (115 g) each lobster, mushrooms, and green peppers
4 fl. oz. (1 dcL) cream sauce

Chambord—Scramble eggs.
Serve on large slices of sautéed
eggplant. Cover each portion with a
thread of demi-glace.
   4 oval slices of eggplant
   4 fl. oz. (1 dcL) demi-glace

Chasseur—Garnish scrambled
eggs with a whole chicken liver that
has been sautéed in butter. Sprinkle
a pinch of fresh chervil over the
portions, and garnish with a thread
of chasseur sauce.
   4 whole chicken livers
   1 oz. (30 g) butter
   chervil as needed
   2 fl. oz. (½ dcL) chasseur sauce

Cheese—Grate fresh Parmesan
and Gruyère cheese. Add to beaten
eggs.
   3 oz. (90 g) each Parmesan and
      Gruyère cheese

Don Juan—Finely slice and
blanch green peppers. Add to
beaten eggs, and cook. Garnish
with thin slices of rinsed anchovies.
Cover each portion with a thread of
Madeira sauce.
   4 oz. (115 g) green peppers
   4 anchovies, halved lengthwise
   4 fl. oz. (1 dcL) Madeira sauce

Fines Herbes—Chop assorted
fresh herbs. If dried herbs must be
used, soak a good pinch of each one
in milk for 30 minutes. Drain and
squeeze them dry before using. Mix
with beaten eggs before cooking.

Georgette—Scoop out three-quarters of a large baked potato. Fill
with cooked scrambled eggs, and
garnish with crayfish sauce and
chopped parsley.
   4 large potatoes
   8 fl. oz. (2¼ dcL) crayfish sauce
   parsley as needed

Joinville—Sauté diced mushrooms and chopped shrimp. Mix
with scrambled eggs. Serve in large
puff pastry shells or vol-au-vents.
Garnish the center of each portion
with whole, sautéed mushrooms
and shrimp.
   4 oz. (115 g) shrimp
   4 oz. (115 g) mushrooms
   4 puff pastry shells or vol-au-
      vents
   4 whole mushrooms
   4 whole shrimp

Magda—Chop mixed fresh herbs.
Add to beaten eggs with a dash of
mustard. Garnish with freshly
grated Parmesan cheese and puff
pastry fleurons.
   1 tsp. (5 mL) each tarragon,
      chives, chervil, and parsley
   2 oz. (60 g) Parmesan cheese
   12 fleurons

Montbarry—Sauté diced mushrooms and asparagus tips in butter,
and add to beaten eggs. Cook.
Serve on a bed of rice mixed with
grated Gruyère cheese and minced,
blanched red peppers.
   4 oz. (115 g) mushrooms
   12 asparagus tips
   3 oz. (90 g) butter
   9 oz. (250 g) rice

4 oz. (115 g) Gruyère cheese
3 oz. (90 g) red peppers

Normandy—Cook scrambled eggs. Serve in a prebaked flan case, and garnish with cooked, shelled mussels and shrimp bound with fish velouté.
1 large or 4 small flan cases
6 oz. (170 g) mussels
6 oz. (170 g) shrimp
4 fl. oz. (1 dcL) fish velouté

Parmentier—Cook scrambled eggs. Garnish with diced, cooked potatoes that have been sautéed in butter and mixed with demi-glace. Sprinkle with chopped parsley.
12 oz. (340 g) potatoes
6 fl. oz. (2 dcL) demi-glace
parsley as needed

Portuguese—Cook scrambled eggs. Seed and chop tomatoes. Mix tomatoes with butter. Place in center of cooked eggs; cover with a thread of meat glaze. Garnish with chopped parsley.
8 oz. (225 g) tomatoes
2 fl. oz. (½ dcL) meat glaze
parsley as needed

Princess—Cook scrambled eggs. Serve in prebaked, short-crust flan cases. Garnish with asparagus tips, slices of chicken breast, and suprême sauce.
1 large or 4 small flan cases
16 asparagus tips
8 oz. (225 g) chicken breast
2 fl. oz. (½ dcL) suprême sauce

Provençale—Beat the eggs. Mix with seeded, chopped tomatoes,

minced garlic, and chopped parsley before cooking.
12 oz. (340 g) tomatoes
garlic and parsley to taste

Raspail—Beat the eggs. Mix with cream, diced celery, and seeded, chopped tomatoes. Cook. Garnish with chopped parsley.
2 fl. oz. (½ dcL) cream
4 oz. (115 g) celery
8 oz. (225 g) whole tomatoes
parsley as needed

Rothschild—Pound crayfish pieces in a mortar or process in a food processor. Add cream. Pass mixture through a sieve. Add to beaten eggs, and cook. Garnish with asparagus tips, crayfish tails, and whole sautéed mushrooms.
6 oz. (170 g) crayfish pieces
2 fl. oz. (½ dcL) cream
16 asparagus tips
8 crayfish tails
8 mushrooms

Saint-Denis—Cook scrambled eggs. Serve on large, lightly grilled mushroom caps with red wine sauce.
8 mushroom caps
4 fl. oz. (1 dcL) red wine sauce

Spanish—Cook scrambled eggs. Sauté seeded, diced tomatoes and chopped red peppers in oil. Drain. Place mixture in center of each portion. Garnish with sautéed onion rings.
8 oz. (225 g) tomatoes
6 oz. (170 g) red peppers
onion rings as needed

Vert-Pré—Cook scrambled eggs. Serve on a bed of creamed spinach. Garnish with chopped mixed herbs.

24 oz. (680 g) creamed spinach
herbs to taste

EGGS EN COCOTTES

All recipes are for 8 eggs.

Basic Preparation: Butter or coat cocottes with a purée. Break the eggs into the cocottes. Place the cocottes into a pan that has been partially filled with water. Cook in oven until set.

Bergère—Line bottom of cocottes with a ⅓ inch of poultry forcemeat. Break eggs into cocottes. Proceed as for basic recipe. Garnish with a thread of meat glaze.

12 oz. (340 g) forcemeat
4 fl. oz. (1 dcL) meat glaze

Bourguignonne—Fill bottom of cocottes one-third full with bourguignonne sauce. Set sauce to boil in cocottes on side of the stove. Break eggs into boiling sauce; finish cooking in the oven.

8 fl. oz. (2¼ dcL) bourguignonne

Commodore—Break eggs into buttered cocottes. Cover cooked eggs with béarnaise sauce, and garnish with blanched tarragon leaves.

8 fl. oz. (2¼ dcL) béarnaise sauce
tarragon leaves

Cuban—Line bottom of cocottes with creamed crab meat. Break eggs into cocottes, and cook. Garnish with chopped parsley.

12 oz. (340 g) creamed crab meat
parsley as needed

Duxelles—Line bottom of cocottes with dry duxelles. Break eggs into cocottes, and cook. Garnish with demi-glace that has been enriched with butter.

8 oz. (225 g) dry duxelles
3 fl. oz. (¾ dcL) demi-glace
1 oz. (30 g) melted butter

Florentine—Line bottom of cocottes with cooked, chopped spinach mixed with finely chopped anchovies. Break eggs into cocottes, and cook. Cover cooked eggs with a little cream and grated cheese; glaze quickly before serving.

8 oz. (225 g) spinach
2 anchovies
3 fl. oz. (¾ dcL) cream
2 oz. (60 g) grated cheese

Forestière—Line bottom of cocottes with diced, fried bacon and mushroom purée. Break eggs into cocottes, and cook. Garnish eggs with chopped parsley.

6 oz. (170 g) bacon
8 oz. (225 g) mushroom purée
parsley as needed

Au Jus—Cook eggs in buttered cocottes. Garnish with threads of reduced veal stock before serving.

4 fl. oz. (1 dcL) veal stock

Léontine—Line bottom of cocottes with a layer of fish forcemeat. Break eggs into cocottes, and cook. Garnish with chopped shrimp and tiny sprigs of parsley.

8 oz. (225 g) fish forcemeat
6 oz. (170 g) shrimp
parsley as needed

Périgueux—Line bottom of cocottes with finely diced foie gras. Break eggs into cocottes, and cook. Garnish with a thread of périgueux sauce.
> 8 oz. (225 g) foie gras
> 5 fl. oz. (1½ dcL) périgueux
>   sauce

Petit-Duc—Line bottom of cocottes with asparagus tips. Break eggs into cocottes, and cook. Garnish with a thread of périgueux sauce.
> 32 asparagus tips
> 5 fl. oz. (1½ dcL) périgueux
>   sauce

Portuguese—Line bottom of cocottes with finely chopped tomatoes and shallots that have been sautéed in butter. Break eggs into cocottes, and cook. Garnish with a thread of tomato sauce.
> 8 oz. (225 g) tomatoes
> 2 oz. (60 g) shallots
> 2 oz. (60 g) butter
> 4 fl. oz. (1 dcL) tomato sauce

Reine—Line bottom of cocottes with minced chicken that has been moistened with cream. Break eggs into cocottes, and cook. Garnish with a thread of fresh cream before serving.
> 8 oz. (225 g) chicken
> 4 fl. oz. (1 dcL) cream

Saint-George—Line bottom of cocottes with onion purée. Break eggs into cocottes, and cook. Cover eggs with cream and grated Parmesan; glaze under broiler.
> 6 fl. oz. (1¾ dcL) onion purée
> 4 fl. oz. (1 dcL) cream
> 2 oz. (60 g) Parmesan cheese

Tartare—Line bottom of cocottes with finely minced raw beef mixed with chopped chives. Break eggs into cocottes, add a little cream, and cook.
> 12 oz. (340 g) raw beef
> chives to taste
> 2 fl. oz. (½ dcL) cream

Zingara—Line bottom of cocottes with ham purée. Break eggs into cocottes, and cook. Cover the cooked eggs with cream and Parmesan cheese; glaze under broiler.
> 8 oz. (225 g) ham purée
> 4 fl. oz. (1 dcL) cream
> 2 oz. (60 g) Parmesan cheese

HARD-BOILED EGGS

All recipes are for 8 eggs.
Basic Preparation: Place eggs in cold water, and bring to a boil. Cook gently for 6 minutes. Remove pan from heat, and let eggs rest in water for 10 more minutes. Remove eggs from water. Crack shells and plunge eggs into cold water. If recipe requires reheating eggs, plunge them in boiling salted water, drain, and dry.

Aurore—Slice eggs into thick round slices. Cover with béchamel sauce flavored with tomato purée. Sprinkle with Gruyère cheese; glaze under broiler. Serve on hot toast or muffins.
> 6 fl. oz. (1¾ dcL) béchamel sauce
> tomato purée to taste
> 2 oz. (60 g) Gruyère cheese

Bagration—Cut eggs in half lengthwise. Place on a bed of risotto. Cover with cream sauce mixed with diced, salted ox tongue, ham, and mushrooms.

8 oz. (225 g) uncooked rice
6 fl. oz. (1¾ dcL) cream sauce
2 oz. (60 g) each ham, ox tongue,
   and mushrooms

Belloy—Cut eggs in half lengthwise. Pass egg yolks through seive. Mix yolks with chopped, cooked shrimp and diced, sautéed mushrooms that have been moistened with Mornay sauce. Glaze under broiler.

2 oz. (60 g) each shrimp and
   mushrooms
6 fl. oz. (1¾ dcL) Mornay sauce

Bretonne—Cut eggs in half lengthwise. Place on a bed of chopped mushrooms, onions, and leeks that have been sautéed in butter. Cover with a béchamel sauce.

4 oz. (115 g) mushrooms
2 oz. (60 g) each onions and leeks
2 oz. (60 g) butter
8 fl. oz. (2¼ dcL) béchamel sauce

Chimay—Cut eggs in half lengthwise. Pass egg yolks through a sieve. Mix yolks with dry duxelles, chopped parsley, and cream. Stuff the egg whites with the mixture. Coat the eggs with a Mornay sauce. Glaze under the broiler.

4 oz. (115 g) dry duxelles
parsley to taste
1 fl. oz. (¼ dcL) cream
6 fl. oz. (1¾ dcL) Mornay sauce

Génoise—Cut eggs in half lengthwise. Pass egg yolks through a sieve. Mix yolks with cream sauce and pounded anchovy fillets. Sprinkle the eggs with herbs and breadcrumbs. Cover with a Mornay sauce. Glaze under a broiler.

2 fl. oz. (½ dcL) cream sauce
3 whole anchovies
parsley, chives, tarragon, and
   breadcrumbs to taste
8 fl. oz. (2¼ dcL) Mornay sauce

Italian—Cut eggs in half lengthwise. Pass egg yolks through a seive. Mix yolks with chopped parsley and mushrooms that have been moistened with tomato sauce. Stuff the egg whites with the mixture. Cover the eggs with cream sauce and grated Parmesan cheese. Glaze under the broiler.

parsley to taste
3 oz. (90 g) mushrooms
1 fl. oz. (30 mL) tomato sauce
14 fl. oz. (4 dcL) cream sauce
3 oz. (90 g) Parmesan cheese

Maintenon—Place whole hard-boiled eggs in prebaked, short-paste tartlets that have been lined with onion purée. Cover the eggs with a Mornay sauce. Sprinkle with grated cheese, and glaze under a broiler.

8 tartlets
4 fl. oz. (1 dcL) onion purée
7 fl. oz. (2 dcL) Mornay sauce
3 oz. (90 g) cheese

Pêcheurs—Cut eggs in half lengthwise. Pass egg yolks through a sieve. Mix egg yolks with salmon purée. Stuff the egg whites with the mixture. Cover the eggs with shrimp sauce. Sprinkle with grated Gruyère cheese, and glaze under the broiler.

4 oz. (115 g) salmon purée
7 fl. oz. (2 dcL) shrimp sauce
4 oz. (115 g) Gruyère cheese

Tripe—Slice eggs into thick round slices. Cover the eggs with onion sauce. Serve on hot toast; garnish with chopped parsley.
8 fl. oz. (2¼ dcL) onion sauce
parsley as needed

SOFT-BOILED EGGS

Basic Preparation: Place eggs in cold water, and bring to a boil. Remove from the stove and allow to rest in the water for 4 minutes. Shell the eggs under cold water, and keep warm in a pan of warm salted water.

POACHED EGGS

All recipes are for 8 eggs.
Basic Preparation: Fill pan with boiling salted water. Add a little vinegar, and bring the water back to a boil. Break eggs into the water, and simmer gently for 3 minutes. Drain and trim whites neatly. Keep in warm water until needed.

Andalouse—Arrange cooked eggs on slices of eggplant sautéed in butter. Cover the eggs with tomato sauce. Sprinkle with diced, blanched green pepper.
8 eggplant slices
2 oz. (60 g) butter
10 fl. oz. (3 dcL) tomato sauce
1 green pepper

Armenonville—Arrange eggs in tartlets that have been lined with creamed asparagus. Cover the eggs

with a suprême sauce, and garnish with chopped parsley.
8 tartlets
4 fl. oz. (1 dcL) creamed asparagus
10 fl. oz. (3 dcL) suprême sauce
parsley as needed

Auber—Arrange cooked eggs in oval tartlets that have been lined with a mixture of minced, cooked beef and mushrooms. Cover the eggs with Madeira sauce.
8 tartlets
12 oz. (340 g) beef and mushroom mixture
10 fl. oz. (3 dcL) Madeira sauce

Aurore—Arrange cooked eggs in puff pastry croustades. Cover the eggs with an aurore sauce. Sprinkle with sieved yolk of hard-boiled eggs and chopped parsley.
8 croustades
10 fl. oz. (3 dcL) aurore sauce
yolks of 2 hard-boiled eggs
parsley as needed

Bagration—Arrange cooked eggs in tartlets that have been lined with cooked macaroni and finely diced, sautéed mushrooms moistened with cream sauce. Garnish with chopped parsley.
8 tartlets
6 oz. (170 g) dry macaroni
4 oz. (115 g) mushrooms
1 oz. (30 g) butter for sautéing
10 fl. oz. (3 dcL) cream sauce
parsley as needed

Bar-le-Duc—Arrange cooked eggs in tartlets that have been lined with chopped artichoke hearts.

Cover the eggs with cream sauce mixed with chopped, fresh tarragon.

8 tartlets
8 artichoke hearts
10 fl. oz. (3 dcL) cream sauce
tarragon to taste

Béarnaise—Surround cooked eggs with gilded duchesse potatoes. Cover the eggs with a reduced demi-glace enriched with butter. Serve with béarnaise sauce as an accompaniment.

1½ lb. (675 g) potatoes
8 fl. oz. (2¼ dcL) demi-glace
1 oz. (30 g) butter
béarnaise sauce to taste

Berlioz—Arrange cooked eggs on large, flat croûtons that have been covered with a purée of game meat. Cover the eggs with chasseur sauce, and garnish with chopped chives.

8 croûtons
8 oz. (225 g) game purée
10 fl. oz. (3 dcL) chasseur sauce
chives as needed

Blanchard—Arrange cooked eggs on slices of toast covered with thinly sliced ox tongue. Cover the eggs with Colbert sauce.

8 shaped toasts
6 oz. (170 g) ox tongue
10 fl. oz. (3 dcL) Colbert sauce

Bohemian—Make nests of duchesse potatoes. Line the nests with pâté. Arrange cooked eggs in the nests. Cover the eggs with chicken velouté. Garnish with diced, cooked ham that has been warmed in Madeira.

1½ lb. (675 g) potatoes
8 oz. (225 g) pâté
10 fl. oz. (3 dcL) chicken velouté
4 oz. (115 g) ham
4 fl. oz. (1 dcL) Madeira

Boston—Arrange cooked eggs in tartlets that have been lined with creamed, smoked cod or haddock. Cover the eggs with cream sauce, and garnish with chopped chives.

8 tartlets
12 oz. (340 g) creamed fish
10 fl. oz. (3 dcL) cream sauce
chives as needed

Boulangère—Arrange cooked eggs on croûtons that have been covered with chopped, sautéed mushrooms. Cover the eggs with Mornay sauce. Sprinkle with grated Parmesan cheese, and glaze under the broiler.

8 croûtons
6 oz. (170 g) mushrooms
2 oz. (60 g) butter for sautéing
10 fl. oz. (3 dcL) Mornay sauce
3 oz. (90 g) Parmesan cheese

Cardinal—Arrange cooked eggs in tartlets that have been lined with finely chopped shrimp or lobster meat moistened with béchamel sauce. Cover the eggs with Cardinal sauce.

8 tartlets
12 oz. (340 g) shrimp or lobster
5 fl. oz. (1½ dcL) béchamel sauce
10 fl. oz. (3 dcL) Cardinal sauce

Cavour—Arrange cooked eggs on beds of buttered noodles. Cover the eggs with Mornay sauce. Sprinkle with Parmesan cheese, and glaze under the broiler.

12 oz. (340 g) dry noodles
3 oz. (90 g) butter
10 fl. oz. (3 dcL) Mornay sauce
2 oz. (60 g) Parmesan cheese

Célia—Arrange cooked eggs on a bed of chopped spinach. Cover the eggs with Mornay sauce. Sprinkle with grated cheese, and glaze under the broiler.

1½ lb. (675 g) cooked spinach
10 fl. oz. (3 dcL) Mornay sauce
2 oz. (60 g) cheese

Chartres—Arrange cooked eggs in tartlets. Cover the eggs with béarnaise sauce, and garnish with blanched tarragon leaves.

8 tartlets
10 fl. oz. (3 dcL) béarnaise sauce
tarragon as needed

Chasseur—Arrange cooked eggs in tartlets that have been lined with chopped, sautéed chicken livers. Cover the eggs with chasseur sauce, and garnish with chopped parsley.

8 tartlets
12 oz. (340 g) chicken livers
3 oz. (90 g) butter for sautéing
10 fl. oz. (3 dcL) chasseur sauce
parsley as needed

Châtelaine—Arrange cooked eggs in tartlets that have been lined with a mixture of unsweetened chestnut purée and creamed onions. Cover eggs with chicken velouté.

8 tartlets
12 oz. (340 g) chestnut purée
4 fl. oz. (1 dcL) creamed onions
20 fl. oz. (6 dcL) chicken velouté

Chivry—Arrange cooked eggs in hollowed croûtons. Cover the eggs with Chivry sauce, and garnish with asparagus tips.

8 croûtons
10 fl. oz. (3 dcL) Chivry sauce
40 asparagus tips

Clamart—Arrange cooked eggs in tartlets that have been lined with a creamed purée of peas. Cover the eggs with suprême sauce, and garnish with chopped parsley.

8 tartlets
8 fl. oz. (2¼ dcL) pea purée
10 fl. oz. (3 dcL) suprême sauce
parsley as needed

Cressonière—Arrange cooked eggs in tartlets that have been lined with 1 small bunch of blanched watercress moistened with fresh cream. Cover the eggs with suprême sauce, and garnish with blanched watercress leaves.

8 tartlets
1 small bunch watercress
3 fl. oz. (¾ dcL) cream
10 fl. oz. (3 dcL) suprême sauce
watercress as needed

Danoise—Arrange cooked egg in tartlets that have been lined with a purée of smoked salmon. Cover the eggs with fish velouté, and garnish with chopped chives.

8 tartlets
8 oz. (225 g) smoked salmon
  purée
10 fl. oz. (3 dcL) fish velouté
chives as needed

Dijonnaise—Arrange cooked eggs in duchesse potato nests. Cover the eggs with red wine sauce. Garnish each egg with a grilled mushroom cap.

1½ lb. (675 g) duchesse potatoes
10 fl. oz. (3 dcL) red wine sauce
8 mushroom caps

Dino—Arrange cooked eggs in tartlets that have been lined with finely diced chicken and mushrooms mixed with a little cream. Cover the eggs with curry sauce.

8 tartlets
12 oz. (340 g) chicken
4 oz. (115 g) mushrooms
2 fl. oz. (½ dcL) cream
10 fl. oz. (3 dcL) curry sauce

Dubarry—Arrange cooked eggs in tartlets that have been lined with creamed cauliflower. Cover with Mornay sauce. Sprinkle with grated cheese, and glaze under the broiler.

8 tartlets
12 oz. (340 g) cauliflower
4 fl. oz. (1 dcL) cream
10 fl. oz. (3 dcL) Mornay sauce
2 oz. (60 g) cheese

Escarlate—Arranged cooked eggs on shaped croûtons. Cover the eggs with tomato sauce enriched with butter. Garnish with chopped ox tongue and chopped parsley.

8 croûtons
10 fl. oz. (3 dcL) tomato sauce
1 oz. (30 g) butter
8 oz. (225 g) smoked ox tongue
parsley as needed

Garcia—Arrange cooked eggs in tartlets that have been lined with chicken purée mixed with blanched, finely chopped red and green peppers. Cover the eggs with Madeira sauce.

8 tartlets
12 oz. (340 g) chicken purée
½ red pepper
½ green pepper
10 fl. oz. (3 dcL) Madeira sauce

Gastronome—Arrange cooked eggs in oval pastry shells that have been lined with asparagus tips in 3 fl. oz. cream sauce. Cover the eggs with 5 fl. oz. cream sauce blended with the same amount of asparagus purée.

8 pastry shells
24 asparagus tips
3 fl. oz. (¾ dcL) cream sauce
5 fl. oz. (1½ dcL) cream sauce
5 fl. oz. (1½ dcL) asparagus
    purée

Gladstone—Arrange cooked eggs in pastry cases or tartlets that have been lined with chestnut purée. Cover the eggs with cream sauce blended with softened liver pâté. Garnish with chopped parsley.

8 tartlets
12 oz. (340 g) chestnut purée
8 fl. oz. (2¼ dcL) cream sauce
2 oz. (60 g) pâté

Indian no. 1—Arrange cooked eggs on a bed of cooked saffron rice. Cover with curry sauce.

10 oz. (280 g) uncooked rice
saffron to color
10 fl. oz. (3 dcL) curry sauce

Indian no. 2—Arrange cooked eggs on a bed of cooked rice that has been flavored with tomato sauce. Cover the eggs with curry sauce, and garnish with chopped chives.

10 oz. (280 g) uncooked rice
tomato sauce to taste
10 fl. oz. (3 dcL) curry sauce
chives as needed

Jean Bart—Arrange cooked eggs in tartlets that have been lined with chopped mussels, mushrooms, and shrimp moistened with béchamel sauce. Cover the eggs with normande sauce, and garnish with sprigs of parsley.

8 tartlets
16 oz. (450 g) mixed chopped mussels, mushrooms, and shrimp
2 fl. oz. (½ dcL) béchamel sauce
10 fl. oz. (3 dcL) normande sauce
parsley as needed

Lafayette—Arrange cooked eggs on croûtons that have been spread with béarnaise sauce. Cover the eggs with stewed, chopped tomatoes.

8 croûtons
3 fl. oz. (¾ dcL) béarnaise sauce
1 lb. (450 g) whole tomatoes

Lénard—Arrange cooked eggs on slices of toast that have been spread with caviar. Cover the eggs with Madeira sauce.

8 slices of toast
5 oz. (140 g) caviar
10 fl. oz. (3 dcL) Madeira sauce

Madrilène—Arrange cooked eggs on croûtons spread with anchovy butter. Cover the eggs with cream sauce mixed with chopped green and black olives.

8 croûtons
3 oz. (90 g) anchovy butter
10 fl. oz. (3 dcL) cream sauce
4 green olives
4 black olives

Massenet—Arrange cooked eggs in nests of duchesse potatoes into which a mixture of minced artichoke bottoms and potatoes has been piped. Cover the eggs with cream sauce mixed with a little tomato sauce. Garnish with sprigs of parsley.

1½ lb. (675 g) potatoes
5 cooked artichoke bottoms
10 fl. oz. (3 dcL) cream sauce
tomato sauce to taste
parsley as needed

Mentonnaise—Arrange cooked eggs on beds of creamed leeks. Cover the eggs with cream sauce. Sprinkle with grated Parmesan cheese, and glaze under the broiler.

2 lb. (900 g) white portion of leeks
cream to bind
10 fl. oz. (3 dcL) cream sauce
3 oz. (90 g) Parmesan cheese

Mirepoix—Arrange cooked eggs on slices of grilled ham set on buttered toast. Cover the eggs with herbed Madeira sauce.

8 slices of ham
8 pieces of buttered toast
10 fl. oz. (3 dcL) Madeira sauce
1 tsp. (5 g) each chives, parsley, and thyme

Navarraise—Arranged cooked eggs on a nest of cooked spaghetti. Cover the eggs with béarnaise sauce, and garnish with finely diced, blanched red and green peppers.

10 oz. (280 g) uncooked spaghetti
10 fl. oz. (3 dcL) béarnaise sauce
red and green peppers as needed

Nicolas—Arrange cooked eggs on pastry shells that have been lined with salmon purée. Cover the eggs with hollandaise sauce, and garnish with caviar.

8 pastry shells
12 oz. (340 g) salmon purée
10 fl. oz. (3 dcL) hollandaise
　　sauce
4 oz. (115 g) caviar

Parmentier—Bake potatoes. Scoop out the pulp and season. Add butter and cream. Stuff this mixture back into potato skins. Arrange one egg on each potato. Cover each egg with Mornay sauce. Sprinkle with Parmesan cheese, and glaze under a broiler.

8 potatoes
salt and pepper
3 oz. (90 g) butter
2 fl. oz. (½ dcL) cream
10 fl. oz. (3 dcL) Mornay sauce
3 oz. (90 g) Parmesan cheese

Perrier—Arrange cooked eggs on a nest of chicken croquette mixture lined with sautéed red peppers. Cover the eggs with parisienne sauce.

1½ lb. (675 g) chicken croquette
　　mixture
8 oz. (225 g) red peppers
10 fl. oz. (3 dcL) parisienne sauce

Scribe—Arrange cooked eggs into pastry shells that have been lined with sautéed, chopped

chicken livers. Cover the eggs with demi-glace.

8 pastry shells
1 lb. (450 g) chicken livers
10 fl. oz. (3 dcL) demi-glace

Suisse—Arrange cooked eggs on slices of toast that have been covered with a thin slice of Gruyère cheese. Cover the eggs with Mornay sauce. Sprinkle with additional grated Gruyère cheese, and glaze under a broiler.

8 slices of toast
8 slices of Gruyère cheese
10 fl. oz. (3 dcL) Mornay sauce
2 oz. (60 g) Gruyère cheese

Voisin—Arrange cooked eggs in tartlets that have been lined with chicken purée. Cover half of each egg with tomato sauce, the other half with cream sauce. Mark the division with a strip of blanched green pepper.

8 tartlets
12 oz. (340 g) chicken purée
5 fl. oz. (1½ dcL) each tomato
　　and cream sauce
8 strips of blanched green pepper

Zingara—Arrange cooked egg in hollowed croûtons that have been lined with thin slices of cooked ham. Cover eggs with Zingara sauce.

8 croûtons
8 oz. (225 g) ham
10 fl. oz. (3 dcL) Zingara sauce

OMELETTES

All recipes are for 2 eggs.
Basic Preparation: Lightly beat

the eggs, add cold water, and season with salt and pepper. Pour the eggs into an omelette pan that contains a small quantity of hot butter. Cook the eggs quickly over a high flame, stirring the center with the back of a fork to allow the remaining liquid egg to reach the heat quickly. Cook until the center is set but still creamy. Fill omelette as desired, and fold over once onto a warmed plate.

2 eggs
1 Tbs. (15 mL) cold water
salt and pepper to taste
½ oz. (15 g) butter

Algerian—Fill the omelette with a mixture of sautéed chopped tomato, green pepper, and onion.

1 oz. (30 g) each chopped tomato, green pepper, and onion

Anchovy—Rub desalted anchovy fillets through a sieve, and add to beaten eggs. Cook as described in the basic recipe. Garnish omelette with anchovy fillets cut into thin strips.

2 anchovies for omelette
1 anchovy for garnish

Argenteuil—Fill the omelette with cooked asparagus tips lightly sautéed in butter. Garnish with more asparagus tips, and cover with a cream sauce.

8 asparagus tips
1 fl. oz. (¼ dcL) cream sauce

Arlequin—Fill the omelette with chopped mushrooms sautéed in butter. Garnish the cooked omelette with bands of tomato sauce, cream sauce, and a velouté colored with purée of spinach.

2 oz. (60 g) mushrooms
1 Tbs. (15 mL) each tomato sauce, cream sauce, and velouté

Arnold Bennett—Fill the omelette with flaked, smoked haddock moistened with a little cream.

3 oz. (90 g) smoked haddock
1 fl. oz. (¼ dcL) cream

Aumale—Fill the omelette with finely diced and sautéed veal kidney that has been moistened with Madeira sauce. Garnish with stewed tomatoes.

2 oz. (60 g) kidney
1 fl. oz. (¼ dcL) Madeira sauce
2 oz. (60 g) stewed tomatoes

Bercy—Add chopped fines herbes to the beaten eggs. Garnish the cooked omelette with grilled chipolata sausages, and cover with tomato sauce.

fines herbes to taste
2 chipolata sausages
1 fl. oz. (¼ dcL) tomato sauce

Bretonne—Sauté chopped leeks, onions, and mushrooms in butter. Drain, and add to beaten eggs.

3 oz. (90 g) assorted vegetables

Chartres—Finely chop tarragon leaves, and add to beaten eggs. Garnish with blanched tarragon leaves.

2 Tbs. (30 g) tarragon leaves
4 whole tarragon leaves

Chasseur—Fill the omelette with chicken livers and chopped mushrooms sautéed in butter. Garnish with the same mixture, and sprinkle with chopped parsley.

    4 oz. (115 g) chicken and mush-
        room mixture
    parsley to taste

Châtelaine—Fill the omelette with chestnut purée that has been moistened with concentrated chicken stock. Serve with a little cream sauce poured over the ends of the omelette.

    4 oz. (115 g) chestnut purée
    1 fl. oz. (¼ dcL) chicken stock
    1 fl. oz. (¼ dcL) cream sauce

Cluny—Fill the omelette with game purée, and garnish with to-mato sauce drizzled over the ends of the omelette.

    3 oz. (90 g) game purée
    1 fl. oz. (¼ dcL) tomato sauce

Dieppoise—Fill the omelette with cooked mussels and shrimp that have been moistened with a little cream. Drizzle white wine sauce over both ends of the omelette.

    1 oz. (30 g) each mussels and
        shrimp
    1 fl. oz. (¼ dcL) white wine sauce

Gasconne—Sauté finely diced ham, chopped garlic and parsley, and sliced onions in butter. Add to the beaten eggs. Serve as a flat om-elette.

    1½ oz. (45 g) diced ham
    small clove garlic
    good pinch chopped parsley
    1 oz. (30 g) onions

Hollandaise—Sauté small strips of smoked salmon in butter. Add

the beaten eggs, and cook. Cover the omelette with hollandaise sauce.

    1½ oz. (45 g) smoked salmon
    1 fl. oz. (¼ dcL) hollandaise
        sauce

Japanese—Fill the omelette with chopped artichoke hearts sautéed in butter and chopped parsley. Gar-nish with cream sauce poured over each end.

    3 oz. (90 g) artichokes
    1 fl. oz. (¼ dcL) cream sauce
    chopped parsley to taste

Lafontaine—Add grated cheese to beaten eggs. Fill cooked omelette with stewed tomatoes. Garnish with a thread of Madeira sauce.

    2 oz. (60 g) cheese
    3 oz. (90 g) tomatoes
    1 fl. oz. (¼ dcL) Madeira sauce

Lorraine—Add finely diced, cooked bacon, grated Gruyère cheese, and chopped scallions to the beaten eggs. Serve as a flat omelette.

    1 oz. (30 g) each bacon, grated
        Gruyère cheese, and scal-
        lions

Mancelle—Fill omelette with a chestnut purée mixed with finely diced, cooked game. Drizzle a thread of chasseur sauce over the omelette.

    2 oz. (60 g) game
    1 oz. (30 g) chestnut purée
    1 fl. oz. (¼ dcL) chasseur sauce

Margaret Friel—Fill the omelette with chopped smoked oysters that have been moistened with a little cream. Drizzle cream sauce on both ends of the omelette, and garnish with parsley in the center.

2 oz. (60 g) oysters
1 Tbs. (15 mL) cream
1 fl. oz. (¼ dcL) cream sauce
parsley as needed

Messinoise—Fill the omelette with fine julienne of smoked sausage that has been mixed with well-drained sauerkraut. Drizzle a thread of demi-glace over the omelette before serving.

1½ oz. (45 g) sausage
2 oz. (60 g) sauerkraut
1 Tbs. (15 mL) demi-glace

Mousseline—Mix the egg yolks with a little cream, and fold in stiffly beaten egg whites. Cook the mixture under the broiler to set the top of the omelette.

Nantaise—Fill the omelette with sardine purée and minced onions. Drizzle a thread of cream sauce on both ends before serving.

2 oz. (60 g) drained sardines
1 oz. (30 g) onion
1 fl. oz. (¼ dcL) cream sauce

Olympia—Fill the omelette with a mixture of crabmeat and minced, sautéed green peppers, moistened with cream. Garnish with cream sauce drizzled over both ends.

2 oz. (60 g) crabmeat
1 Tbs. (15 g) green pepper
1 Tbs. (15 mL) cream
1 fl. oz. (¼ dcL) cream sauce

Poissonnière—Fill the omelette with cooked white fish that has been moistened with white wine sauce. Coat both ends of the

cooked omelette with additional sauce.

3 oz. (90 g) white fish
3 fl. oz. (¾ dcL) white wine sauce

Prélat—Mix finely shredded lettuce with beaten eggs. Fill the omelette with diced, cooked fish or shellfish. Coat both ends of the omelette with cream sauce.

lettuce to taste
2 oz. (60 g) assorted fish
1 fl. oz. (¼ dcL) cream sauce

Rouennaise—Fill the omelette with chopped duck liver that has been sautéed in butter. Garnish with heated red currant jelly drizzled over both ends of the omelette.

2 oz. (60 g) duck liver
1 fl. oz. (¼ dcL) red currant jelly

Savoyarde—Add thinly sliced, cooked potatoes and grated cheese to the beaten eggs. Serve as a flat omelette.

3 oz. (90 g) potatoes
1 Tbs. (15 g) cheese

SHIRRED EGGS

All recipes are for 2 eggs.

Basic Preparation: Shirred eggs are similar to eggs en cocotte, except that two eggs are always served in each cassolette. Butter a cassolette and season it lightly. Lay the base garnish, if required, in the buttered dish. Break two eggs into the dish, and bake in the oven at 350°F (180°C). Garnish the dish according to recipe instructions.

Américaine—Break eggs on a thin slice of lean, cooked ham. Surround

the cooked eggs with a thread of tomato sauce.

2 oz. (60 g) ham
1 Tbs. (15 mL) tomato sauce

Anchovy—Break eggs over a
sprinkling of chopped anchovies.
Garnish cooked eggs with crossed
anchovy fillets.

2 anchovy fillets for base
2 anchovy fillets for garnish

Beurre Noir—Cook eggs as in
the basic preparation. Garnish
with beurre noir poured over the
eggs.

1 Tbs. (15 mL) beurre noir

Duchesse—Lay a base of creamed
potatoes in the dish. Break eggs
onto base, coat with cream, and
bake. Garnish with lightly sautéed
button mushrooms.

6 oz. (170 g) potatoes
1 fl. oz. (¼ dcL) cream
2 oz. (60 g) mushrooms

Egyptian—Break eggs onto a
base of minced, sautéed leeks and
onions. Garnish cooked eggs with a
thread of tomato sauce.

4 oz. (115 g) leek and onion mixture
1 Tbs. (15 mL) tomato sauce

Florentine—Break eggs onto a
base of chopped, cooked spinach.
Sprinkle with grated cheese. Coat
eggs with Mornay sauce, and bake
in the oven.

3 oz. (90 g) chopped spinach
1 Tbs. (15 g) grated cheese
1 Tbs. (15 mL) Mornay sauce

Au Gratin—Break eggs onto a
base of Mornay sauce. Cover with
additional sauce, and bake.

2 fl. oz. (½ dcL) Mornay sauce

Lorraine—Line a dish with crisp
fried bacon and grated Gruyère
cheese. Cover the eggs with cream,
and bake.

3 oz. (90 g) uncooked bacon
1 oz. (30 g) Gruyère cheese
1 fl. oz. (¼ dcL) cream

Maximillian—Place baked tomato
halves in dish, and break eggs into
the tomatoes. Cover the eggs with
breadcrumbs and grated cheese;
bake.

1 tomato
1 oz. (30 g) breadcrumbs
1 oz. (30 g) cheese

Mirabeau—Line the bottom of a
dish with anchovy butter. Break
eggs onto the base. Top the cooked
eggs with anchovy fillets, and garnish with stuffed olives.

1 oz. (30 g) anchovy butter
3 anchovy fillets
olives as needed

Miror—Break eggs into a dish,
coat with thick cream, and bake.

2 Tbs. (30 mL) cream

Monégasque—Line the bottom of
a dish with stewed tomatoes and a
pinch of tarragon. Break the eggs
onto the base. Garnish cooked eggs
with anchovy fillets and a thread of
tomato sauce.

1 oz. (30 g) tomatoes
pinch of tarragon

3 anchovy fillets
1 fl. oz. (¼ dcL) tomato sauce

Normandy—Line the bottom of a dish with raw oysters. Mix the oyster liquor with a little cream, and pour the mixture over the base. Break the eggs onto the base. Surround the cooked eggs with normande sauce.

4 oysters
1 Tbs. (15 mL) cream
1 fl. oz. (¼ dcL) normande sauce

Saint-Hubert—Line the bottom of a dish with minced game that has been moistened with cream. Break eggs onto the base. Garnish cooked eggs with a thread of poivrade sauce.

3 oz. (90 g) minced game
1 Tbs. (15 mL) cream
1 fl. oz. (¼ dcL) poivrade sauce

Trouville—Line the bottom of a dish with mussels, shrimp, and mushrooms that have been moistened with fish fumet. Break the eggs onto the base. Cover the cooked eggs with shrimp sauce.

1 oz. (30 g) each mussels, shrimp, and mushrooms
1 fl. oz. (¼ dcL) fish fumet
1 fl. oz. (¼ dcL) shrimp sauce

All recipes are for 2 lb. (900 g) fish, unless otherwise noted.

BASS

See also recipes under Carp.

Lemon Butter—Baste fish with melted butter, and broil in pre-heated oven or under broiler for 10 minutes per inch of thickness for fresh fish. Turn the fish once it has browned on one side. Brush with melted butter again, and finish broiling. Melt butter, mix in lemon juice, and pour over cooked fish.

    4 oz. (115 g) butter
    lemon juice to taste

Pan-fried—Remove head and tail of fish; clean well. Dip the fish in flour, then in milk, and roll them in breadcrumbs or cornmeal. Sauté in butter, oil, or bacon fat.

    4 oz. (115 g) flour
    4 fl. oz. (1 dcL) milk
    4 oz. (115 g) breadcrumbs or cornmeal
    4 oz. (115 g) butter, oil, or bacon fat

Parsley Butter—Proceed as for broiled bass with lemon butter, sub-stituting 4 oz. (115 g) chopped pars-ley for lemon juice.

Tartar Sauce—Clean and wash bass. Place it on an oiled baking dish. Dot with butter, season with salt and pepper, and bake at 450°F (230°C) until cooked. Baste fre-quently while cooking. Mix mayon-naise, chopped onion, lemon juice, chopped dill pickle, and chopped parsley. Serve with cooked fish.

    1 oz. (30 g) butter
    salt and pepper to taste
    16 oz. (450 g) mayonnaise
    2 Tbs. (30 g) each chopped onion, dill pickle, and parsley
    2 tsp. (10 mL) lemon juice

BLUEFISH

Cognac—Baste the fish with melted butter, and broil in a pre-heated oven or under broiler for 10 minutes per inch of thickness for fresh fish. Turn the fish once it has browned. Brush with melted butter again, and finish broiling. Serve the fish on a bed of dried thyme, fennel, bay leaf, and parsley. Pour Cognac over the fish, and ignite. Let Co-gnac burn until the herbs are smok-ing.

1 oz. (30 g) butter
thyme, fennel, bay leaf, and parsley to taste
2 fl. oz. (60 mL) Cognac

Crabmeat—Stuff the bluefish
with seasoned crabmeat. Tie up the
fish, and place it on an oiled baking
dish. Dot with butter, and season
with salt and black pepper. Bake
the fish at 425°F (220°C) until
cooked. Serve with lemon butter.
    12 oz. (360 g) crabmeat
    salt and pepper to taste
    1 oz. (30 g) butter
    2 oz. (60 g) lemon butter

Meunière—Heat butter in a frying
pan until very hot. Fry fish fillets
until golden on one side; turn and
brown on the other side. Remove
fish to a hot platter. Pour butter
from pan over the fish. Serve with
lemon juice and chopped parsley.
    2 oz. (60 g) butter
    lemon juice and chopped parsley
        to taste

Rémoulade—Dip fish fillets into
flour, beaten egg, and breadcrumbs.
Sauté in butter or bacon fat. Season
with salt and pepper to taste. Mix
mayonnaise, chopped garlic, hard-
boiled eggs, parsley, tarragon, capers, dry mustard, and anchovy
paste. Serve with fish.
    flour, as needed to bread
    eggs, beaten, as needed to bread
    breadcrumbs, as needed to bread
    butter, as needed to sauté
    salt and pepper, to taste
    16 oz. (480 g) mayonnaise
    2 cloves garlic, chopped
    2 hard-boiled eggs, finely
        chopped

1 Tbs. (15 g) chopped parsley
1 Tbs. (15 g) finely chopped tarragon
1 Tbs. (15 g) capers
1 tsp. (5 g) dry mustard
1 tsp. (5 g) anchovy paste

BUTTERFISH

Almonds and Cream—Dust the
fish with flour, and sauté it in butter
and oil until browned. Remove to a
hot platter. Add almonds to the fat
remaining in the pan, and toast until
golden brown. Stir in cream and
nutmeg; simmer. Pour sauce over
fish, and garnish with chopped scallions.
    4 oz. (115 g) flour
    2 oz. (60 g) butter
    4 Tbs. (60 mL) oil
    4 oz. (115 g) slivered almonds
    4 fl. oz. (1 dcL) heavy cream
    ¼ tsp. (1 g) nutmeg
    finely chopped scallions as
        needed

Apples and Cider—Peel, core,
and dice the apples. Toss with
lemon juice. Butter a baking dish,
and sprinkle it with tarragon, salt,
and pepper. Add a layer of apple.
Top each piece of butterfish with
chopped tomato. Pour cider over
fish, and bake in preheated oven at
425°F (220°C) for approximately 20
minutes. Garnish with chopped
parsley.
    2 apples
    juice of 1 lemon
    tarragon to taste
    salt and pepper to taste
    1 ripe tomato, peeled, seeded,
        and chopped

8 fl. oz. (2¼ dcL) apple cider
finely chopped parsley

Curry and Tomatoes—Sauté
finely chopped onions in butter. Dip
butterfish fillets in flour seasoned
with curry powder and salt. Sauté
fish in the pan with the onion. Remove fish to a hot platter. Deglaze
pan with white wine and pour liquid
over fish. Serve with tomato sauce
mixed with a pinch of curry powder.
  1 onion, chopped
  2 oz. (60 g) butter
  2 Tbs. (30 g) curry powder
  salt to taste
  8 fl. oz. (2¼ dcL) tomato sauce

Niçoise—Sauté butterfish in olive
oil. Grill or sauté tomatoes in olive
oil, and season with tarragon and
garlic. Arrange the fish on a bed of
tomatoes, and top with strips of anchovies. Garnish with ripe olives.
  2 fl. oz. (60 mL) olive oil
  3 ripe tomatoes, sliced
  2 cloves garlic, chopped
  tarragon to taste
  8 anchovy fillets
  ripe olives as needed

Sesame Seed—Dip fish fillets in
seasoned flour, then in beaten egg;
roll in sesame seeds. Sauté fish in
butter with whole peeled slices of
orange until done.
  4 oz. (115 g) seasoned flour
  2 eggs, beaten
  8 oz. (240 g) sesame seeds,
      toasted
  1 orange, sliced

CARP

See also recipes under Bass.
  Beer—First, brown carp cutlets
in butter. Remove to 400°F (200°C)
oven and braise with chopped onions, celery, and diced gingerbread.
Cover with light ale, and bake for
approximately 15 minutes. Thicken
cooking liquid with beurre manié.
Strain, and pour over fish.
  2 oz. (60 g) each onions, celery,
      and gingerbread
  12 fl. oz. (3½ dcL) light ale
  2 oz. (60 g) beurre manié

  Bleu—Cook carp in salted water
and vinegar, and remove to a hot
platter. Pour beurre noisette over
fish and serve with grated fresh
horseradish or raifort sauce.
  Canotière—Stuff the carp with
forcemeat, and place it in a buttered
baking dish sprinkled with chopped
shallots. Surround the fish with button mushrooms. Moisten with white
wine, sprinkle with breadcrumbs,
dot with butter, and bake in pre-
heated 450°F (230°C) oven for 15–20
minutes. Garnish with crayfish tails
or large shrimp and fleurons. Serve
with crayfish or shrimp sauce.
  8 oz. (240 g) forcemeat
  1 oz. (30 g) shallots
  4 oz. (115 g) mushrooms
  4 fl. oz. (1 dcL) white wine
  breadcrumbs to cover
  2 oz. (60 g) butter
  2 crayfish or 2 shrimp and 2 fleu-
      rons per portion

  Jutlandaise—Marinate fillets in
tarragon vinegar and water with
ground cloves. Bake in light ale

with a little of the marinade and the grated lemon zest. Remove the fish to a hot platter. Reduce liquid by one-third, thicken with gingerbread, and enrich with butter. Add raisins, and pour over fish.

- 1 tsp. (5 g) clove for each pint of marinade
- 3 fl. oz. (¾ dcL) marinade (equal parts tarragon vinegar and water)
- 10 fl. oz. (3 dcL) light ale
- zest of 1 lemon
- 4 oz. (115 g) gingerbread
- 2 oz. (60 g) butter
- 1 oz. (30 g) raisins

Oriental—Poach carp fillets in white wine and fish stock with chopped onion and shallots. Add bouquet garni and crushed garlic. Remove fish to a hot platter. Reduce cooking liquid by one-third, and add saffron, a pinch of cayenne pepper, and chopped almonds. Cover carp with sauce.

- 5 fl. oz. (1½ dcL) white wine
- 8 fl. oz. (2 dcL) fish stock
- 1 oz. (30 g) each onions and shallots
- bouquet garni
- 2 cloves garlic
- saffron to color
- pinch of cayenne pepper
- 2 oz. (60 g) chopped almonds

Raisins—Proceed as for Oriental recipe, but add sugar, raisins, sultanas, and currants that have been soaked in warm water and brandy to the sauce.

- 1 oz. (30 g) each sugar and dried fruits

Red Wine—Poach small whole fish in red wine flavored with mushroom essence and chopped shallot. Remove fish to a hot platter. Reduce cooking liquid by one-half, and thicken with beurre manié. Pour sauce over fish, and garnish with fleurons.

- 12 fl. oz. (3½ dcL) red wine
- 1 fl. oz. (¼ dcL) mushroom essence
- 1 oz. (30 g) shallot
- 1 oz. (30 g) beurre manié

Sainte-Menehould—Blanch fillets in fish stock. After fillets have cooled, dip them in beaten egg and breadcrumbs mixed with crushed almonds. Pan-fry. Garnish with chopped, pickled gherkins and cucumbers. Serve with hash sauce mixed with chopped anchovies, on the side.

- fish stock to cover
- 2 eggs
- 1 oz. (30 g) almonds in 5 oz. (140 g) breadcrumbs
- gherkins and cucumbers as needed
- 4 anchovies in 10 fl. oz. (3 dcL) hash sauce

COD

Alentejana—Layer poached, flaked cod fillet; diced, fried lean pork; and chopped onions in a baking dish alternately with sliced, cooked potatoes and chopped tomatoes. Moisten with milk, sprinkle with breadcrumbs, and bake.

- 8 oz. (225 g) pork
- 6 oz. (170 g) onions
- 1½ lb. (675 g) potatoes

12 oz. (340 g) tomatoes
milk as needed
breadcrumbs to cover

Bandong—Marinate thick fillets
in oil, lemon juice, curry powder,
and chopped shallots. Coat fish with
flour, and pan-fry. Serve on plain,
boiled rice with sweet chutney and
Indian relish.
Marinade:
2 fl. oz. (½ dcL) oil
6 fl. oz. (1½ dcL) lemon juice
1 tsp. (5 g) curry powder
1 oz. (30 g) shallots
Cream au Gratin—Poach and
flake fillets. Place fish in a casserole
over the 5 fl. oz. Mornay sauce.
Surround with piped, creamed potatoes, and coat with the 7 fl. oz.
sauce. Sprinkle with grated cheese,
and glaze.
5 fl. oz. (1½ dcL) Mornay sauce
2 lb. (900 g) potatoes
7 fl. oz. (2 dcL) Mornay sauce
3 oz. (90 g) cheese

Diaz—Mix poached, flaked fillets
with chopped mushrooms and
blanched, diced green peppers.
Moisten with tomato sauce. Put in
baking dish, sprinkle with breadcrumbs, dot with butter, and bake.
6 oz. (170 g) mushrooms
6 oz. (170 g) green peppers
7 fl. oz. (2 dcL) tomato sauce
breadcrumbs to cover
2 oz. (60 g) butter

Dimitri—Cover poached steaks
with white wine sauce mixed with
anchovy butter and chopped anchovies.

12 fl. oz. (3½ dcL) white wine
sauce
1½ oz. (45 g) anchovy butter
3 anchovies

Flamande—Poach in white wine
flavored with chopped shallots and
ground fennel. Remove fish to a hot
platter. Reduce liquid by one-third,
and thicken with white breadcrumbs. Cover fish with sauce, and
garnish with peeled, sliced lemon.
12 fl. oz. (3½ dcL) white wine
1 oz. (30 g) shallots
ground fennel to taste
2 oz. (60 g) white breadcrumbs or
as needed
lemon slices as needed

Portuguese—Place cod fillets in a
buttered baking pan with chopped
onions, garlic, and sliced, raw potatoes. Cover with fish fumet. Bake.
Garnish with chopped parsley.
1½ oz. (45 g) onions
garlic to taste
1½ lb. (675 g) potatoes
fish fumet as needed
chopped parsley as needed

Printanière—Pan-fry cod fillets in
butter. Cover with a cream sauce
blended with purée of asparagus.
Serve with boiled new potatoes,
spring carrots, and buttered green
peas.
10 fl. oz. (3 dcL) cream sauce
2 fl. oz. (½ dcL) asparagus purée
vegetables as desired

DRUM

Cold Bayou—Poach fish in water
mixed with sliced onion. Cool and

debone. Add bones to broth, and reduce by one-third. Break fish into pieces, and mix with green onion, green pepper, and celery. Mix mustard with lemon juice, and stir into fish mixture. Soak gelatin in the water. Add strained broth and fish mixture to gelatin, and pour into mold. Chill.

1 onion, sliced, for poaching
2 oz. (60 g) each chopped onion, green pepper, and celery
1 tsp. (5 g) dry mustard
1 Tbs. (15 mL) lemon juice
½ oz. (15 g) gelatin
2 oz. (60 mL) water

Creole—Fry bacon. Add butter to bacon fat, and sauté onions and garlic. Add sieved tomatoes, bay leaf, cloves, thyme, salt, and pepper. Clean the fish, leaving it whole. Place it in an oiled baking pan. Cover it with sauce. Garnish the cooked fish with bacon slices, sliced eggs, and black olives.

4 slices bacon
3 Tbs. (45 g) butter
2 onions, chopped
garlic to taste
24 fl. oz. (7 dcL) cooked tomatoes
1 bay leaf
2 cloves
½ tsp. (2 g) thyme
salt and pepper to taste
sliced, hard-boiled eggs
black olives

EEL

Catalan—Skin the eel, cut it in pieces, and pan-fry in oil. Arrange the eel on a bed of sautéed green peppers, onions, tomatoes, and garlic. Season, add cayenne pepper, and finish with chopped parsley.

6 oz. (170 g) green peppers
6 oz. (170 g) onions
8 oz. (225 g) tomatoes
2 cloves garlic
salt and pepper
cayenne pepper and parsley

Gourmet—Skin the eel, cut it in pieces, and poach it in white wine and fish stock. Arrange the eel on a bed of rice garnished with crayfish tails or jumbo shrimp. Cover with cream sauce finished with crayfish or shrimp butter.

7 fl. oz. (2 dcL) each white wine and fish stock
6 oz. (170 g) uncooked rice
8 crayfish tails
8 fl. oz. (2¼ dcL) cream sauce
1½ oz. (45 g) crayfish butter

Italian—Skin, and cut eel into pieces. Fry in oil to stiffen. Remove pieces. Brown chopped onions, and add shallots and mushrooms. Return eel to pan. Moisten with white wine and tomato sauce; simmer until cooked. Arrange in casserole, and sprinkle with chopped tarragon and parsley.

1 oz. (30 g) onion
1 oz. (30 g) shallots
4 oz. (115 g) mushrooms
4 fl. oz. (1 dcL) white wine
7 fl. oz. (2 dcL) tomato sauce
tarragon and parsley to taste

Rioja—Skin the eel, and cut it into pieces. Cook eel in red wine with a dash of tarragon vinegar, chopped onions, red peppers, bay leaf, and garlic. Strain the cooking liquid, and mix the cooked aromatics with the cooked rice. Serve fish on this rice base.

dash of tarragon vinegar
6 oz. (170 g) onions
6 oz. (170 g) red pepeprs
1 bay leaf
2 cloves garlic
6 oz. (170 g) uncooked rice

FLOUNDER

All recipes are also suitable for sole.

All recipes are for approximately 2 lb. (900 g) fillets or 2¼ lb. (1 kg) whole fish.

Alexandrine—Poach fillets in fumet and white wine. Arrange on a bed of stewed tomatoes and mushrooms. Cover with Bercy sauce, and garnish with thin slices of lobster meat.

12 fl. oz. (3½ dcL) fish fumet
5 fl. oz. (1½ dcL) white wine
1 lb. (450 g) tomatoes
8 oz. (225 g) mushrooms
12 fl. oz. (3½ dcL) Bercy sauce
lobster meat as needed

Alsacienne—Poach fillets in fumet. Arrange fish on a bed of well-drained sauerkraut, and cover with Mornay sauce. Sprinkle with cheese, and glaze under broiler.

2 lb. (900 g) sauerkraut
12 fl. oz. (3½ dcL) Mornay sauce
cheese as needed

Amandine—Dredge fillets in flour. Pan-fry in butter with slivered almonds. Remove to a hot platter. Scatter almonds over fish. Mix pan butter with lemon juice, and pour over fillets.

flour as needed
6 oz. (170 g) butter
8 oz. (225 g) slivered almonds
2 fl. oz. (½ dcL) lemon juice

Américaine—Fold fillets, and poach in fumet and white wine. Arrange on a hot platter. Place a slice of lobster meat on each fillet. Cover with américaine sauce.

12 fl. oz. (3½ dcL) fish fumet
5 fl. oz. (1½ dcL) white wine
12 slices lobster meat
16 fl. oz. (4½ dcL) américaine
    sauce

D'Artois—Roll out puff pastry, cut into rectangles, and spread with forcemeat. Place folded fillets onto rectangles, and cover with second rectangle of pastry. Brush with egg yolk, and bake at 400°F (200°C) for approximately 30 minutes.

2 lb. (900 g) puff paste
1¼ lb. (575 g) forcemeat

Batalière—Spread fillets with forcemeat. Fold, and poach in fumet. Arrange each fillet on a pastry barquette lined with a mixture of chopped shrimp and mussels moistened with white wine sauce. Coat each fillet with parsley sauce.

12 oz. (340 g) forcemeat
12 barquettes
12 oz. (340 g) shrimp
6 oz. (170 g) mussels
white wine sauce to moisten
12 fl. oz. (3½ dcL) parsley sauce

Bonaparte—Fold fillets and poach in fumet and white wine. Remove to a hot platter. Reduce cooking liquid by one-third, enrich with butter and cream, and pour over fillets. Garnish with boiled, baby new potatoes and chopped parsley.

12 fl. oz. (3½ dcL) fish fumet
12 fl. oz. (3½ dcL) white wine
1½ oz. (45 g) butter
2 fl. oz. (½ dcL) cream
boiled, baby new potatoes as
    needed
chopped parsley as needed

Cancalaise—Fold fillets, and poach in fumet and oyster liquor. Remove to a hot platter. Reduce cooking liquid by one-third, add chopped oysters and shrimp, and mix with normande sauce. Cover fillets with this sauce.

20 fl. oz. (6 dcL) fish fumet
oyster liquor as available
12 oysters
6 oz. (170 g) shrimp
5 fl. oz. (1½ dcL) normande sauce

Caprice—Dip fillets in butter and breadcrumbs, and grill. Serve on fried banana halves. Cover with bâtarde sauce mixed with lemon juice, or Robert sauce.

Carmen—Pan-fry fillets in butter. Garnish with julienned red peppers and blanched tarragon leaves. Serve with béarnaise sauce.

Casanova—Roll fillets, and poach in fumet and mushroom essence. Arrange on a hot platter covered with a base of peeled, cored, and poached apples. Reduce cooking liquid by one-half, and mix with hollandaise sauce. Cover fillets with sauce, and garnish with julienne of blanched red peppers.

12 fl. oz. (3½ dcL) fish fumet
3 fl. oz. (¾ dcL) mushroom es-
    sence
12 apples
9 fl. oz. (2½ dcL) hollandaise
    sauce
julienned red peppers as needed

Cecelia—Pan-fry fillets in butter; pour browned butter over fillets; garnish with asparagus tips.

Cingalèse—Poach fish fillets in fumet. Arrange on a bed of rice pilaf mixed with finely diced red and green peppers. Cover with white sauce flavored with curry.

15 fl. oz. (4½ dcL) fish fumet
12 oz. (340 g) uncooked rice
red and green peppers to taste
9 fl. oz. (2½ dcL) white sauce
curry powder to taste

Circassienne—Lay slices of peeled zucchini in buttered baking dish. Place fillets on top, moisten with white wine, and dot with butter. Cover, and bake in oven.

16 oz. (450 g) zucchini
7 fl. oz. (2 dcL) white wine
2 oz. (60 g) butter

Clarence—Poach fillets in fumet. Arrange on ovals of duchesse potatoes. Cover with américaine sauce mixed with diced lobster and curry powder. Garnish each fillet with a grilled mushroom.

fish fumet as needed
duchesse potatoes as needed
12 fl. oz. (3½ dcL) américaine
    sauce
5 oz. (140 g) lobster meat
curry powder to taste
12 mushroom caps

Czarina—Fold and poach fillets. Arrange on a hot platter. Coat with white wine sauce mixed with fresh cream and grated horseradish. Garnish with circles of toast spread with caviar.

Deauvillaise—Poach fillets in fumet, cream, and minced onions. Arrange on a hot platter. Reduce cooking liquid by one-fourth, and enrich with butter. Pour sauce over fish, and garnish with fleurons.

16 fl. oz. (4½ dcL) fish fumet
5 fl. oz. (1½ dcL) cream
4 oz. (115 g) onions
1½ oz. (45 g) butter
fleurons as needed

Dorée—Pan-fry fillets in butter; serve with slices of peeled lemon.

Edouard IV—Marinate fillets in brandy for a half-hour. Drain fillets, and coat with flour. Pan-fry in butter. Arrange on a hot platter. Mix white wine sauce with meat glaze and anchovy paste; enrich with butter. Pour sauce over fillets.

brandy as needed
12 fl. oz. (3½ dcL) white wine sauce
2 fl. oz. (½ dcL) meat glaze
1 oz. (30 g) anchovy paste
1½ oz. (45 g) butter

François I—Poach fillets in white wine with butter, chopped onion, diced tomato, and minced mushrooms. Arrange on a hot platter. Reduce cooking liquid by one-third, and coat fillets with the sauce.

16 fl. oz. (4½ dcL) white wine
1½ oz. (45 g) butter
3 oz. (90 g) onions

6 oz. (170 g) tomatoes
4 oz. (115 g) mushrooms

Gismond—Poach fillets in fumet and port wine. Arrange on a hot platter. Reduce cooking liquid by one-third, and thicken with egg yolks and cream. Add cayenne pepper. Pour over fillets, and glaze under broiler.

12 fl. oz. (3½ dcL) fish fumet
5 fl. oz. (1½ dcL) port
2 egg yolks
2 fl. oz. (½ dcL) cream
cayenne pepper to taste

Grand-Hôtel—Pan-fry fillets in butter. Garnish with diced, sautéed potatoes and artichoke bottoms. Pour browned butter over fillets.

Havaraise—Poach fillets in fumet. Arrange on a hot platter. Cover with Bercy sauce. Garnish with mussels stuffed with forcemeat (or minced mushrooms) that have been dipped in beaten egg and bread crumbs and deep-fried.

Ismaîl—Poach fillets in fumet flavored with curry. Arrange on a hot platter. Reduce cooking liquid by one-fourth, enrich with butter, and add white grapes. Cover fillets with the sauce, and glaze under the broiler.

16 fl. oz. (4½ dcL) fish fumet
curry powder to taste
2 oz. (60 g) butter
6 oz. (170 g) grapes

Livornaise—Layer stewed tomatoes, onions, and garlic on the bottom of a baking dish. Lay fillets on base. Moisten with white wine, sprinkle with breadcrumbs, and drizzle with oil. Bake in the oven. Add lemon juice and parsley before serving.

12 oz. (340 g) tomatoes
5 oz. (140 g) onions
2 cloves garlic
5 fl. oz. (1½ dcL) white wine
breadcrumbs and oil as needed
lemon juice and chopped parsley
    as needed

Louisiana—Pan-fry fillets in butter. Garnish with slices of fried banana and diced, cooked red peppers. Pour browned butter over fillets before serving.

6 bananas
4 oz. (115 g) red peppers
3 oz. (90 g) butter

Marianette—Fold fillets, and poach in fumet. Arrange on slices of baked eggplant covered with minced mushrooms. Coat fillets with Mornay sauce, and glaze under the broiler.

Mathilde—Poach fillets in white wine. Arrange fillets on a hot platter. Cover with white wine sauce blended with onion purée and cream. Garnish with slices of zucchini sautéed in butter.

12 fl. oz. (3½ dcL) white wine
    sauce
5 fl. oz. (1½ dcL) onion purée
2 fl. oz. (½ dcL) cream
zucchini slices as desired

Mercédès—Poach fillets in white wine with shallots, butter, and meat glaze or oyster sauce. Remove to a hot platter. Reduce cooking liquid by one-third, and enrich with cream. Cover fillets with sauce.

16 fl. oz. (4½ dcL) white wine
2 oz. (60 g) shallots
1½ oz. (45 g) butter
2 fl. oz. (½ dcL) meat glaze
2 fl. oz. (½ dcL) cream

Meunière—Coat fillets with flour, and pan-fry in butter. Pour browned butter over fillets, and garnish with chopped parsley and lemon.

Monaco—Poach fillets in fumet. Remove fillets to a hot platter. Cover with white wine sauce mixed with tomato purée, chopped parsley, and basil. Garnish with poached oysters and croûtons.

16 fl. oz. (4½ dcL) fish fumet
16 fl. oz. (4½ dcL) white wine
    sauce
1 Tbs. (15 mL) tomato purée
parsley and basil to taste
24 oysters
croûtons as needed

Montespan—Poach fillets in fumet and white wine with minced mushrooms and chopped parsley. Arrange on a hot platter. Reduce liquid by one-third; enrich with cream and butter. Coat fillets with the sauce.

12 fl. oz. (3½ dcL) fish fumet
12 fl. oz. (3½ dcL) white wine
6 oz. (170 g) mushrooms
chopped parsley to taste
2 fl. oz. (½ dcL) cream
1½ oz. (45 g) butter

Murat—Cut fillets into goujons, roll and dredge with seasoned flour, and pan-fry in butter. Arrange on dish with diced, sautéed potatoes and artichoke bottoms. Pour browned butter over fillets.

Olga—Poach fillets in fumet. Arrange each fillet on a baked potato that has been scooped out and lined with a mixture of shrimp and mushrooms. Coat with white wine sauce, and glaze under broiler.

fish fumet as needed
1 baked potato for each fillet
12 Tbs. (180 g) shrimp and mushroom mixture
12 fl. oz. (3½ dcL) white wine sauce

Orly—Dip fillets in a light batter, and deep-fry. Serve with tomato sauce.

Sully—Dip fillets in beaten egg and breadcrumbs; deep-fry. Spread anchovy butter on each fillet; serve béarnaise sauce separately.

Thérèse—Roll fillets in paupiettes; poach in fumet. Arrange fillets on a hot platter. Cover in white sauce mixed with lobster coral.

fish fumet as needed
12 fl. oz. (3½ dcL) white sauce
lobster coral to taste

Verdi—Poach fillets in fumet, and arrange them on a bed of macaroni mixed with chopped shrimp. Coat with Mornay sauce, and glaze under the broiler.

fish fumet as needed
14 oz. (400 g) macaroni
10 oz. (280 g) shrimp
16 fl. oz. (4½ dcL) Mornay sauce

GROUPER

All recipes are also suitable for seabass.

Italian—Put vegetables, herbs, garlic, seasonings, wine, and water in a Dutch oven; bring mixture to a boil. Add fish, and cook. Serve with white sauce mixed with lemon juice.

8 oz. (225 g) each chopped onions, carrots, and celery
parsley and thyme to taste
1 bay leaf
2 cloves of garlic, chopped
1 tsp (5 g) each salt and pepper
14 fl. oz. (4 dcL) red wine
14 fl. oz. (4 dcL) water
8 fl. oz. (2¼ dcL) white sauce
lemon juice to taste

Lettuce—Cook chopped scallions in butter in a skillet. Add wine, then lettuce. Season fish. Add fish to skillet, and cook. Garnish with thyme, parsley, and lemon wedges.

1 oz. (30 g) butter
3 scallions, chopped
2 fl. oz. (½ dcL) white wine
1 large head of Boston lettuce, chopped
salt and pepper to taste
thyme, parsley, and lemon wedges as needed

Sweet and Sour—Poach fish fillets. Mix vinegar, water, garlic, and cornstarch-soy sauce mixture in saucepan. Bring to a boil, and cook until thickened. Add bamboo shoots, green pepper, pineapple, and tomato. Pour over fish.

2 fl. oz. (½ dcL) cider vinegar
8 fl. oz. (2¼ dcL) water
1 clove garlic, chopped
1½ Tbs. (22 g) cornstarch mixed in 2 Tbs. (30 mL) soy sauce
8 oz. (225 g) bamboo shoots
1 green pepper, cut into squares
8 oz. (225 g) pineapple chunks

1 tomato, peeled, seeded, and
chopped

HADDOCK

All recipes are also suitable for cod.

Ancienne—Poach fillets in white
wine or fumet, and arrange on a
platter. Cover lightly with caper
sauce mixed with chopped gherkins.

16 fl. oz. (4½ dcL) poaching liquid
12 fl. oz. (3½ dcL) caper sauce
1½ oz. (45 g) gherkins

Buena Vista—Poach fillets in
fumet, and arrange fish on a platter.
Cover fillets with matelote sauce
mixed with diced shrimp, tomatoes,
and mushrooms.

fumet as needed
12 fl. oz. (3½ dcL) matelote sauce
3 oz. (90 g) shrimp
4 oz. (115 g) tomatoes
3 oz. (90 g) mushrooms

Butter Sauce—Poach fillets in
salted water; drain. Garnish fish
with parsley and boiled potatoes;
serve with melted butter.

Flamande—Poach fillets in white
wine with button mushrooms and
baby white onions. Arrange fish on
a platter. Reduce cooking liquid by
one-third, and add chopped parsley.
Coat fish.

16 fl. oz. (4½ dcL) white wine
4 oz. (115 g) each button mushrooms and baby white onions
chopped parsley to taste

Herbs—Place fillets in a buttered
gratin dish sprinkled with chopped

mushrooms, onions, and parsley.
Moisten with white wine, cover
with breadcrumbs, and dot with
butter. Bake.

4 oz. (115 g) mushrooms
3 oz. (90 g) onions
parsley to taste
8 fl. oz. (2¼ dcL) white wine
3 oz. (90 g) breadcrumbs
1 oz. (30 g) butter

Lyonnaise—Fry fillets in butter,
and arrange on a dish. Cover with
browned butter with a dash of tarragon vinegar added. Sprinkle with
chopped parsley, and garnish with
fried onions.

3 oz. (90 g) butter
dash of tarragon vinegar
parsley to taste
fried onions as needed

Maître d'Hôtel—Fry fillets, and
arrange on a hot platter. Serve
maître d'hôtel butter on each
portion.

Oysters—Poach fillets in white
wine or fumet. Serve with oyster
sauce. Garnish with poached oysters and chopped parsley.

16 fl. oz. (4½ dcL) poaching liquid
12 fl. oz. (3½ dcL) oyster sauce
12 to 16 oysters
parsley as needed

Poached—Poach fillets in white
wine. Drain, and serve on a hot
platter with an appropriate sauce,
such as anchovy, lobster, or
parsley.

Portuguese—Cut fillets into large
squares, and place them in a buttered baking dish over a bed of

stewed onions, tomatoes, garlic, and chopped parsley. Moisten with white wine, cover, and bake in hot oven (400°F, 200°C).

6 oz. (170 g) onions
6 oz. (170 g) tomatoes
garlic to taste
parsley to taste
7 fl. oz. (2 dcL) white wine

HALIBUT

Au Gratin—Poach halibut, and place in a buttered baking dish. Cover with Mornay sauce. Sprinkle with buttered breadcrumbs and finely grated Swiss cheese, and pass under the broiler until brown.

8 fl. oz. (2¼ dcL) Mornay sauce
4 oz. (115 g) buttered bread-
    crumbs
4 oz. (115 g) Swiss cheese, grated

Lobster—Poach the lobster in court bouillon, and cool. Remove the lobster meat. Return the shells to the bouillon. Poach the halibut in the bouillon. Remove the fish to a hot platter, and strain the bouillon. Reduce the poaching liquid by one-half. Make velouté using reduced bouillon. Arrange the lobster meat on one of the steaks; top with the other steak. Pour velouté sauce over the fish, and garnish with parsley.

1 large lobster
16 fl. oz. (4½ dcL) court bouillon
8 fl. oz. (2¼ dcL) velouté sauce
chopped parsley as needed

Spinach—Cook celery and scallions in butter, and add spinach. Cook until water is evaporated,

then add cream cheese. Stir until melted. Add parsley, mace, tarragon, and breadcrumbs; stir. Add beaten egg, and stuff fillets with mixture. Brush with melted butter, and bake.

3 Tbs. (45 g) butter
1 stalk celery, finely chopped
2 scallions, finely chopped
10 oz. (280 g) frozen spinach,
    thawed and pressed dry
3 oz. (90 g) cream cheese
2 oz. (60 g) parsley, finely
    chopped
½ tsp. (2 g) mace
1½ tsp. (7 g) tarragon
4 oz. (150 g) breadcrumbs
1 egg, beaten

HERRING, FRESH

The following recipes are for 12 fish.

Boulangère—Lay fish in a well-greased, ovenproof dish. Season, and surround with thinly sliced potatoes and chopped onion. Sprinkle with thyme, bay leaf, and pepper. Pour melted butter over the fish. Add water to cover, and bring dish to a boil. Transfer to oven, and bake. Garnish with parsley, and serve from the dish.

salt and pepper to taste
4 potatoes
2 onions
pinch each of thyme, bay leaf,
    and pepper
3 oz. (90 g) butter
parsley as needed

Calaisienne—Split and bone herrings. Stuff with chopped roes, shallots, and parsley and mushrooms mixed with softened maître d'hôtel butter. Cook in papillotes.

roes as available
8 oz. (225 g) shallots
parsley to taste
16 oz. (450 g) mushrooms
4 oz. (115 g) maître d'hôtel butter

Devilled—Clean whole fish, and slit along the back and belly. Season, spread with mustard, and sprinkle with white breadcrumbs and a trickle of oil. Grill slowly. Serve with mustard or ravigote sauce on the side.

Flamande—Clean and fillet fish. Poach in white wine with chopped shallots, butter, and peeled lemon slices. Arrange on a hot platter. Strain, and reduce liquid by one-third. Thicken with breadcrumbs; pour over fish.

16 fl. oz. (4½ dcL) white wine
1 oz. (30 g) shallots
1 oz. (30 g) butter
2 whole lemons
breadcrumbs to thicken

Nantaise—Clean and season herrings. Roll in flour, dip in beaten egg, then breadcrumbs. Fry herrings in clarified butter. Coat with a sauce made with purée of roes and mustard, enriched with butter.

flour as needed
2 eggs
breadcrumbs as needed
Sauce:
16 oz. (450 g) roes
1 Tbs. (15 mL) mustard
1 oz. (30 g) butter

JOHN DORY

Most often filleted.

Père Lachaise—Coat fillets with beaten egg and breadcrumbs. Pan-fry. Arrange on pilaf. Surround with chopped onions and seeded tomatoes gently sautéed in butter.

MACKEREL

Anglaise—Poach in court bouillon with fennel. Serve with boiled potatoes and a purée of green gooseberries.

Boulonnaise—Cut fish into thick slices, and poach in court bouillon with vinegar added. Drain and skin. Arrange cooked fish on a dish with poached mussels as garnish. Cover with bâtarde sauce, extended with a little cooking liquid from the mussels.

1 Tbs. (15 mL) vinegar added to
    each 16 fl. oz. (4½ dcL)
    court bouillon
24 mussels
10 fl. oz. (3½ dcL) bâtarde sauce
2 fl. oz. (½ dcL) reserved cooking
    liquid

Eggplant—Season, and pan-fry fillets in butter. Arrange fish on a hot platter, and sprinkle with lemon juice. Surround with sliced eggplant sautéed in butter.

4 oz. (115 g) butter
lemon juice to taste
16 oz. (450 g) eggplant

Flamande—Poach fillets. Arrange fish on a hot platter. Serve with fish velouté mixed with a little mustard.

Francillon—Poach fillets. Arrange fillets on long, fried croûtons spread with anchovy butter. Serve with straw potatoes and tomato sauce on the side.

Lyonnaise—Line ovenproof dish with finely chopped onions that have been gently sautéed in butter. Lay fillets on onions, and cover with equal quantity of sautéed onions. Moisten with white wine, sprinkle with breadcrumbs, and dot with butter. Bake in oven.

  1 lb. (450 g) onions
  3 oz. (90 g) butter
  5 fl. oz. (1½ dcL) white wine
  breadcrumbs as needed
  2 oz. (60 g) butter

Printanière—Poach fillets. Coat with bâtarde sauce enriched with printanière butter. Garnish with bouquet of assorted young vegetables.

PERCH

May also be prepared like fresh haddock.

Asparagus—Cut back of fish, and remove backbone. Poach in white wine. Remove skin. Arrange on a hot platter. Garnish with asparagus tips, and serve with hollandaise sauce.

Joinville—Spread fillets with forcemeat. Fold, and poach in fumet and wine. Garnish with mushrooms and chopped shrimp. Pour Joinville sauce over fish and garnish.

  8 oz. (225 g) forcemeat
  7 fl. oz. (2 dcL) white wine
  4 fl. oz. (1 dcL) fish fumet
  3 oz. (90 g) mushrooms
  3 oz. (90 g) shrimp
  10 fl. oz. (3 dcL) Joinville sauce

Suédoise—Fold fillets, and place them in a buttered baking dish. Sprinkle with a mixture of white breadcrumbs, lemon zest, and chopped parsley. Moisten with fish fumet. Drizzle melted butter on top, and bake in oven.

  breadcrumbs, lemon zest, and
      parsley to taste
  fish fumet as needed
  2 oz. (60 g) butter

PIKE

All recipes are also suitable for Pickerel fillets.

Anglaise—Dip pike fillets in beaten egg and breadcrumbs. Bake in oven in a gratin dish.

Benoiton—Pan-fry fillets. Serve with wine sauce.

Bordelaise—Cut fillets in pieces. Place on a mirepoix, and cook in red wine. Remove fish, and reduce cooking liquid by one-third. Thicken with beurre manié. Coat fish with sauce.

  6 oz. (170 g) mirepoix
  16 fl. oz. (4½ dcL) red wine
  2 oz. (60 g) beurre manié

Gayarre—Poach fillets in white stock. Arrange fish on a platter. Cover with a fish velouté colored with saffron and flavored with sherry. Garnish with a julienne of blanched red peppers.

7 fl. oz. (2 dcL) velouté
2 Tbs. (30 mL) Amontillado
   sherry

Grillé—Marinate small, whole
fish for 1 hour. Dry, and grill
slowly, basting with a little oil and
some of the marinade mixture.
Serve with mayonnaise mixed with
chopped walnuts.
Marinade:
equal parts vinegar and water
minced onion
2 cloves, crushed
1 oz. (30 g) walnuts to each 10 fl.
   oz. (3 dcL) mayonnaise

Italian—Stiffen fillets in butter.
Place in a baking dish. Cover with
Italian sauce, sprinkle with breadcrumbs, and dot with butter. Brown
in oven.
12 fl. oz. (3½ dcL) Italian sauce
breadcrumbs as needed
2 oz. (60 g) butter

Meunière—Cut fillets in pieces,
and cook in butter with chopped
shallots. Arrange fillets on a hot
platter. Deglaze the pan with white
wine and fish fumet. Thicken with
cream and egg yolk. Garnish with
chopped parsley.
3 oz. (90 g) butter
1 oz. (30 g) shallots
7 fl. oz. (2 dcL) each wine and
   fumet
1 fl. oz. (¼ dcL) cream
1 egg yolk
parsley as needed

Normande—Stuff small, whole
fish with forcemeat. Braise in white
wine with bouquet garni and

chopped shallots. Remove fish, and
skin. Coat fish with normande
sauce.
8 oz. (225 g) forcemeat
white wine as needed
bouquet garni
1 oz. (30 g) shallots
12 fl. oz. (3½ dcL) normande
   sauce

Oysters—Bake fillets in oven.
Moisten and baste with white wine.
Arrange fish on a hot platter. Reduce cooking liquid by one-half;
mix with white wine sauce. Garnish
with poached oysters.
10 fl. oz. (3 dcL) white wine
7 fl. oz. (2 dcL) white wine sauce
12 oysters

Parmesan—Pan-fry fillets with
chopped shallots. Flame with
brandy. Arrange on a platter, and
cover with cream sauce. Sprinkle
with grated Parmesan, dot with anchovy butter, and glaze.
1 oz. (30 g) shallots
1 fl. oz. (¼ dcL) brandy
12 fl. oz. (3½ dcL) cream sauce
2 oz. (60 g) Parmesan cheese
2 oz. (60 g) anchovy butter

Persil—Poach fillets in salted
water. Arrange fillets on a dish, and
pour beurre noisette over them.
Garnish with lemon slices and
chopped parsley.
2 fl. oz. (½ dcL) beurre noisette
lemon slices and parsley as
   needed

Provençale—Poach fillets in white
wine. Sauté tomatoes, chopped
garlic, shallots, parsley, and mush-

rooms in a little oil. Arrange fish on a hot platter, and cover with vegetables. Add a little stock if too thick.

7 fl. oz. (2 dcL) white wine
8 oz. (225 g) tomatoes
2 cloves garlic
1 oz. (30 g) shallots
parsley to taste
3 oz. (90 g) mushrooms
1 fl. oz. (¼ dcL) oil
stock as needed

Raifort—Poach fillets in court bouillon. Remove to hot platter, and cover with horseradish mixed with cream. Sprinkle with breadcrumbs, dot with butter, and brown under grill.

court bouillon as needed
3 oz. (90 g) horseradish
6 fl. oz. (1¾ dcL) cream
breadcrumbs as needed
1 oz. (30 g) butter

Saint-Germain—Dip fillets in melted butter, then in breadcrumbs. Grill, and serve with béarnaise sauce and noisette potatoes.

Sevillana—Dip fillets in melted butter and breadcrumbs, and grill. Serve with tomato sauce to which finely chopped anchovies, gherkins, and capers have been added.

butter and breadcrumbs as
        needed
12 fl. oz. (3½ dcL) tomato sauce
2 anchovies
2 oz. (60 g) gherkins
1 oz. (30 g) capers

POMPANO

Cranberries—Cook cranberries with water, sugar, and a pinch of salt until soft, and set aside. Sauté onion in butter, and stir into cranberry mixture. Arrange fish in a buttered baking dish. Spoon cranberry mixture over fish, cover with white wine, and bake. Sprinkle with chopped parsley before serving.

12 oz. (360 g) cranberries
4 fl. oz. (1 dcL) water
1 Tbs. (45 g) sugar
pinch of salt
1 small onion, grated
2 Tbs. (30 g) butter
5 fl. oz. (1½ dcL) white port wine
2 oz. (60 g) chopped parsley

Papillote—Sauté mushrooms in butter. Butter the fillets, and place on papillotes. Cover with duxelles and sautéed mushrooms. Dot with additional butter, and sprinkle with chopped parsley. Fold parchment, and bake.

8 oz. (225 g) duxelles
8 whole mushroom caps
butter as needed
chopped parsley to taste

Paysanne—Cook the mushrooms in 4 Tbs. each of oil and butter. Add the almonds, pickles, and capers. Dredge the fillets in flour, and sauté in the remaining oil and butter. Arrange fillets on a hot platter, and cover with mushroom and almond mixture. Pour juices over fish, and garnish with chopped parsley.

8 oz. (225 g) mushrooms,
        chopped
8 Tbs. (120 mL) oil
8 Tbs. (120 g) butter
4 oz. (115 g) almonds, blanched
        and slivered
6 dill pickles, chopped

2 oz. (60 g) capers
flour as needed
chopped parsley

RED MULLET

Note: Small fish may be broiled;
large fish (over 1¼ kg/3 lb.) are best
stuffed and baked.

Bercy—Proceed as for Bordelaise
recipe, but serve with softened
Bercy butter.

Bordelaise—Make a few shallow
cuts across the back of small fish.
Brush with oil, and broil under
moderate heat. Garnish with lemon
and parsley.

Epicurean—Pan-fry small fish.
Coat with tomato pulp mixed with
espagnole sauce.

Per fish:
1 fl. oz. (¼ dcL) each tomato
    pulp and espagnole sauce

Fennel—Make incisions along the
back of each fish. Put in ovenproof
dish, and sprinkle with sautéed,
chopped onions and fresh, chopped
fennel. Cover with breadcrumbs,
sprinkle with melted butter, and
bake in moderate oven. Garnish
with lemon and parsley.

Per fish:
1 oz. (30 g) onions
1 Tbs. (15 g) fennel
breadcrumbs as needed
melted butter as needed
lemon and parsley as needed

Francillon—Grill small fish. Arrange fish on pieces of toast spread
with anchovy butter and cut the
same length as the fish. Serve with
straw potatoes. Sprinkle tomato
sauce mixed with a little anchovy
essence over each fish.

Grenoble—Pan-fry small fish. Arrange on a platter with capers,
chopped parsley, and lemon slices.
Pour beurre noir over each portion.

Italian—Season and grill small
fish. Place in buttered papillotes
with duxelles and diced tomato.
Coat with Italian sauce, and sprinkle with breadcrumbs. Set in oven
to reheat and to brown the paper
case.

Per fish:
1 oz. (30 g) duxelles
2 oz. (60 g) tomato
1 fl. oz. (¼ dcL) Italian sauce
1 Tbs. (15 g) breadcrumbs

Maître d'Hôtel—Season and grill
fish. Arrange on a dish with noisette
potatoes. Place a knob of maître
d'hôtel butter on each fish.

Montague—Season fillets. Dip in
melted butter, and roll in minced
onion and chopped parsley. Pan-fry
in butter and lemon juice.

Niçoise—Grill small fish. Mix tomato pulp with tarragon. Lay fish
on top. Garnish with thin strips of
desalted anchovy, black olives, and
quarters of lemon.

Per fish:
3 oz. (90 g) tomato pulp
tarragon to taste
1 anchovy
4 olives
lemon

Papillote—Grill small fish. Lay
fish on thin slices of ham. Coat with
chopped mushrooms mixed with espagnole sauce. Wrap in oiled paper,

and put in hot oven to swell and brown.

Per fish:
1½ oz. (45 g) ham
1½ oz. (45 g) mushrooms
1 fl. oz. (¼ dcL) espagnole sauce

Théodore—Stuff large fish with chopped mushrooms, and poach in white wine. Coat with wine sauce.

Trouville—Open a large fish along the back, and remove the backbone. Stuff fish with force-meat. Wrap in waxed paper and tie. Poach in white wine and water. Remove wrapping, arrange fish on a platter, and cover with Colbert sauce.

For a 3-lb. (1¼ kg) fish:
1 lb. (450 g) moist forcemeat
7 fl. oz. (2 dcL) white wine and
    water combined
12 fl. oz. (3½ dcL) Colbert sauce

Venetian—Sauté fillets in oil. Garnish with stuffed olives and sautéed mushrooms. Arrange on a platter, and coat with Venetian sauce.

RED SNAPPER

Archiduc—Sprinkle buttered baking dish with shallots. Fold fillets in half, and arrange them in a single layer. Add wine and enough fumet to almost cover the fish. Bring the mixture to a boil. Cover and bake. Remove fillets to a hot platter. Reduce cooking liquid by one-half. Add cream, and cook gently until sauce thickens. In another pan, combine carrots, celery, leeks, brandy, Madeira, and port; cook over high heat until vegetables are

cooked and the liquid is evaporated. Blend vegetables into sauce, and pour over fish.

6 shallots, finely chopped
4 fl. oz. (1 dcL) dry white wine
16 fl. oz. (4½ dcL) fish fumet
24 fl. oz. (7 dcL) whipping cream
4 oz. (115 g) each finely diced
    carrots, celery, and leeks
2 Tbs. (30 mL) each brandy, Madeira, and port

Ginger Sauce—Poach fillets. Combine 4 fl. oz. (1 dcL) of the broth, sherry, sugar, and soy sauce. Combine the remaining 2 fl. oz. of broth with the cornstarch. Heat the oils in a wok, and stir-fry the ginger. Add sherry mixture and red pepper. Reduce heat and simmer. Cook until the sauce thickens. Add green onions, and pour sauce over fish.

6 fl. oz. (1½ dcL) chicken broth
2½ Tbs. (37 mL) dry sherry
1 tsp. (5 g) sugar
2 tsp. (10 mL) soy sauce
2 tsp. (10 mL) cornstarch
2 Tbs. (30 mL) vegetable oil
½ tsp. (2 mL) sesame oil
chopped, fresh gingerroot to taste
1 small red pepper, sliced into
    strips
8 green onions, snipped

Mustard Sauce—Marinate fillets in salt, sugar, fennel, peppercorns, and all but 2 Tbs. (30 g) of the dill. Rinse fillets. Pan-fry or broil. Combine mustard and vinegar; add the oil a drop at a time. Whisk sauce until it thickens. Stir in the remaining 2 Tbs. (30 g) dill and salt and pepper. Serve sauce on the side.

3 Tbs. (45 g) each salt and sugar
1 Tbs. (15 g) crushed fennel seed
10 white peppercorns, crushed
8 oz. (225 g) snipped, fresh dill
2 Tbs. (30 mL) Dijon mustard
1 tsp. (5 mL) malt vinegar
4 fl. oz. (1 dcL) oil
salt and pepper to taste

Tomato Vinaigrette—Poach fillets. Heat olive oil, and add garlic, crushed red pepper, and basil. Cook for 1 minute. Add lemon peel, tomatoes, and sugar, breaking tomatoes into small chunks. Simmer. Stir in vinegar, salt, and parsley. Remove lemon peel, and pour sauce over fillets.
1 Tbs. (15 mL) olive oil
1 garlic clove, crushed
⅛ tsp. (⅝ g) crushed red pepper
1 Tbs. (15 g) chopped, fresh basil
1 3-inch strip of lemon peel
16 oz. (480 g) tomatoes with juice
½ tsp. (2½ g) sugar
1 Tbs. (15 mL) wine vinegar
salt to taste
1 Tbs. (15 g) chopped parsley

SALMON

Allemande—Dip middle-cut fillets or steaks in melted butter, beaten egg, and breadcrumbs. Pan-fry in butter. Arrange on hot platter, and garnish with creamed mushrooms.
6 oz. (170 g) butter
2 eggs
breadcrumbs as needed
1 lb. (450 g) mushrooms

Bourguignonne—Halve salmon steaks down the middle, and remove bone. Trim the two pieces to resemble cutlets. Braise in red wine and fish fumet. Drain, and set on cutlet-shaped croûtons. Garnish with button mushrooms and glazed onions. Reduce cooking liquid by one-third, and thicken with beurre manié. Enrich with cream, and pour over fish.
7 fl. oz. (2 dcL) red wine and fish fumet combined
croûtons as needed
4 oz. (115 g) each mushrooms and onions
1 oz. (30 g) beurre manié
1 fl. oz. (¼ dcL) cream

Champère—Poach cutlets in white wine and fish stock. Arrange on pilaf of rice, and cover with normande sauce. Garnish with glazed button onions and chopped parsley.
7 fl. oz. (2 dcL) white wine
16 fl. oz. (4½ dcL) fish stock
10 fl. oz. (3 dcL) normande sauce
onions as needed
·parsley as needed

Condorcet—Poach cutlets in white wine and stock. Sauté chopped tomatoes and peeled, sliced cucumber in butter. Cover fish with this mixture. Coat with white wine sauce, and garnish with chopped parsley.
16 fl. oz. (4½ dcL) fish stock
7 fl. oz. (2 dcL) white wine
12 oz. (340 g) tomatoes
8 oz. (225 g) cucumbers
3 oz. (90 g) butter
12 fl. oz. (3½ dcL) white wine sauce

Coquilles de Saumon—Pipe a border of mashed potatoes around edge of each scallop shell. Line base with

Mornay sauce. Divide cooked, flaked fish among shells; place on top of sauce. Cover fish with more Mornay sauce, and sprinkle with Parmesan and melted butter. Brush potato border with beaten egg, and set in hot oven to brown.

For each coquille:
potatoes as needed
1 fl. oz. (¼ dcL) Mornay sauce
    for the base
3½ oz. (100 g) fish, approximately
1 fl. oz. (¼ dcL) Mornay sauce to
    cover
1 Tbs. (15 mL) Parmesan cheese
melted butter as needed
beaten egg as needed

Cream—Dredge steaks in flour, and cook in butter. Add whole button mushrooms to pan, and finish cooking. Drain fish, and set on shaped croûtons with mushrooms on top. Deglaze pan with Madeira. Enrich sauce with cream, add fish velouté, and reduce cooking liquid by one-third. Strain sauce, and pour over fish.

flour as needed
3 oz. (90 g) butter
2 mushrooms per cutlet
croûtons as needed
4 fl. oz. (1 dcL) Madeira
1 fl. oz. (¼ dcL) cream
1 fl. oz. (¼ dcL) velouté

Danoise—Poach middle-cut fillets in court bouillon. Garnish with boiled new potatoes. Cover with bâtarde sauce mixed with a little anchovy butter.

potatoes as needed
12 fl. oz. (3½ dcL) bâtarde sauce
1 oz. (30 g) anchovy butter

Ecossaise—Poach middle-cut fillets. Arrange on a hot platter, and coat with white wine sauce. Garnish with a brunoise of vegetables.

Epicurean—Poach middle-cut fillets in white wine, fish stock, and Madeira. Arrange on a hot platter. Reduce cooking liquid by one-half; thicken with beurre manié. Mix finished sauce with anchovy essence and lemon juice. Garnish with chopped parsley.

7 fl. oz. (2 dcL) white wine
12 fl. oz. (3½ dcL) fish stock
4 fl. oz. (1 dcL) Madeira
2 oz. (60 g) beurre manié
anchovy essence and lemon juice
    to taste
parsley as needed

Florentine—Proceed as for Coquilles de Saumon recipe, but line each shell with chopped, cooked spinach moistened with butter. Finish as for Saint-Jacques.

Froid Chambertin—Whole fish poached in Chambertin; cool and chill. Decorate as desired; coat with aspic. Dress and surround with jelly made from fish fumet.

Froid Champagne—Proceed as for froid Chambertin, using Champagne as poaching liquid.

Froid en Darnes—Poach, cool, then chill. Dress on dish with parsley sprigs. Serve with mayonnaise or sauce Tartare.

Italian—Coat cutlets on one side with thick mushroom purée. Dip in beaten egg and breadcrumbs mixed with Parmesan cheese. Deep-fry.

8 oz. (225 g) mushroom purée

Crumb mix:
2 parts breadcrumbs
1 part Parmesan cheese

Kedgeree—Flake cooked salmon, and heat in butter. Mix cooked rice with a thin béchamel flavored with a little curry powder. Alternate layers of salmon and rice in a deep dish. Sprinkle with chopped, hard-boiled egg on last layer of salmon. Put final layer of rice over egg, and coat with more béchamel. Heat thoroughly in oven.
 4 oz. (115 g) butter
 2¼ lb. (1 kg) cooked rice
 32 fl. oz. (9 dcL) béchamel sauce
 curry powder to taste
 4 hard-boiled eggs

Marcel Prévost—Poach cutlets, and arrange on chopped, cooked spinach moistened with butter. Cover fish with marinière sauce, and garnish with poached mussels.
 1½ lb. (675 g) spinach
 butter as needed
 12 fl. oz. (3½ dcL) marinière
   sauce
 24 mussels

Medici—Dip medallions in melted butter, then breadcrumbs. Grill. Garnish with small grilled tomatoes filled with béarnaise sauce.

Oysters—Poach middle-cut fillets in white wine with mirepoix. Arrange on a hot platter. Reduce stock by one-half. Mix with fish velouté and oyster liquor. Garnish with poached oysters. Pour sauce over fish.
 7 fl. oz. (2 dcL) white wine
 2 oz. (60 g) mirepoix
 12 fl. oz. (3½ dcL) stock
 3 fl. oz. (¾ dcL) velouté
 24 oysters

Pilaf—Sauté flakes of cooked salmon in butter. Drain, and keep warm. Pour white wine into pan. Add fish glaze and tomato purée, and deglaze. Heat, but do not boil. Add the fish flakes, and mix. Butter a turban ring, fill with cooked rice, and unmold. Pour fish mixture in center, and surround with sautéed mushrooms.
 5 oz. (140 g) butter
 10 fl. oz. (3 dcL) white wine
 12 fl. oz. (3½ dcL) fish glaze
 2 Tbs. (30 mL) tomato purée
 1 lb. (450 g) raw rice
 8 oz. (225 g) mushrooms

Pojarski—Mash raw salmon with softened butter and breadcrumbs soaked in milk. Squeeze dry. Season, and add nutmeg. Divide mixture, shape into cutlets, and cook in butter.
 8 oz. (225 g) butter
 9 oz. (250 g) dry breadcrumbs
 milk as needed
 salt and pepper to taste
 ½ tsp. (5 g) nutmeg

Provençale—Arrange flakes of cooked salmon, pitted and chopped green olives, and finely sliced mushrooms in coquilles. Cover with provençale sauce, sprinkle with breadcrumbs, and drizzle with oil. Brown under grill. Garnish the center of each shell with rolled anchovy fillet, and sprinkle with parsley.

For each coquille:
fish as needed (approximately
   5–7 oz./140–200 g)
2 olives
1 oz. (30 g) mushrooms
1 fl. oz. (¼ dcL) provençale
   sauce
breadcrumbs as needed
oil as needed
1 anchovy fillet per coquille
parsley as needed

Réjane—Poach medallions in
stock. Cover with white wine sauce
enriched with watercress butter.
Garnish with nests of duchesse potatoes filled with peas.
   10 fl. oz. (3 dcL) white wine
      sauce
   2 oz. (60 g) watercress butter
   nests and peas as needed

Turenne—Poach medallions.
Coat with white wine sauce mixed
with anchovy essence, and garnish
with slices of cucumber and tomato
   12 fl. oz. (3½ dcL) white wine
      sauce
   1 Tbs. (15 mL) anchovy essence
   cucumber and tomato slices as
      needed

Vol-au-Vent—Sliced smoked
salmon cut in strips and bound with
hollandaise sauce and served in puff
pastry cases. Garnish with poached
oysters.

SALT COD

All recipes are for 2 lb. (900 g) fish.
   Bénédictine—Soak fish. Poach,
drain, and flake. Mix with mashed
potatoes. Work oil and milk very
gradually into the mixture. When it
is smooth, put it in buttered baking
dish. Drizzle with melted butter,
and bake in oven.
   1 lb. (450 g) potatoes
   5 fl. oz. (1½ dcL) oil
   10 fl. oz. (3 dcL) boiled milk
   2 oz. (60 g) butter

Benoiton—Slice onions, and
brown in butter. Add flour. Mix,
and moisten with red wine and fish
fumet. Cook for 15 minutes. Add
sliced, boiled potatoes and the
poached, flaked fish. Place mixture
in buttered dish, sprinkle with
breadcrumbs and melted butter, and
brown in oven.
   5 oz. (140 g) onions
   1 oz. (30 g) flour
   16 fl. oz. (4½ dcL) red wine
   4 fl. oz. (1 dcL) fish fumet
   8 oz. (225 g) potatoes
   breadcrumbs as needed
   melted butter as needed

Brandade—Proceed as for Bénédictine recipes, using half the quantity of potatoes. Add minced garlic
and cayenne pepper. Cook in a timbale. Serve with croûtons.
   Cream—Poach fish, and flake.
Coat with cream sauce, and garnish
with chopped parsley.
   Fishcakes—Cook and flake fish.
Mix with an equal quantity of
mashed potatoes. Shape into patties. Coat with beaten eggs and
breadcrumbs. Pan-fry. Serve with
tomato sauce.
   Lyonnaise—Poach and flake fish.
Mix with lyonnaise potatoes sautéed in butter. Deglaze pan with
vinegar, and add to mixture. Cook
in a timbale. Garnish with parsley.

1 lb. (450 g) lyonnaise potatoes
2 oz. (60 g) butter
2 tsp. (10 mL) vinegar
parsley as needed

Portuguese—Poach and flake fish. Mix with cold, minced, french-fried potatoes and beaten eggs. Bake in oven. Garnish with black olives.
 1 lb. (450 g) potatoes
 4 eggs
 black olives as needed

SHAD

Bercy—Bake fillets in a well-oiled container. Arrange on a hot platter, and serve with Bercy sauce.
 12 fl. oz. (3½ dcL) Bercy sauce

En Cocottes—Line cocottes with tomato purée. Place small cooked fillets on top. Cover with tomato sauce, sprinkle with grated Parmesan, and brown under grill.
 4 fl. oz. (1 dcL) tomato purée
 6 fl. oz. (1¾ dcL) tomato sauce
 3 oz. (90 g) Parmesan cheese

Farcie—Stuff whole fish with forcemeat mixed with chopped herbs. Wrap in oiled paper and bake. Serve with Bercy sauce.
 12 fl. oz. (3½ dcL) Bercy sauce

Au Gratin—Place fillets in buttered gratin dish lined with minced onions and half the Mornay sauce. Add dry white wine. Cover fish with remainder of sauce. Sprinkle with breadcrumbs, dot with butter, and bake.
 6 oz. (170 g) onion
 21 fl. oz. (6 dcL) Mornay sauce

2 fl. oz. (½ dcL) white wine
breadcrumbs as needed
2 oz. (60 g) butter

Grilled—Marinate fish in oil, vinegar, bay leaf, parsley, and thyme. Remove and drain. Grill. Serve with an appropriate compound butter such as anchovy, maître d'hôtel, or watercress.
 16 fl. oz. (4½ dcL) marinade
 3 oz. (90 g) compound butter

Hollandaise—Poach fillets in salted water mixed with a touch of vinegar and chopped parsley. Serve with hollandaise sauce.
Milanaise—Marinate fillets. Dip in beaten egg, then in breadcrumbs that have been mixed with grated Parmesan. Deep-fry. Serve with spaghetti Milanese as a side dish.
Raifort—Clean and score small, whole fish. Pan-fry. Cover with horseradish sauce extended with cream.
 4 fl. oz. (1 dcL) horseradish sauce
 6 fl. oz. (1½ dcL) cream

SMELT

All recipes are for 1 lb. (450 g) of fish.

This small fish lends itself only to a limited number of preparation styles. The rule is: the simpler, the better.
Anglaise—Split the fish along the back; open gently. Dip in beaten egg and breadcrumbs and pan-fry.
Grillés à l'Anglaise—Proceed as for Anglaise, but dip in melted butter and breadcrumbs and grill.
Orly—Split; bone. Dip in egg and

breadcrumbs and deep-fry. Serve with tomato sauce.

Ravigote—Bone and poach in court bouillon. Dress on dish and cover with a sauce composed of apple purée, grated horseradish, tarragon vinegar, sugar, and salt.

court bouillon to cover
8 fl. oz. (2¼ dcL) apple purée
1 oz. (30 g) horseradish
1 Tbs. (15 mL) tarragon vinegar
1 Tbs. (15 g) sugar
pinch salt

SOLE

The following recipes for whole fish are for 2¼ lb. (1 kg). The recipes for fillets are for 12 fillets from 3 fish weighing approximately 16 oz. (450 g) each.

Aiglon—Poach whole fish in white wine. Place on a bed of mushroom purée. Coat with white wine sauce mixed with Soubise. Drizzle a thread of meat glaze over each fish, and garnish with fleurons.

16 fl. oz. (4 ½ dcL) white wine
8 oz. (225 g) mushroom purée
10 fl. oz. (3½ dcL) white wine
    sauce
5 fl. oz. (1½ dcL) Soubise
meat glaze as needed
fleurons as needed

Amélie—Poach whole fish in fish fumet. Arrange on a hot platter. Border with sliced, sautéed mushrooms and boiled new potatoes. Coat with Nantua sauce.

16 fl. oz. (4½ dcL) fish fumet
16 mushrooms
potatoes as needed
16 fl. oz. (4½ dcL) Nantua sauce

Amiral—Poach whole fish in fumet; arrange on a hot platter; garnish with button mushrooms and baby onions sautéed in butter; coat fish with white wine sauce.

16 fl. oz. (4½ dcL) fish fumet
10 mushrooms
10 onions
16 fl. oz. (4½ dcL) white wine
    sauce

Archiduc—Poach fillets in fumet mixed with whiskey and port. Arrange on a hot platter. Reduce stock by one-third. Add butter and cream, then cooked brunoise of vegetables. Coat fish with sauce.

20 fl. oz. (6 dcL) fish fumet
2 fl. oz. (½ dcL) whiskey
2 fl. oz. (½ dcL) port
2 oz. (60 g) butter
5 fl. oz. (1½ dcL) cream
6 oz. (170 g) cooked brunoise

Arlésienne—Poach fillets in fumet with chopped shallots, diced tomato, crushed garlic, and parsley. Sauté sliced artichoke hearts in butter; finish with cream. Remove fish, and reduce cooking liquid by one-half. Add aspic jelly, and coat fish. Arrange artichokes around the fish.

28 fl. oz. (8 dcL) fish fumet
1 oz. (30 g) shallots
6 oz. (170 g) tomatoes
1 clove garlic
parsley to taste
12 artichoke hearts
1½ oz. (45 g) butter
2 fl. oz. (½ dcL) cream
1 Tbs. (15 mL) aspic jelly

Bedfort—Grill fillets. Arrange on a hot platter. Cover with Mornay sauce, and glaze. Garnish with puff pastry bouchées filled with mushroom purée first and then creamed spinach.

16 fl. oz. (4½ dcL) Mornay sauce
bouchées and fillings as needed

Bercy—Sweat chopped shallots in 1 oz. butter. Place fish on top; moisten with white wine and fumet. Bake. Remove cooked fish, and reduce cooking liquid by one-half. Add 2 oz. butter. Pour sauce over fish, and glaze under broiler.

2 oz. (60 g) shallots
1 oz. (30 g) butter
10 fl. oz. (3 dcL) white wine
16 fl. oz. (4½ dcL) fish fumet
2 oz. (60 g) butter

Note: This recipe is also suitable for smelt.

Boistelle—Proceed as for Bercy recipe, with the addition of sliced, sautéed mushrooms.

Bordelaise—Place soles on chopped shallots and parsley. Moisten with red wine, and poach. Remove fish and reduce cooking liquid by one-half, and add to bordelaise sauce. Cover sole with sauce.

2 oz. (60 g) shallots
parsley to taste
12 fl. oz. (3½ dcL) red wine
10 fl. oz. (3 dcL) bordelaise sauce

Bourguignonne—Poach fillets in red wine with button onions and small mushrooms. Remove fish; reduce cooking liquid by one-third. Make wine sauce with roux and

cooking liquid; finish with butter. Coat fish.

28 fl. oz. (8 dcL) red wine
6 oz. (170 g) button onions
4 oz. (115 g) small mushrooms
1 oz. (30 g) each butter and flour
for roux
1½ oz. (45 g) butter to finish
sauce

Bretonne—Poach fillets in dish with vegetable fondue and fish fumet. Remove fish and reduce cooking liquid by one-fourth. Add fresh cream, and coat fish.

7 fl. oz. (2 dcL) fondue of choice
16 fl. oz. (4½ dcL) fish fumet
5 fl. oz. (1½ dcL) cream

Champagne—Poach fillets in dry champagne. Remove fish, and reduce cooking liquid by one-fourth. Make sauce with roux, and pour it over fish. Garnish with peeled, seeded black and green grapes.

24 fl. oz. (7 dcL) dry champagne
1 oz. (30 g) each butter and flour
for roux
6 oz. (170 g) black and green
grapes

Colbert—Open the soles by cutting along the backbone with a sharp knife. Cut toward the outer edges of the fish on both sides (as for filleting), but be sure the outer edges remain attached. Fold back the fillets. Break backbone at head, center, and tail and remove. With fillets still folded back, dip fish in beaten egg and breadcrumbs. Deep fry. Serve with Colbert butter and maître d'hôtel butter. This recipe is also suitable for smelt.

Desmoulins—Poach fillets in white wine and fumet with diced tomatoes, minced mushrooms, and parsley. Remove fish, and reduce cooking liquid by one-third. Pass sauce through a sieve, and add butter. Coat fish.

 10 fl. oz. (3 dcL) white wine
 10 fl. oz. (3 dcL) fish fumet
 6 oz. (170 g) tomatoes
 6 oz. (170 g) mushrooms
 parsley to taste
 2 oz. (60 g) butter

Duguesclin—Poach fillets in fumet. Remove fish, and cover with shrimp sauce. Garnish with artichoke hearts filled with peeled shrimp.

 12 fl. oz. (3½ dcL) fish fumet
 16 fl. oz. (4½ dcL) shrimp sauce
 10 artichoke hearts
 5 oz. (140 g) shrimp

Dumas—Poach fillets. Remove fish, and cover with a white wine sauce mixed with chopped fresh herbs and finely diced tomatoes.

 16 fl. oz. (4½ dcL) white wine
    sauce
 herbs and tomatoes as needed

Eggplant—Pan-fry fillets in butter. Surround with slices of eggplant gently cooked in butter. Sprinkle with chopped parsley and lemon juice. Pour butter over fish.

Fines Herbes—Poach fillets. Arrange on a hot platter, and coat with white wine sauce. Sprinkle with chopped parsley.

Flaubert—Poach fillets in fumet. Remove fish. Coat with white wine sauce containing brunoise of vegetables. Garnish with chopped shrimp and mushrooms in tartlets.

 10 fl. oz. (3 dcL) fish fumet
 16 fl. oz. (4½ dcL) white wine
    sauce
 5 oz. (140 g) brunoise
 2 tartlets per portion, each containing 1 shrimp and 1 mushroom

Florentine—Poach fillets in fumet. Arrange on a bed of chopped and buttered spinach. Coat fish with Mornay sauce; glaze.

 10 fl. oz. (3 g) fish fumet
 spinach as needed
 16 fl. oz. (4½ dcL) Mornay sauce

Gourmets—Poach fillets in fumet, mushroom liquid, and port wine. Arrange on a dish. Reduce cooking liquid by one-half. Enrich with butter, and pour over fish.

 20 fl. oz. (6 dcL) fish fumet
 5 fl. oz. (1½ dcL) mushroom liquid
 5 fl. oz. (1½ dcL) port wine
 2 oz. (60 g) butter

Hélène—Poach fillets in fumet. Set fish on bed of buttered noodles, cover with Mornay sauce, and glaze.

 12 fl. oz. (3½ dcL) fish fumet
 1 lb. (450 g) cooked noodles
 16 fl. oz. (4½ dcL) Mornay sauce

Louis XV—Poach fillets in fumet. Arrange on a hot platter, and cover with white wine sauce. Garnish with lobster coral and sliced mushrooms sautéed in butter.

 12 fl. oz. (3½ dcL) white wine
    sauce

lobster coral as needed
6 oz. (170 g) mushrooms

Mâconnaise—Poach fillets in red wine with chopped onions and mushrooms. Arrange on a hot platter. Strain cooking liquid. Make roux, and extend with cooking liquid. Pour sauce over fish. Serve with croûtons.
   20 fl. oz. (6 dcL) red wine
   6 oz. (170 g) onions
   6 oz. (170 g) mushrooms
   1½ oz. (45 g) each flour and butter for roux
   croûtons as needed

Marchand de Vin—Proceed as for Bercy recipe, using red wine instead of white.
   Marguery—Poach fillets in fumet. Arrange on a hot platter, and cover with white wine sauce. Glaze. Garnish with shrimp, mussels, and fleurons.
   12 fl. oz. (3½ dcL) fish fumet
   16 fl. oz. (4½ dcL) white wine sauce
   6 oz. (170 g) shrimp
   10 oz. (280 g) mussels
   fleurons as needed

Marinière—Proceed as for Marguery recipes, adding oysters and chopped mushrooms. Do not glaze.
   16 oysters
   6 oz. (170 g) mushrooms

Marseillaise—Poach fillets in fumet with chopped onion and garlic. Arrange on a hot platter. Coat with white wine sauce colored with saffron. Garnish with peas.
   Mornay—Poach fillets. Arrange on a hot platter, coat with Mornay sauce, and glaze.
   16 fl. oz. (4½ dcL) Mornay sauce

Mushrooms—Poach fillets in fumet with minced mushrooms. Remove fish. Reduce cooking liquid by one-half, and mix with white wine sauce. Coat fish. Garnish with fleurons.
   12 fl. oz. (3½ dcL) fish fumet
   8 oz. (225 g) mushrooms
   10 fl. oz. (3 dcL) white wine sauce
   fleurons as needed

Noilly—Poach fillets in Noilly Prat vermouth, fish stock, and minced mushrooms. Arrange on a hot platter. Reduce cooking liquid by one-half. Add white wine sauce, and enrich with butter. Coat fish.
   5 fl. oz. (1½ dcL) vermouth
   16 fl. oz. (3½ dcL) fish stock
   6 oz. (170 g) mushrooms
   5 fl. oz. (1½ dcL) white wine sauce
   1½ oz. (45 g) butter

Paysanne—Poach fillets in fish fumet with brunoise of vegetables. Arrange on a hot platter. Reduce cooking liquid by one-third. Strain, and enrich with butter. Coat fish.
   20 fl. oz. (6 oz. dcL) fish fumet
   8 oz. (225 g) brunoise
   1½ oz. (45 g) butter

Princess—Poach fillets, and arrange them on a hot platter. Cover with white wine sauce mixed with asparagus purée. Surround with duchesse potato nests filled with asparagus tips, and garnish with sautéed mushroom caps.

    16 fl. oz. (4½ dcL) white wine
        sauce
    6 fl. oz. (1¾ dcL) asparagus
        purée
    nests, mushrooms, and asparagus
        tips as needed

Saint-Germain—Dip fillets in butter and breadcrumbs; grill. Serve with béarnaise sauce and noisette potatoes.

Saint-Valéry—Poach fillets in fumet. Arrange fillets on a hot platter. Cover with white wine sauce, garnish with shrimp and diced mushrooms, and glaze.

    12 fl. oz. (3½ dcL) white wine
        sauce
    4 oz. (115 g) shrimp
    6 oz. (170 g) mushrooms

Schneider—Proceed as for Bercy recipe. Garnish with mussels, and sprinkle with brown breadcrumbs.

    20 mussels

Spanish—Sauté fillets in butter. Arrange on bed of stewed tomatoes. Garnish with sautéed onion rings and julienne of stewed red and green peppers.

    4 oz. (115 g) butter
    1 lb. (450 g) tomatoes
    8 oz. (225 g) onions
    6 oz. (170 g) mixed peppers

Thermidor—Proceed as for Bercy recipe. Do not glaze. Add a thread of meat glaze over the fish.

Traviata—Proceed as for Bercy recipe. Surround with small baked tomatoes filled with Nantua sauce.

    12–14 tomatoes
    5 fl. oz. (1⅝ dcL) Nantua sauce

Valois—Poach fillets. Coat with white wine sauce mixed with béarnaise sauce. Garnish with asparagus tips and mushrooms.

    10 fl. oz. (3 dcL) white wine
        sauce
    5 fl. oz. (1½ dcL) béarnaise sauce
    asparagus tips and mushrooms as
        needed

Van den Berg—Poach fillets, and arrange them on a hot platter. Coat with wine sauce mixed with fine dice of tomato flesh and minced mushrooms.

    15 fl. oz. (4½ dcL) wine sauce
    6 oz. (170 g) each chopped toma-
        toes and mushrooms

Véronique—Poach fish fillets in fumet with orange Curaçao. Arrange fillets on a hot platter. Garnish with peeled and seeded Muscat grapes. Reduce cooking liquid by one-third, and enrich with butter. Coat fish, and glaze.

    12 fl. oz. (3½ dcL) fish fumet
    2 fl. oz. (½ dcL) Curaçao
    grapes as needed
    2 oz. (60 g) butter

White Wine—Poach fillets in white wine. Cover with reduced cooking liquid mixed with white wine sauce. Garnish as desired.

    12 fl. oz. (3½ dcL) wine
    8 fl. oz. (2¼ dcL) white wine
        sauce

Yvette—Proceed as for Fines Herbes recipe. Garnish with small baked tomatoes stuffed with fish forcemeat.

SWORDFISH

Castilian—Sauté the peppers in oil; drain, add lemon juice. Sauté onion and garlic in oil. Add tomatoes, oregano, chili powder, parsley, and coriander. Add peppers, mix, and simmer. Place swordfish steaks in an oiled baking dish, dot with butter, and bake. Top with vegetable mixture.

4 green peppers, shredded
olive oil as needed
1 tsp. (5 mL) lemon juice
3 medium onions, chopped
3 garlic cloves, chopped
16 fl. oz. (4½ dcL) stewed tomatoes
1 tsp. (5 g) oregano
1 Tbs. (15 g) chili powder
2 Tbs. (30 g) chopped parsley
fresh coriander to taste
butter as needed

Rosemary—Dredge the swordfish steaks in flour. Press rosemary into the fish, brush with oil, and sauté steaks in 6 Tbs. (90 g) of butter, turning once while cooking. Add 2 more Tbs. (30 g) of butter to the pan. Add wine; swirl sauce. Serve with lemon quarters.

flour as needed
2 oz. (60 g) fresh or dried rosemary, chopped
oil as needed
4 oz. (115 g) butter
4 fl. oz. (1 dcL) dry white wine or 1 fl. oz. (¼ dcL) sherry

lemon quarters as needed

Teriyaki—Mix mustard with hot water. Dissolve cornstarch in sherry. Combine mustard mixture, soy sauce, chicken broth, and sugar in small saucepan; simmer. Add sherry and cornstarch mixture, brush swordfish with mixture, and broil fish, basting often.

2 tsp. (10 g) dry mustard
1 tsp. (5 mL) hot water
1 tsp. (5 g) cornstarch
2 Tbs. (30 mL) dry sherry
2 fl. oz. (½ dcL) soy sauce
4 fl. oz. (1 dcL) chicken broth
1 tsp. (5 g) sugar
vegetable oil

TROUT

All recipes are for 4 medium trout.

Amandine—Dip fillets in cold milk. Roll in seasoned flour. Sauté in the first 3 oz. of butter. Arrange fish on a dish and pour the lemon juice over them. Add the second 3 oz. of butter to the pan. Heat and stir in blanched, chipped almonds. Cook briefly. Pour butter almond sauce over trout.

milk as needed
seasoned flour as needed
3 oz. (90 g) butter
2 fl. oz. (½ dcL) lemon juice
3 oz. (90 g) butter
3 oz. (90 g) almonds

Boulevardier—Fillet trout, and roll into paupiettes. Put in a pan with chopped onion, parsley, and thyme. Moisten with fish stock and oil. Cover, and bake in hot oven.

Arrange on a dish. Serve with hollandaise sauce.

2 oz. (60 g) onion
sprig of parsley
pinch of thyme
4 fl. oz. (1 dcL) fish stock
2 fl. oz. (½ dcL) oil
hollandaise sauce as needed

Bourguignonne—Lay fish in a dish with finely chopped shallots and bouquet garni. Moisten with red wine. Cover, and bake in oven. Arrange fish on a hot platter, and squeeze lemon over each fish. Reduce cooking liquid by one-third. Strain, and thicken with beaten yolks. Pour sauce over fish, and garnish with parsley and lemon slices.

1 oz. (30 g) shallots
bouquet garni
12 fl. oz. (3½ dcL) red wine
lemon juice to taste
2 egg yolks
parsley and lemon slices as
    needed

Felix—Skin and flour fillets; cook in butter. Remove to a hot platter, and coat with américaine sauce.

Hussarde—Clean fish, and remove backbone. Stuff with fish forcemeat mixed with 2 oz. of sautéed, minced onion. Line a baking dish with 6 oz. onions. Add bouquet garni, white wine, and fish. Dot with butter, and bake in oven. Arrange fish on a dish. Reduce cooking liquid by one-third. Thicken with velouté, and enrich with butter. Strain, and pour over fish.

8 oz. (225 g) fish forcemeat
2 oz. (60 g) onions

6 oz. (170 g) onions
bouquet garni
5 fl. oz. (1½ dcL) white wine
1 fl. oz. (¼ dcL) velouté
1 oz. (30 g) butter

Red Wine—Chop onion and carrot, and lightly cook in butter. Line heatproof dish with this mixture, and place trout on top. Moisten with red wine, and bake in oven. Arrange on a dish. Reduce cooking liquid by one-third. Thicken with beurre manié, and enrich with cream. Strain, and pour over fish.

2 onions
2 carrots
2 oz. (60 g) butter
12 fl. oz. (3½ dcL) red wine
1 oz. (30 g) beurre manié
1 fl. oz. (¼ dcL) cream

Russian—Poach fillets in court bouillon. Arrange on a hot platter. Cover with hollandaise sauce; sprinkle with caviar.

TUNA

Amandine—Blanch and sliver almonds. Melt the butter. Dredge the fish steaks in seasoned flour. Brown. Add almonds and chopped parsley; serve with lemon wedges.

8 oz. (225 g) almonds
6 Tbs. (90 g) butter
salt and pepper to taste
flour as needed
2 Tbs. (30 g) chopped parsley
lemon wedges as needed

Green Olives—Dredge the fish steaks in flour. Brown in 6 fl. oz. of the oil. Arrange steaks in a buttered baking dish. Cook the onions in the remaining 2 fl. oz. of oil. Add tomatoes, and season with salt and pepper. Cook uncovered until the sauce is thickened. Add capers, green olives, and chopped parsley. Serve over fish steaks.

8 fl. oz. (2¼ dcL) olive oil
1 medium onion, peeled and chopped
1 lb. (450 g) tomatoes with their juice
salt and pepper to taste
2 Tbs. (30 g) capers
8 oz. (225 g) green olives, sliced
2 oz. (60 g) chopped parsley

Tomatoes and Onions—Place fish steaks, skinned side down, in a greased baking dish. Overlap tomato and onion slices on top. Season with salt and pepper, drizzle with oil, and bake. Sprinkle cooked fish with chopped parsley.

1 large tomato, sliced very thin
1 large onion, sliced very thin
salt and pepper to taste
4 Tbs. (60 mL) vegetable oil
2 Tbs. (30 g) chopped parsley

Tomatoes and Raisins—Cook onions in olive oil. Stir in tomatoes, oregano, and pepper. Bring liquid to a boil; simmer. Add tuna steaks, and simmer until cooked. Add raisins.

3 large onions, sliced thin
4 Tbs. (60 mL) olive oil
1½ lb. (675 g) tomatoes with their juice
¾ tsp. (3 g) each oregano and pepper
3 oz. (90 g) white raisins

TURBOT

All recipes are for 6½ lb. (3 kg) whole fish, or 3 lb. (1.35 kg) fillets. Recipes for fillets are also suitable for halibut and John Dory.

Aïda—Poach fillets. Arrange on a bed of chopped, buttered spinach seasoned with paprika. Coat with Mornay sauce, sprinkle with cheese and breadcrumbs, and brown in oven.

2¼ lb. (1 kg) spinach
3 oz. (90 g) butter
16 fl. oz. (4½ dcL) Mornay sauce
6 oz. (170 g) cheese
breadcrumbs as needed

Andalouse—Place whole fish in buttered dish on a bed of sliced onions that have been lightly sautéed beforehand, chopped tomatoes, minced mushrooms, and a fine julienne of red and green peppers. Sprinkle with breadcrumbs, and dot with butter. Moisten carefully with white wine and stock; braise in oven.

4 oz. (115 g) onions
6 tomatoes
6 oz. (170 g) mushrooms
1 each red and green pepper
breadcrumbs as needed
3 oz. (90 g) butter
5 fl. oz. (1½ dcL) each white wine and fish stock

Antoinette—Poach fillets, and remove to a hot platter. Cover with cream sauce mixed with chopped capers and shrimp.

16 fl. oz. (4½ dcL) cream sauce
2 oz. (60 g) capers
6 oz. (170 g) shrimp

Bouilli—Poach slices of fillet in court bouillon. Arrange on a hot platter. Serve with any appropriate sauce such as caper, hollandaise, shrimp, or egg; or accompany with a compound butter such as anchovy or lobster. Use a simple garnish such as chopped parsley. Boiled potatoes are always served with this dish.

Madame Hylton—Braise whole fish. Remove fillets, discard bones, but retain head and tail. Spread lower fillets with forcemeat. Place top fillets on forcemeat. Arrange on long dish with head and tail in position. Coat with Nantua sauce. Surround with boiled potatoes alternating with small tartlets containing green peas. Serve hollandaise sauce separately.

1 lb. (450 g) fish forcemeat
12 fl. oz. (3½ dcL) Nantua sauce
potatoes and tartlets as needed
hollandaise sauce as needed

Nelson—Poach fillets in stock with chopped onions, tomatoes, shallots, and parsley. Remove to a platter. Reduce stock by one-third and enrich with butter. Coat fish with stock, and garnish with croquette potatoes.

16 fl. oz. (4½ dcL) fish stock
6 oz. (170 g) onions
8 oz. (225 g) tomatoes
2 oz. (60 g) shallots
parsley to taste
3 oz. (90 g) butter
potatoes as needed

WHITING

All recipes are for 2½ lb. (1 kg) whole fish.

Bercy—Split fish up the back, and remove the backbone. Lay in buttered dish with chopped shallots, white wine, and lemon juice. Bake in oven. Reduce stock by one-half, and pour over fish. Glaze under broiler.

3 oz. (90 g) shallots
7 fl. oz. (2 dcL) white wine
juice of 1 lemon

Cecelia—Sauté fillets in butter. Garnish with asparagus tips that have been sprinkled with grated cheese.

Doria—Fry fillets in butter. Garnish with sautéed, sliced zucchini.

10 oz. (280 g) zucchini

Hôtelière—Remove backbone. Dip fish in beaten egg and breadcrumbs; deep-fry. Serve with maître d'hôtel sauce mixed with demiglace; garnish with diced, sautéed mushrooms.

beaten egg as needed
breadcrumbs as needed
7 fl. oz. (2 dcL) maître d'hôtel
  sauce
1 fl. oz. (¼ dcL) demi-glace
3 oz. (90 g) mushrooms

Lorgnette—Spread small fillets with forcemeat, and roll them into scrolls. Set scrolls on a dish sprinkled with chopped shallots; surround with sliced mushrooms. Top each scroll with a mushroom cap; moisten with white wine. Cover with Mornay sauce, breadcrumbs, and melted butter. Bake in a very hot oven.

4 oz. (115 g) forcemeat
2 oz. (60 g) chopped shallots

6 oz. (170 g) mushrooms
mushroom caps as needed
4 fl. oz. (1 dcL) white wine
6 fl. oz. (1½ dcL) Mornay sauce
breadcrumbs as needed
2 oz. (60 g) butter

Medici—Remove backbone. Dip
fish in beaten egg and breadcrumbs;
pan-fry. Garnish with small, grilled
tomatoes that have been scooped
out and filled with béarnaise sauce.

Quenelles à la Soubise—Shape
whiting forcemeat with tablespoons.
Poach in fumet; arrange on a hot
platter. Serve with Soubise sauce.
  2 lbs. (900 g) whiting forcemeat
  12 fl. oz. (3½ dcL) Soubise sauce

Mollusks, Crustacea, and Other Seafood

CLAMS

Casino—Mix whole clams with green pepper, onion, celery, hot pepper sauce, and Worcestershire sauce. Spoon into reserved clam shells. Sprinkle with cheese, cover with bacon slices, and bake for 10 minutes. Broil until bacon is crisp.

1 pt. (4½ dcL) whole clams
1 tsp (5 g) each minced green pepper, onion, and celery
hot pepper sauce to taste
¼ tsp. (1 mL) Worcestershire sauce
grated Parmesan cheese as needed
bacon strips as needed

Fritters—Shell clams and mince. Beat egg yolks until light. Add clams, cracker crumbs, salt and pepper, and cayenne. Moisten with enough clam juice to make a heavy batter. Fold in stiffly beaten egg whites, and drop the mixture by spoonfuls into hot oil. Sauté until brown.

2 eggs, separated
1 pt. (4½ dcL) whole clams
8 oz. (225 g) cracker crumbs
salt and pepper to taste
cayenne pepper to taste
clam juice as needed
oil for sautéing

Herbed Butter—Mash butter until soft; mix in parsley, oregano, garlic, Worcestershire sauce, and salt and pepper. Refrigerate until chilled. Mold butter into a log. Shuck clams. Cut butter into ¼-inch slices, and place one slice on each clam. Sprinkle with breadcrumbs; broil until browned.

4 oz. (115 g) butter
1 oz. (30 g) chopped parsley
½ oz. (15 g) each oregano and chopped garlic
1 tsp. (5 mL) Worcestershire sauce
salt and pepper to taste
2¼ pt. (1 L) clams in their shells
4 oz. (115 g) fresh breadcrumbs

Wine Broth—Wash clam shells thoroughly. Place wine and 1 oz. (30 g) butter in a large pot fitted with a rack. Arrange clams on top. Steam until clams open. Serve with the cooking juice, melted butter, and lemon wedges.

2¼ pt. (1 L) clams in their shells
4 fl. oz. (1 dcL) white wine
1 oz. (30 g) butter

4 fl. oz. (1 dcL) melted butter
1 lemon, quartered

CONCH

Fritters—Grind conch meat. Combine with onion, tomato, garlic, salt, parsley, cracker crumbs, and beaten egg yolks. Beat egg whites until stiff; fold into a batter. Drop by spoonfuls onto a well-buttered pan; cook until brown. Serve with lemon wedges.

  1 lb. (450 g) conch meat
  4 oz. (115 g) each chopped onion
    and tomato
  2 cloves garlic, chopped
  salt to taste
  2 oz. (60 g) chopped parsley
  8 oz. (225 g) cracker crumbs
  3 eggs, separated
  1 lemon, quartered

Tomato Sauce—Tenderize the conchs. Sauté the onions and garlic in oil. Add the basil, salt, tomato sauce, and wine; simmer. Add the conch, and cook until tender. Serve with rice.

  1 lb. (450 g) conch meat
  2 onions, chopped
  3 cloves garlic, chopped
  6 Tbs. (90 mL) olive oil
  1 tsp (5 g) each basil and salt
  16 fl. oz. (4½ dcL) tomato sauce
  8 fl. oz. (2¼ dcL) red wine

CRAB

These shellfish are cooked in salted water, and the white and soft brown meat is removed from the shell and claws. In the following recipes, 1½ lb. (675 g) of meat is the standard production unit. Only the white meat should be used.

Baltimore—Sauté flaked meat in butter with chopped shallots, a dash of Worcestershire sauce, cayenne pepper, and dry mustard. Coat scallop shells or empty crab shells with 4 fl. oz. of the Mornay sauce. Cover with crab mixture, then with 12 fl. oz. of Mornay sauce. Sprinkle with Parmesan cheese, dot with butter, and glaze under broiler.

  3 oz. (90 g) butter
  1 oz. (30 g) shallots
  Worcestershire sauce, cayenne
    pepper, and dry mustard to
    taste
  16 fl. oz. (4½ dcL) Mornay sauce
  Parmesan cheese as needed
  breadcrumbs as needed
  3 oz. (90 g) butter

Bordelaise—Flake crabmeat, and mix with sautéed mushrooms. Moisten with bordelaise sauce. Spoon mixture into vol-au-vents.

  5 oz. (140 g) mushrooms
  1½ oz. (45 g) butter
  12 fl. oz. (3½ dcL) bordelaise
    sauce
  vol-au-vents as needed

Dewey—Heat flaked crabmeat in butter with lemon juice and cayenne pepper. Add rich cream sauce flavored with sherry. Serve on a base of creamed potatoes. Garnish with poached oysters and sautéed button mushrooms.

  3 oz. (90 g) butter
  1 fl. oz. (¼ dcL) lemon juice
  cayenne pepper to taste
  12 fl. oz. (3½ dcL) cream sauce

2 fl. oz. (½ dcL) Amontillado
  sherry
potatoes as needed
12 poached oysters
6 oz. (170 g) button mushrooms

Diable—Sweat minced onions in butter until soft. Add flaked crab-meat, and mix. Add cream sauce mixed with Cognac, cayenne pep-per, dry mustard, and Worcester-shire sauce to taste. Spoon mixture into scallop shells. Sprinkle with breadcrumbs, dot with butter, and brown in oven.

2 oz. (60 g) onions
1 oz. (30 g) butter
12 fl. oz. (3½ dcL) cream sauce
Cognac, cayenne pepper, dry
  mustard, and Worcestershire
  sauce
breadcrumbs as needed
3 oz. (90 g) butter

Italian—Sweat finely chopped onions in butter with garlic; add chopped parsley and a little tomato sauce. Mix in flaked crabmeat; sprinkle with grated Gruyère mixed with breadcrumbs. Dot with butter, and brown in oven.

2 oz. (60 g) onions
2 oz. (60 g) butter
garlic to taste
parsley to taste
1 fl. oz. (¼ dcL) tomato sauce
4 oz. (115 g) each breadcrumbs
  and Gruyère cheese

Maryland—Gently fry flaked crabmeat in butter. Simmer in cream. Mix in cayenne pepper, and add Cognac at the end. Serve from chafing dish on triangles of hot toast.

2 oz. (60 g) butter
10 fl. oz. (3 dcL) cream
pinch of cayenne pepper
1 fl. oz. (¼ dcL) Cognac

Mexican—Sauté chopped onions, diced green peppers, and garlic in butter. Add Worcestershire sauce and flaked crabmeat; mix well. Fill shells, coat with Mornay sauce, and glaze.

1 oz. (30 g) butter
1 oz. (30 g) each onions and green
  peppers
garlic to taste
1 fl. oz. (¼ dcL) Worcestershire
  sauce
12 fl. oz. (3½ dcL) Mornay sauce

Salad—Mix finely chopped celery with flaked crabmeat. Moisten with mayonnaise. Arrange on a bed of lettuce and garnish with capers, chopped anchovies, black olives, and hard-boiled eggs.

3 oz. (90 g) celery
5 fl. oz. (2½ dcL) mayonnaise
capers, anchovies, black olives,
  and hard-boiled eggs as
  needed

CRAYFISH

All recipes are for 24 crayfish tails, each weighing about 4 oz.

Aneth—Cook shelled tails. Bind with fish velouté, and finish with cream flavored with dill. Serve on rice pilaf.

Bordelaise—Clean the crayfish. Toss in ½ oz. of butter with cooked mirepoix until the crayfish have a fine, red color. Moisten with white wine and flamed brandy. Reduce cooking liquid by one-third; add espagnole sauce, tomato purée, and fish fumet. Cook for 10 minutes. Remove crayfish, and arrange on platter. Reduce sauce by one-fourth; add meat glaze, 2 oz. of butter, chopped chervil, and tarragon. Blend, and pour over fish.

1½ oz. (45 g) butter
2 oz. (60 g) mirepoix
7 fl. oz. (2 dcL) white wine
3 fl. oz. (¾ dcL) brandy
2 fl. oz. (½ dcL) espagnole sauce
2 fl. oz. (½ dcL) tomato purée
5 fl. oz. (1½ dcL) fish fumet
1 fl. oz. (¼ dcL) meat glaze
2 oz. (60 g) butter
pinch of chervil
pinch of tarragon

Georgette—Scoop out baked potatoes. Fill potato shells with roughly chopped tails. Coat with Nantua sauce, sprinkle with grated cheese, and glaze under a broiler.

Lafayette—Sauté tails in butter with lemon juice. Remove and shell; add cream to pan. Thicken with egg yolks, and stir in brandy and dry sherry.

2 oz. (60 g) butter
1 fl. oz. (¼ dcL) lemon juice
12 fl. oz. (3½ dcL) cream
2 egg yolks
1 Tbs. (15 mL) each brandy and
    dry sherry

Liègeoise—Cook crayfish in court bouillon. Dish into a timbale, and keep warm. Strain court bouillon, and reduce by one-fourth. Add butter; pour over fish.

24 fl. oz. (6½ dcL) court bouillon
2 oz. (60 g) butter

Marinière—Toss cleaned crayfish in butter over high flame to obtain good color. Add finely chopped shallots, thyme, and bay leaf. Moisten with white wine. Cover, and cook for 10 minutes. Arrange on a hot platter. Reduce cooking liquid by one-half. Thicken with fish velouté, enrich with butter, and pour over fish.

1½ oz. (45 g) butter
1 oz. (30 g) shallots
pinch of thyme
pinch of bay leaf
7 fl. oz. (3 dcL) white wine
5 fl. oz. (1½ dcL) fish velouté
2 oz. (60 g) butter

Mousse—Cook crayfish *à la mirepoix*. Drain and shell. Pound shells in mortar with mirepoix; add butter, cold fish velouté, and melted aspic jelly. Rub through a fine sieve into saucepan; add lightly whipped cream and the diced tails. Line charlotte mold with buttered paper, and fill with mixture; set in refrigerator. Just before serving, garnish as desired.

2 oz. (60 g) mirepoix
1½ oz. (45 g) butter
5 fl. oz. (1½ dcL) fish velouté
3 fl. oz. (¾ dcL) melted aspic
7 fl. oz. (2 dcL) cream

Ragoût à la Nantua—Cook tails in white wine with mirepoix for 10 minutes. Drain, and remove shells. Put tails in pan with butter; heat without browning. Sprinkle with flour, and mix. Moisten with brandy and cream; mix again. Simmer very gently for 10 minutes, then add Nantua sauce.

- 5 fl. oz. (1½ dcL) white wine
- 1 oz. (30 g) mirepoix
- 1 oz. (30 g) butter
- 1 oz. (30 g) flour
- 1 fl. oz. (¼ dcL) brandy
- 2 fl. oz. (½ dcL) cream
- 12 fl. oz. (3½ dcL) Nantua sauce

Voltaire—Lightly sauté thick slices of mushrooms in very hot butter. Mix with crayfish tails. Cook in cream and lemon juice. Flavor with brandy; thicken with yolks.

- 6 oz. (170 g) mushrooms
- 2 oz. (60 g) butter
- 12 fl. oz. (3½ dcL) cream
- 1 fl. oz. (¼ dcL) lemon juice
- 1 fl. oz. (¼ dcL) brandy
- 2 egg yolks

FROGS' LEGS

All recipes are for 24 legs.

Basic Preparation: Cut off feet, then skewer legs and immerse in very cold water. Change water every hour and allow three changes of water; this will swell and whiten the legs.

Béchamel—Season legs and pan-fry in a covered pan in butter and white wine. Simmer for 1 minute. Enrich the sauce with butter; dress and serve.

- butter and white wine as needed
- *Sauce:*
- 1 fl. oz. (¼ dcL) cream
- 1 oz. (30 g) butter

Fricassée—Poach legs in white wine and butter. Remove and dress. Reduce liquid by one-half. Add fish or chicken velouté; enrich with cream. Add finely sliced blanched mushrooms. Pour sauce over legs.

- 16 fl. oz. (4½ dcL) white wine
- 2 oz. (60 g) butter
- *Sauce:*
- 2 fl. oz. (½ dcL) velouté
- 1 fl. oz. (¼ dcL) cream
- 4 oz. (115 g) mushrooms

Gratinée—Proceed as for fricassée but do not add mushrooms. Place legs in a casserole bordered with duchesse potatoes. Cover with sauce, cheese, and breadcrumbs. Bake.

- 2 oz. (60 g) cheese
- breadcrumbs as needed

Lyonnaise—Dip preseasoned legs in flour, then sauté in butter over a high flame. When browned, add minced onion to pan. Cook for 6 minutes. Add chopped parsley. Remove legs, keeping warm. Add lemon juice to pan; pour liquid over legs.

- 4 oz. (115 g) butter
- 1 oz. (30 g) onion
- parsley as needed
- juice of 1 lemon

Malagueña—Fry legs in butter. Cover with a mixture of sautéed onions, garlic, green peppers, sliced eggplant, and chopped tomatoes. Dress on dish and garnish with chopped parsley.

- 4 oz. (115 g) butter
- 2 oz. (60 g) onions
- 2 cloves garlic

2 oz. (60 g) green peppers
4 oz. (115 g) eggplant
12 oz. (340 g) tomatoes
parsley as needed

Mirepoix—Sauté preseasoned and floured legs in butter until tender. Add softened vegetable mirepoix. Mix well and heat over a high flame. Finish with concentrated meat stock poured into the pan; serve in this sauce.

4 oz. (115 g) butter
4 oz. (115 g) vegetable mirepoix
2 fl. oz. (½ dcL) concentrated meat stock

Mornay—Cook preseasoned legs in butter; moisten with white wine and lemon juice. Place legs in baking dish lined with 4 oz. Mornay sauce and bordered with duchesse potatoes. Brush potatoes with egg yolk. Add pan juices to remaining sauce; pour over legs. Sprinkle with cheese and brown under grill.

4 oz. (115 g) butter
2 fl. oz. (½ dcL) white wine
squeeze of lemon
16 fl. oz. (4½ dcL) Mornay sauce
1 egg yolk
3 oz. (90 g) cheese

Poulette—Poach legs in seasoned white wine and lemon juice. Add chopped onion and bouquet garni. When boiling, add mushrooms; simmer until legs are tender. Drain legs and mushrooms and strain liquid, reducing by one-half; thicken with egg yolk and cream. Return legs and mushrooms to thickened sauce. Heat.

16 fl. oz. (4½ dcL) seasoned white wine
juice of two lemons
1 oz. (30 g) onion
bouquet garni as needed
6 oz. (170 g) whole mushrooms
1 egg yolk
2 fl. oz. (½ dcL) cream

LOBSTER

All recipes are for 1 lobster weighing approximately 2 lb. (900 g).

Note: A lobster *queen* is the little bag near the head, often containing gravel.

Américaine—Remove and crack claws; separate tail from body. Cut body in half lengthwise, and remove queen. Cut tail into sections; season with salt and cayenne pepper. Set aside creamy section and the coral. Fry in oil and 2 oz. of butter mixed with chopped onion and garlic. Add chopped shallots at last moment; moisten with flamed brandy, white wine, and fumet. Add chopped tomatoes and tomato purée; cook for 20 minutes. Arrange lobster on silver platter. Reduce cooking liquid to about 7 fl. oz.; add creamy parts of lobster and chopped coral. Enrich with 1 oz. of butter, strain sauce, and coat lobster.

Salt and cayenne pepper to taste
1 fl. oz. (¼ dcL) oil
2 oz. (60 g) butter
1 oz. (30 g) onion
1 clove garlic
1 oz. (30 g) shallots
2 fl. oz. (½ dcL) brandy
7 fl. oz. (2 dcL) white wine
2 fl. oz. (½ dcL) fish fumet
8 oz. (255 g) ripe tomatoes

1 Tbs. tomato purée
1 oz. (30 g) butter

Bohemian—Cook live lobster in court bouillon. Cut in half, and remove meat from tail and claws. Cut meat into thin slices, and return it to empty tail shells that have been lined with foie gras. Lay filled shells in buttered baking dish. Cover with Bohemian sauce, sprinkle with cheese, and brown in oven.
    court bouillon to cover
    3 oz. (90 g) foie gras
    8 fl. oz. (2¼ dcL) Bohemian
        sauce
    2 oz. (60 g) cheese

Bordelaise—Cut live lobster as for Américaine recipe. Sauté tail and body in 2 oz. of butter to stiffen and color. Remove; pour away about half the butter. Add chopped shallots, garlic, white wine, and brandy; cook together for 5 minutes to reduce. Add fumet, espagnole sauce, tomato sauce, bouquet garni, and cayenne pepper; mix. Return lobster to the pan, and cook, covered, for 20 minutes. Remove meat from tail and claws, and keep warm. Add coral and liver to sauce; reduce to 7 fl. oz. Pass through a tammy. Return lobster pieces to the sauce; heat without boiling. Add chopped chervil and tarragon, and enrich with 3 oz. of butter. Pour into serving dish.
    2 oz. (60 g) butter
    1 oz. (30 g) shallots
    1 clove garlic
    4 fl. oz. (1 dcL) white wine
    1 fl. oz. (¼ dcL) brandy
    10 fl. oz. (3 dcL) fish fumet

7 fl. oz. (2 dcL) espagnole sauce
2 fl. oz. (½ dcL) tomato sauce
bouquet garni
cayenne pepper to taste
chervil and tarragon to taste
3 oz. (90 g) butter

Cardinal—Cook the live lobster whole in court bouillon for about 20 minutes. Cut lengthwise, and remove meat from tail. Slice the meat, and keep it hot. Moisten with a little Cardinal sauce. Open claws, remove meat, and cut into dice. Add liver. Line the two empty half-shells with Cardinal sauce; rest lobster meat on them. Cover with same sauce, sprinkle with grated cheese, and glaze under the broiler.
    court bouillon to cover
    10 fl. oz. (3 dcL) Cardinal sauce
    2 oz. (60 g) cheese

Churchill—Split live lobster lengthwise. Coat with a mixture of softened butter, dry mustard, salt, and cayenne pepper. Set on tray, and bake in oven.
Clarence—Cook whole, live lobster in court bouillon. Split in half. Sprinkle with curry powder, and toss halves in melted butter. Remove meat, and cut into thin slices. Fill empty tail shell with boiled rice mixed with a little Mornay sauce. Place the slices of lobster on rice, and coat with Mornay sauce slightly flavored with curry. Glaze under the broiler.
    court bouillon to cover
    curry powder to taste
    2 oz. (60 g) raw rice
    10 fl. oz. (3 dcL) Mornay sauce

Dumas—Cook lobster in court bouillon. Remove meat, and cut into thin slices. Sauté meat in butter; remove. Deglaze pan with white wine; add tomato-flavored demi-glace. Arrange in a timbale, and garnish with fleurons.
court bouillon to cover
1½ oz. (45 g) butter
2 fl. oz. (½ dcL) white wine
2 fl. oz. (½ dcL) demi-glace
3 fleurons

Grammont—Cook lobster in court bouillon. Cut in half lengthwise. Remove and chop the meat. Fill half-shells with lobster mousse, and arrange thin slices of lobster meat on top, alternating with cold, poached oysters and truffle slices. Coat with aspic jelly, arrange on dish, and chill.
court bouillon to cover
5 Tbs. (5 mL) lobster mousse
oysters and truffle as needed
3½ fl. oz. (1 dcL) aspic jelly

Henri Duvernois—Split lobster, and joint it. Season with salt and paprika; sauté in 2 oz. of butter. Remove from pan. Add julienne of leeks and button mushrooms tossed in butter; return lobster. Moisten pan with sherry and brandy; reduce liquid by one-fourth. Add cream, cover pan, and simmer for 20 minutes. Arrange lobster on dish in the center of rice pilaf. Reduce sauce by one-fourth, enrich with 1 oz. of butter, and pour over lobster.
2 oz. (60 g) butter
2 oz. (60 g) each leeks and mushrooms

5 fl. oz. (1½ dcL) Amontillado sherry
1 fl. oz. (¼ dcL) brandy
2 fl. oz. (½ dcL) cream
3 oz. (90 g) raw rice
1 oz. (30 g) butter

Hungarian—Proceed as for Newburg recipe, adding chopped onion and paprika sautéed in butter, and omitting sherry.
3 oz. (90 g) onions
1 oz. (30 g) butter
paprika to taste

Lord Randolph—Cut live lobster in half; grill. Remove meat. Dice the meat, and mix it with anchovy butter and chopped parsley. Refill shells. Coat with Mornay sauce, sprinkle with grated parmesan, and glaze.
2 oz. (60 g) anchovy butter
parsley to taste
4 fl. oz. (1 dcL) Mornay sauce
2 oz. (60 g) Parmesan cheese

Mousse—Cook lobster in court bouillon; allow to cool. Split lobster, crack claws, and remove meat. Pound meat in mortar, adding cold fish velouté little by little. Rub mixture through a sieve. Mix well, and chill. Add fish aspic that has been melted and cooled. Add lightly whipped cream. Correct seasoning. Spoon into molds, and chill until set.
court bouillon to cover
10 fl. oz. (3 dcL) fish velouté
2 fl. oz. (½ dcL) fish aspic
6 fl. oz. (1½ dcL) cream

Newburg—Cut live lobster as for Américaine recipe. Season; sauté in the first 1 oz. of butter and oil for 15 minutes. Remove lobster. Deglaze pan with brandy and sherry; reduce by one-third. Season, and add cream and fumet. Return lobster to the pan, cover, and cook for 20 minutes. Remove lobster, and take meat from shell. Arrange on a dish, and keep warm. Thicken sauce with liver, coral, and the second 1 oz. of butter. Heat sauce again. Run through a tammy, and pour over pieces of lobster. (Sauce should coat back of spoon.)

Salt and pepper to taste
1 oz. (30 g) butter
1 Tbs. (15 mL) oil
1 fl. oz. (¼ dcL) brandy
7 fl. oz. (2 dcL) Amontillado
    sherry
10 fl. oz. (3½ dcL) cream
3 fl. oz. (¾ dcL) fish fumet
1 oz. (30 g) butter

Port—Use 2 small lobsters for this recipe. Split lobsters; remove meat, and sauté in butter with salt and paprika. Cover with port wine, and cook until tender. Remove meat from pan; cut into slices, and reduce liquid by one-third. Thicken with egg yolk and cream. Arrange thin slices of meat on dish, and pour sauce over them.

2 oz. (60 g) butter
salt and paprika to taste
port as needed
1 or 2 egg yolks
1 fl. oz. (¼ dcL) cream

Ragoût à la Trouville—Cut boiled lobster into thin slices. Mix with sliced, sautéed mushrooms, poached oysters, mussels, and truffle pieces. Moisten with normande sauce. Arrange a dish with a border of risotto; put lobster mixture in center. Cover with Mornay sauce and grated cheese; glaze.

1 oz. (30 g) butter
4 oz. (115 g) mushrooms
6 oysters
6 mussels
truffle pieces as needed
5 fl. oz. (1½ dcL) normande
    sauce
risotto as needed
8 fl. oz. (2¼ dcL) Mornay sauce
2 oz. (60 g) cheese

Scalloped (Mornay, Parisienne, etc.)—Border silver shells or scallop shells with duchesse potatoes. Brown potatoes in oven. Coat base with appropriate sauce. Place thin slices of lobster over the base. Cover with same sauce, and glaze.

Soufflé—Note weight of lobster meat used in this recipe. Pound cooked lobster, and rub through a sieve. Mix béchamel sauce with a little court bouillon, and add to lobster. Season as usual, adding nutmeg. Blend in egg yolks, then stiffly beaten whites. Put mixture in buttered soufflé molds, and cook for 25 to 30 minutes.

11 oz. (310 g) lobster meat
6 fl. oz. (1½ dcL) béchamel sauce
court bouillon as needed
4 eggs, separated

Suchet—Cook lobster in court bouillon; allow to cool. Remove meat from shell and claws; cut into thin slices. Sauté julienne of lightly cooked vegetables in butter, adding a dash of white wine; strain. Put vegetables in half-shells; top with slices of lobster. Cover with white wine sauce, and glaze.

    court bouillon to cover
    6 oz. (170 g) appropriate vegeta-
       bles (mushrooms and celery,
       for example)
    1 oz. (30 g) butter
    2 fl. oz. (½ dcL) white wine
    5 fl. oz. (1½ dcL) white wine
       sauce

Thermidor—Cook lobster in court bouillon; halve lengthwise. Slice lobster meat, and line shells with a mixture of Bercy sauce, Mornay sauce, and dry mustard. Fill shells with meat; cover with same sauce mixture. Sprinkle with grated cheese, and glaze.

    court bouillon to cover
    5 fl. oz. (1½ dcL) Bercy sauce
    3 fl. oz. (¾ dcL) Mornay sauce
    ½ oz. (2½ mL) dry mustard
    2 oz. (30 g) cheese

Vol-au-Vent—Assortment of lobster, shrimp, and crayfish bound with Américaine sauce and served in puff pastry cases.

Xavier—Proceed as for Ragoût à la Trouville, substituting Nantua sauce for the Mornay sauce. Fill half-shells, cover with grated cheese, and glaze.

    10 fl. oz. (3 dcL) Nantua sauce
    2 oz. (60 g) cheese

MUSSELS

All recipes are for 4 quarts of mussels.

Bonne Femme—Wash and beard mussels. Cook in white wine with aromatics; remove mussels. Discard bouquet garni and garlic; reduce cooking liquid slightly. Beat in egg yolks and cream; add melted butter. Put mussels in deep dish, and pour sauce over them.

    32 fl. oz. (9 dcL) white wine
    4 oz. (115 g) chopped onion
    4 oz. (115 g) julienne of mush-
       rooms
    4 oz. (115 g) chopped celery
    bouquet garni
    2 cloves garlic, left whole
    4 egg yolks
    7 fl. oz. (2 dcL) cream
    2 oz. (60 g) butter

Commodore—Clean, poach, and chop mussels. Arrange in scallop shells. Sprinkle with herb butter and finely diced bacon; bake in oven.

    8 oz. (225 g) herb butter
    6 oz. (170 g) bacon

Fritters—Poach mussels. Remove from shells, and marinate in oil, lemon juice, and parsley for 1 hour. Drain, dip in batter, and deep-fry.

    5:1 oil to lemon juice
    parsley to taste

Mouclade—Heat cleaned mussels in a dry pan over a high flame until they open. Discard empty half-shells. Strain mussel liquid, and put in another pan. Heat gently, and add butter, garlic, parsley, curry powder, and seasoning. Add mussels; simmer 5 minutes. Add cream; heat through and serve.

    8 oz. (225 g) butter
    2 cloves garlic
    parsley to taste

pinch of curry powder
salt and pepper to taste
10 fl. oz. (3 dcL) cream

Nantua—Cook mussels *à la bonne femme,* but add cooked, shelled mussels to Nantua sauce. Serve on toast or in casseroles.
20 fl. oz. (6 dcL) Nantua sauce

Provençale—Heat mussels in a dry pan over a high flame until they open. Remove one half of each shell. In another pan, heat oil with finely chopped parsley, chives, mushrooms, and garlic; sauté for a few minutes. Add wine, strained liquid from mussels, and fish fumet; heat until liquid thickens slightly. Add black pepper and the mussels. When serving, sprinkle with lemon juice and grated nutmeg.
2 fl. oz. (½ dcL) oil
1 oz. (30 g) each parsley, chives, and mushrooms
1 clove garlic
12 fl. oz. (3½ dcL) wine
5 fl. oz. (1½ dcL) fish fumet
black pepper, lemon juice, and nutmeg to taste

OYSTERS

All recipes are for 24 oysters.
Basic Preparation: Poach oysters in their own liquor. Drain, dry, and cool. Remove beards. Proceed with recipe. Retain liquor for other use.
Américaine—Poach; lay oysters in deep halves of their shells. Set on baking dish lined with rock salt to keep shells firm. Sprinkle with lemon juice, a dash of cayenne pepper, and fried breadcrumbs. Sea-

son. Drizzle a little melted butter over each shell, and brown in hot oven.
Andalouse—Poach oysters. Allow to cool and garnish each with a sliver of truffle. Take 12 deep half shells and line them generously with tomato mousse. Set two oysters in each shell and mask completely with half-set truffle aspic.
½ oz. (15 g) truffles
12 Tbs. (180 mL) tomato mousse
12 Tbs. (180 mL) truffle aspic

Anglaise—Thread oysters and squares of lean bacon alternately on small metal skewers. Dust with cayenne pepper, and grill.
Barquettes—Poach oysters, and mask with glazing mayonnaise. Decorate with truffles or truffle aspic, and crayfish coral. Set decoration in place with aspic. Place oysters in pairs in oval barquettes, and garnish as desired.
Barquettes à l'Américaine—Poach oysters. Lay 3 oysters in each barquette lined with américaine sauce. Cover with fried breadcrumbs; season with cayenne pepper. Drizzle a little butter over oysters, and brown in hot oven.
8 barquettes
4 fl. oz. (1 dcL) américaine sauce
12 Tbs. (180 g) breadcrumbs
cayenne pepper to taste
2 oz. (60 g) melted butter

Bouchettes Villeroi—Poach oysters, and thread them on small metal skewers. Cover with Villeroi sauce. Dip in beaten egg and breadcrumbs; deep-fry.
Bourguignonne—Beard oysters,

and arrange them on the half-shell. Coat with garlic butter. Sprinkle with breadcrumbs and melted butter; glaze.

Caviar—Set uncooked oysters in small pastry barquettes lined with caviar. Garnish with parsley; serve with lemon.

24 barquettes
6 oz. (170 g) caviar
parsley and lemon as needed

Cream—Detach oysters from shell; remove beard. Line each half-shell with cream. Replace oysters. Sprinkle with butter and grated cheese; grill under fairly high flame.

8 fl. oz. (2¼ dcL) cream
4 oz. (115 g) butter
4 oz. (115 g) cheese

Delmonico—Poach oysters. Arrange in half-shell. Coat with cream sauce thickened with egg yolk and mixed with lemon juice.

12 fl. oz. (3½ dcL) cream sauce
1 egg yolk
juice of 1 lemon

Dubarry—Poach oysters. Arrange in scooped-out, baked potatoes. Cover with cream sauce, sprinkle with grated cheese, and glaze under broiler. Use 3 or 4 oysters per potato.

6–8 baked potatoes
7 fl. oz. (2 dcL) cream sauce
4 oz. (115 g) cheese

Florentine—Poach oysters. Line each half-shell with cooked, chopped spinach mixed with a little melted butter. Lay an oyster on each. Cover with Mornay sauce,

sprinkle with cheese, and brown in hot oven.

12 oz. (340 g) cooked spinach
2 oz. (60 g) butter
12 fl. oz. (3½ dcL) Mornay sauce
4 oz. (115 g) cheese

Fricassée Baltimore—Lightly brown butter in pan. Add flour, pepper, and chopped parsley; mix well. Add bearded oysters, and cook slowly until edges begin to curl. Add beaten yolks, stirring constantly until set. Arrange on a dish. Surround with a ring of fried breadcrumbs, chopped parsley, and lemon quarters.

1½ oz. (45 g) butter
1 oz. (30 g) flour
pepper to taste
chopped parsley to taste
2 egg yolks
breadcrumbs, parsley, and lemon
    quarters as needed

Grilled—Poach oysters, and thread them on small metal skewers. Dip in melted butter mixed with lemon juice, salt, and pepper; then in fine breadcrumbs. Grill over a low flame.

2 oz. (60 g) butter
lemon juice to taste
salt and pepper to taste
breadcrumbs as needed

Louis—Beard oysters; arrange on the half-shell. Cover with breadcrumbs mixed with paprika and chopped shallots sautéed in 1 oz. butter. Drizzle 2 oz. melted butter on top of each, and bake in oven.

breadcrumbs as needed
paprika to taste

6 oz. (170 g) shallots
1 oz. (30 g) butter
2 oz. (60 g) butter

Manhattan—Beard oysters; arrange on the half-shell. Mix together chopped, fried, lean bacon pieces; blanched, minced red and green peppers; sliced mushrooms; chopped onions; and a little oregano. Cover oysters with this mixture. Drizzle a little butter over each oyster, and bake in oven.
4 oz. (115 g) bacon
3 oz. (90 g) each vegetable
oregano
butter as needed

Quenelles à la Reine—Make a mousseline with pounded chicken breasts, raw oysters, egg white, and cream. Shape this mixture with a tablespoon into quenelles, placing two cold, poached oysters in the center of each quenelle. Poach the quenelles. Drain, and arrange on a dish. Cover with highly seasoned suprême sauce. Garnish the top of each quenelle with a tiny piece of truffle or decoratively shaped truffle aspic, and garnish the center of the serving dish with asparagus tips. This recipe will produce 6 very large quenelles, each sufficient for one portion.
Mousseline:
8 oz. (225 g) chicken breast
12 raw, bearded oysters
seasoning for suprême sauce
1 egg white
10 fl. oz. (3 dcL) thick cream
5 fl. oz. (1½ dcL) suprême sauce
asparagus tips as needed

Soufflé—Poach oysters, and set 12 aside. Pound remaining 12 in mortar. Mix in the egg white little by little. Rub mixture through a sieve. Stir in cream, mixing over a bowl of ice. Line 12 half-shells with a little forcemeat; put a cooked oyster on top. Cover with a layer of soufflé mixture, forming it into a dome. Bake in oven.
1 egg white
7 fl. oz. (2 dcL) cream
8 oz. (225 g) forcemeat

Stewed—Poach oysters in milk almost to cover. Add 1 fl. oz. cream, and season with salt, pepper, and nutmeg.
Valpariso—Beard oysters, and arrange them on the half-shell, covered with raw, chopped, tender celery and mushrooms. Coat with cream sauce, and glaze under a broiler.
6 oz. (170 g) each celery and
   mushrooms
6 fl. oz. (1½ dcL) cream sauce

SCALLOPS

All recipes are for 2¼ lb. (1 kg) scallops.
Curry—Blanch and dice scallops; sauté in butter with chopped onions and a dash of tomato purée. Add curry sauce, and finish cooking. Serve on a rice pilaf.
4 oz. (115 g) butter
4 oz. (115 g) onions
tomato purée to taste
21 fl. oz. (6 dcL) curry sauce
rice as needed

Fritters—Poach scallops in court bouillon; drain and slice. Marinate in oil, lemon juice, and chopped parsley for 30 minutes. Dip in light batter, and deep-fry.

Fritters with Tartar Sauce—Proceed as for fritters. Serve tartar sauce separately. Scallops fried this way can be served with a variety of sauces, such as béarnaise, Portuguese, or Hungarian, and will take the name of the accompanying sauce.

Au Gratin—Blanch, slice, and braise scallops in white wine and mushroom essence. Arrange scallops in their shells on a little duxelles bound with tomato sauce. Coat with Mornay sauce, sprinkle with breadcrumbs, and brown under the broiler.

    12 fl. oz. (3½ dcL) white wine
    1 fl. oz. (¼ dcL) mushroom essence
    duxelles as needed
    2 fl. oz. (½ dcL) tomato sauce
    12 fl. oz. (3½ dcL) Mornay sauce
    breadcrumbs as needed

Marinade—Sprinkle over fish or other seafood. Moisten only with olive oil and a good squeeze of lemon juice. Turn fish over every ½ hour.

    2 oz. (60 g) minced onion
    8 sprigs parsley, chopped coarse
    2 bay leaves, crushed
    1 clove garlic, minced
    2 fl. oz. (½ dcL) olive oil

Mayonnaise—Line each shell with finely chopped, seasoned lettuce. Place poached scallops that have been preseasoned with oil, vinegar, and chopped parsley on this base. Coat with mayonnaise, and garnish with crossed slices of anchovy fillets. Sprinkle a few capers between the angles.

    lettuce as needed
    salt and pepper to taste
    12 fl. oz. (3½ dcL) mayonnaise
    anchovies and capers as needed

Nantaise—Proceed as for scallops au gratin, but surround scallops in their shells with poached, chopped oysters and mussels. Coat with white wine sauce, and glaze under the broiler.

    1 oyster and 2 mussels for each
        shell, approximately

Newburg—Slice scallops. Gently sauté in butter to stiffen them. Cook in a rich cream sauce flavored with cayenne pepper and sherry.

    3 oz. (90 g) butter
    24 fl. oz. (7 dcL) cream sauce
    cayenne pepper to taste
    2 fl. oz. (½ dcL) sherry

Ostendaise—Proceed as for Nantaise recipe, but garnish with shrimp and chopped mushrooms. Coat with Nantua sauce, and garnish with parsley.

    6 oz. (170 g) shrimp
    3 oz. (90 g) mushrooms
    12 fl. oz. (3½ dcL) Nantua sauce

Parisienne—Proceed as for Ostendaise recipe, but border each shell with duchesse potatoes. Coat with white wine sauce, and glaze.

    1½ lb. (675 g) potatoes
    12 fl. oz. (3½ dcL) white wine
        sauce

SHRIMP

All recipes are for 1½ lb. (675 g) of shrimp.

Coquilles—Line the bottom of scallop shells with cooked asparagus tips. Place cooked shrimp on top. Line border with duchesse potatoes. Cover with Mornay sauce, sprinkle with grated Parmesan, and glaze.

5 asparagus tips per shell
1½ lb (675 g) potatoes
10 fl. oz. (3 dcL) Mornay sauce
3 oz. (90 g) Parmesan cheese

Creole—Sauté shrimp in butter and lemon juice. Mix with creole sauce. Serve on bed of plain, boiled rice.

4 oz. (115 g) butter
1 fl. oz. (¼ dcL) lemon juice
12 fl. oz. (3½ dcL) creole sauce

Curry—Proceed as for Creole recipe, substituting curry sauce for creole sauce.

Mousse—Cook shrimp in white wine with mirepoix. Peel shrimp, and pass them through a sieve. Add fish velouté, then aspic, and a little lightly whipped cream. Line molds with aspic, fill with mousse, garnish, and top with aspic to seal.

12 fl. oz. (3½ dcL) white wine
6 oz. (170 g) mirepoix
Make purée and use one-quarter
    of its volume of velouté
1 Tbs. (15 mL) cream
12 fl. oz. (3½ dcL) aspic
decorative aspics or vegetable
    stars as needed for garnish

Puffs—Roughly chop cooked shrimp. Add to the batter, and deep-fry. Serve tartar sauce separately.

Batter:
1 lb. (450 g) flour
1 oz. (30 g) baking powder
pinch of salt, nutmeg, and thyme
2 eggs
16 fl. oz. (4½ dcL) milk

Vol-au-Vent—Diced cooked shrimp and oysters bound with shrimp sauce and served in puff pastry cases. Garnish with poached oysters.

SNAILS

All recipes are for 24 snails that have been prewashed, blanched, cleaned, and poached.

Bourguignonne—Place a piece of chilled snail butter inside each shell. Return cooked snails to shell and seal entrance with butter. Sprinkle with breadcrumbs moistened with a little olive oil. Put in oven and warm thoroughly.

Chablisienne—Pour a few drops of sauce made with chopped shallots and parsley stewed in Chablis and enriched with meat demi-glace into each empty shell. Return snails to shells; seal entrance with snail butter.

1 oz. (30 g) shallots
parlsey as needed
4 fl. oz. (1 dcL) Chablis
2 fl. oz. (½ dcL) demi-glace
snail butter as needed

Grenobloise—Proceed as for bourguignonne, but add crushed hazelnuts to the butter.

Mode de l'Abbaye—Fry minced onions in butter and add snails. Sprinkle with flour and moisten with cream. Simmer for 15 minutes. Thicken with egg yolk and enrich with butter. Serve snails in this sauce, not in their shells.

4 oz. (115 g) onions
2 oz. (60 g) butter
½ oz. (15 g) flour
7 fl. oz. (2 dcL) cream
1 egg yolk
1½ oz. (45 g) butter

Provençale—Make stuffing by heating olive oil and adding minced mushrooms, green peppers, shallots, garlic, and chopped parsley and cooking for 5 minutes. Mix in flour and moisten with white wine. Add salt, nutmeg, and cayenne pepper; cook for 5 minutes more. Stir in beaten egg yolk. Add snails and heat through. Fill each shell with some stuffing and one snail. Cover entrance with thin layer of breadcrumbs moistened with olive oil. Brown in hot oven.

1 fl. oz. (¼ dcL) olive oil
1 oz. (30 g) mushrooms, green peppers, shallots
1 clove garlic
parsley as needed
½ oz. (15 g) flour

7 fl. oz. (2 dcL) white wine
salt, nutmeg, and cayenne pepper as needed
1 egg yolk
2 oz. (60 g) breadcrumbs
olive oil as needed

Vigneronne—Toss cooked, shelled snails in butter mixed with chopped shallots, garlic, seasonings, and nutmeg. Dip in batter and deep-fry. Dress on dish and sprinkle with parsley.

3 oz. (90 g) butter
1 oz. (30 g) shallots
1 clove garlic
salt, pepper, and nutmeg as needed
batter as needed
parsley as needed

Villebernier—Simmer cooked, shelled snails in a mixture of red wine, minced shallots, tarragon vinegar, and pepper for 5 minutes. Remove snails. Reduce liquid by one-half. Enrich with butter. Return snails to sauce and serve very hot.

10 fl. oz. (3 dcL) red wine
1 oz. (30 g) shallots
1 tsp. (5 mL) tarragon vinegar
pepper as needed
2 oz. (60 g) butter

Garnishes for Meats

The following garnishes are appropriate for fillets, ribs, sirloins, and barons of beef; loins, legs, shoulders, and saddles of lamb and mutton; shoulders, loins, and legs of pork; and roast chicken.

At special functions, such as a banquet, one serving platter is presented to the guest of honor for approval. Usually, only one platter is prepared "whole" for presentation. The remaining cuts are carved in the kitchen, arranged on platters surrounded by the appropriate garnish, and taken into the dining room by the waiters.

The correct number of garnish items to correspond to the portions on each service platter are disposed around the rim of the platter. They should not rest in any gravy or sauce, but should be presented absolutely dry.

African (for joints of lamb)—Mushroom caps, sliced eggplant, quartered tomatoes tossed in oil; served with château potatoes. *Sauce:* Pan juices extended with Madeira and thickened veal stock.

Algerian (for joints of lamb)—Small tomatoes, peeled and gently sautéed in oil; served with sweet potato croquettes. *Sauce:* Clear veal stock flavored with tomato paste.

Alsacienne (for pork and game)—Tartlets filled with sauerkraut, set on a rondel of ham. *Sauce:* Veal stock or thin demi-glace.

Ambassadeur (for large cuts of beef)—Duchesse potatoes, artichoke hearts filled with mushroom purée; served with horseradish cream. *Sauce:* Pan juices, deglazed with red wine, with thickened veal stock added.

Ancienne (for chicken)—Small onions, braised without coloring, and mushroom caps. *Sauce:* Suprême sauce flavored with Madeira.

Andalouse (for beef and lamb)—Red and green peppers cut julienne and braised; mounds of rice *à la grecque* and cubes of eggplant cooked in oil. *Sauce:* Thickened veal stock flavored with sherry.

Anglaise (for chicken)—Carrots, turnips, cauliflower, and french beans cooked in salted water; plain, boiled potatoes. *Sauce:* Concentrated chicken stock thickened with beurre manié.

Anversoise (for lamb and pork)—Tartlets filled with diced apples and almonds. *Sauce:* Thickened veal gravy.

Arlésienne (for beef)—Sliced eggplant fried in oil; onion rings and diced tomatoes stewed in oil. *Sauce:* Veal gravy with a little mustard added.

Armenonville (for beef and pork)—Quarters of braised artichoke hearts, tomatoes, and french beans; served with cocotte potatoes or small château potatoes. *Sauce:* Pan juices from roast, deglazed with white wine; veal stock added.

Badoise (for boiled pork)—Braised red cabbage, diced lean bacon, creamed potatoes. *Sauce:* Concentrated braising stock.

Beatrix (for pork, beef, and lamb)—Mushrooms or morels tossed in butter; new carrots, artichoke hearts; fondantes potatoes. *Sauce:* Pan juices diluted with appropriate stock.

Belle-Hélène (for lamb)—Grilled mushrooms filled with stewed tomatoes; served with croquette potatoes and baby carrots. *Sauce:* Demi-glace mixed with béarnaise sauce.

Berrichonne (for beef)—Braised cabbage formed into balls; small onions and whole, braised chestnuts; slices of bacon. *Sauce:* Pan juices deglazed with brandy and red wine; finished with veal stock.

Bordelaise no. 1 (for beef)—Mushrooms or cèpes cooked *à la bordelaise;* served with cocotte potatoes. *Sauce:* Pan juices from the roast.

Bordelaise no. 2 (for poultry)—Sautéed potatoes, quartered artichokes stewed in butter; fried onion rings; chopped parsley. *Sauce:* Pan juices deglazed with white wine and chicken stock.

Boulangère (for lamb)—Sliced, seasoned onions and potatoes, moistened with consommé cooked in the same dish as the lamb. *Sauce:* Pan juices, extended with consommé if required.

Bouquetière (for beef and lamb)—Artichoke hearts filled with small carrot and turnip balls; french beans and green peas, boiled separately, then mixed together and bound with butter; cauliflower covered with suprême sauce. *Sauce:* Pan juices, extended with concentrated stock.

Bourgeoise (for braised beef and veal)—Shaped carrots, glazed baby onions, and diced lean bacon. *Sauce:* Braising liquor, reduced by half.

Bourguignonne (for beef)—Glazed onions, quartered mushrooms sautéed in butter; and diced ham. Add all ingredients to the pan a short time before the roast has finished cooking. *Sauce:* Bourguignonne.

Brabançonne (for lamb)—Tartlets filled with a purée of brussels sprouts, lightly coated with Mornay sauce and glazed; served with flat, croquette potatoes. *Sauce:* Reduced veal stock.

Brehan (for lamb and beef)—Artichoke hearts filled with cauliflower, coated with hollandaise sauce. *Sauce:* Demi-glace for lamb; pan gravy for beef.

Bretonne (for leg of lamb)—Haricot beans moistened with bretonne sauce; chopped parsley. *Sauce:* Roast pan juices or veal stock flavored with tomato paste.

Bruxelloise (for lamb and pork)—
Braised chicory and brussels
sprouts; served with château potatoes. *Sauce:* clear veal stock or
thinned demi-glace.

Byzantine (for lamb and beef)—
Nests of duchesse potatoes filled
with cauliflower purée; usually accompanied by braised lettuce.
Sauce: Demi-glace.

Châtelaine no. 1 (for lamb, veal,
and beef)—Braised celery, quartered artichoke hearts, tomato
halves, and château potatoes.
Sauce: Thickened veal stock, or
pan juices deglazed with white
wine; veal stock added.

Châtelaine no. 2 (also for lamb,
veal, and beef)—Artichoke hearts
lined with Soubise, whole braised
chestnuts on top; served with noisette potatoes. *Sauce:* As for Châtelaine no. 1.

Chipolata (for pork)—Braised
button onions, chipolata sausages,
chestnuts cooked in consommé, and
diced, cooked bacon. *Sauce:* Pan
juices deglazed with white wine;
stock added; thickened with beurre
manié if necessary.

Clamart (for lamb, veal, and beef)
—Tartlets or artichoke hearts filled
with peas *à la française* or a purée
of peas; served with small château
potatoes. *Sauce:* Pan gravy blended
with veal stock.

Conti (for boiled, salt beef)—
Thick purée of lentils and pieces of
lean, unsmoked bacon cooked together. *Sauce:* Reduced stock from
pan.

Dauphine (for lamb and beef)—
Croquettes of dauphine potatoes.
Sauce: Thickened gravy.

Descar (for lamb and pork)—Artichoke hearts filled with chicken;
croquette potatoes. *Sauce:* Pan
juices for roast; clear stock otherwise.

Dubarry (for beef)—Cauliflower
shaped into mounds, covered with
Mornay sauce and glazed. *Sauce:*
Diluted pan juices.

Dubley (for lamb, veal, beef, and
chicken)—Croustades of duchesse
potatoes filled with mushroom
purée; grilled mushrooms to accompany. *Sauce:* Pan juices, extended
with appropriate stock.

Favorite (for lamb and pork)—
Quartered artichoke hearts and
chopped, braised celery; served
with small château potatoes. *Sauce:*
Pan juices suitably extended or
demi-glace.

Fermière (for lamb and chicken)
—Paysanne of carrots, turnips, on-
ions, and celery; mixed with butter.
Sauce: Demi-glace.

Ferval (for pork, chicken, or
braised veal)—Artichoke hearts and
potato croquettes stuffed with
minced ham. *Sauce:* Demi-glace
with tomato paste.

Flamande (for boiled meats)—
Balls of braised cabbage, chopped
carrots, and turnips; rondels of
spiced sausage and boiled potatoes.
Sauce: Reduced stock from pan.

Florian (for lamb and pork)—
Braised lettuce, glazed button onions, baby carrots, and fondantes
potatoes. *Sauce:* Demi-glace.

Forestière (for lamb and chicken)
—Cèpes or morels according to season. If not available, use mushrooms sautéed in butter with dice of
lean ham; Parmentier potatoes.

Sauce: Demi-glace, reduced stock, or diluted pan juices.

Française (for beef)—Leaf spinach and Anna potatoes. *Sauce:* Pan gravy extended with stock.

Frascati (for beef and chicken)—Thick slices of foie gras sautéed in butter, used as croûtons; mushroom caps filled with asparagus tips; crescents of gilded duchesse potatoes. *Sauce:* Thin demi-glace or pan gravy.

Gastronome (for chicken)—Whole chestnuts cooked and glazed. Chopped mushrooms and onions with chicken livers, sautéed in butter and red wine, and reduced to purée; spooned over chicken pieces. *Sauce:* Demi-glace or pan juices.

Gorenflot (for braised beef and pork)—Red cabbage, braised with slices of spiced sausage. *Sauce:* Reduced braising stock.

Grand-Duc (for chicken)—Asparagus tips and sliced truffles. *Sauce:* Suprême sauce with a chicken stock base.

Grecque (for boned and stuffed lamb or chicken)—Rice *à la grecque* used as stuffing; garnished with artichoke hearts and sliced eggplant sautéed in butter. *Sauce:* Demi-glace with tomato paste.

Hungarian (for lamb, pork, beef, and chicken)—Cauliflower shaped into balls, coated with a mixture of Mornay sauce, minced ham, and paprika, and glazed; served with boiled potatoes. *Sauce:* Demi-glace with a dash of paprika.

Hussarde (for beef)—Small jacket potatoes scooped out and stuffed with horseradish cream; eggplant sections stuffed with stewed tomatoes. *Sauce:* Demi-glace or pan gravy.

Ismail Bayaldi (for beef)—Slices of eggplant fried in oil, set on a bed of rice mixed with chopped, stewed tomatoes. *Sauce:* Demi-glace with tomato purée to which finely diced red and green peppers are added.

Italian (for pork, beef, and chicken)—Quartered artichoke hearts cooked *à l'italienne* and set on a nest of buttered macaroni. *Sauce:* Italian.

Japanese (for beef, pork, lamb, and chicken)—Croustades of puff pastry filled with chopped Japanese artichokes; served with croquette potatoes. *Sauce:* Demi-glace with beef; demi-glace and paprika with lamb, pork, or chicken.

Jardinière (for roasts, braised meats, and chicken)—An assortment of young vegetables, plainly boiled and set around dish separately and by contrasting colors; similar in style to bouquetière garnish; cauliflower is coated with hollandaise. *Sauce:* Demi-glace.

Judic (for pork, lamb, beef, and chicken)—Braised lettuce, stuffed tomatoes, and château potatoes. *Sauce:* Demi-glace.

Jules Verne (for all roast meats and poultry)—Potatoes and white turnips scooped and stuffed as desired, then braised; serve with quarters of mushrooms tossed in butter. *Sauce:* Pan juices deglazed with wine and extended with appropriate stock.

Languedocienne (for lamb,

chicken, pork, and braised veal)—
Rondels of eggplant and minced
mushrooms fried in oil, then mixed
with chopped, stewed tomatoes and
chopped parsley until a stiff paste is
formed; served with château potatoes. *Sauce:* Demi-glace with tomato.

Ligurienne (for pork, lamb, and
chicken)—Tomatoes stuffed with risotto colored with saffron. *Sauce:*
Demi-glace with tomato paste.

London House (for a whole fillet
of beef)—Open lengthwise; line inside with foie gras and truffles;
braise with veal stock and Madeira;
glaze, surround with sautéed mushrooms. *Sauce:* Well-reduced braising liquor.

Lorette (for chicken, braised beef,
and veal)—Chicken croquettes, asparagus tips, and sautéed mushrooms. *Sauce:* Reduced stock or
extended pan gravy.

Lorraine (for roast or braised
pork, lamb, and chicken)—Braised
red cabbage and fondantes potatoes. *Sauce:* Diluted demi-glace, extended pan gravy, or reduced
braising stock.

Louisiana (for roast chicken)—
Sweet corn in nests of duchesse potatoes and rondels of fried bananas.
Sauce: Pan gravy extended with
chicken stock.

Madeleine (for lamb, beef, and
chicken)—Artichoke hearts filled
with Soubise and purée of haricot
beans mixed with egg yolk, poured
into molds, and poached. *Sauce:*
Demi-glace flavored with Madeira.

Maillot (for lamb, chicken, and
braised meats)—Glazed carrots,
turnips, and onions; french beans
and green peas tossed in butter; arrange around platter in two distinct
groups. *Sauce:* Thickened pan
gravy.

Maraîchère (for lamb and pork)—
Sautéed oyster-plant (salsify); brus-
sels sprouts; château potatoes.
Sauce: Thickened gravy.

Marie-Louise (for roast or braised
beef or veal)—Artichoke hearts
filled with mushroom purée, covered with grated cheese and glazed;
served with noisette potatoes.
Sauce: Thickened gravy.

Mascotte (for lamb and chicken)
—Sliced artichoke hearts sautéed in
butter; potato scallops served from
a separate dish. *Sauce:* Thickened
gravy.

Mentonnaise (for pork and
chicken)—Thick slices of vegetable
marrow or zucchini stuffed with tomato-flavored rice; small artichokes
cut in quarters and braised; serve
with croquette potatoes. *Sauce:*
Demi-glace.

Mercédès (for chicken)—Grilled
mushrooms, grilled tomatoes,
braised lettuce, and croquette potatoes. *Sauce:* Thickened gravy.

Mexican (for lamb, beef, pork,
and chicken)—Grilled mushrooms
filled with stewed tomatoes; julienne of red and green peppers sautéed in oil; slices of eggplant grilled.
Sauce: Thinned demi-glace with tomato paste.

Moderne (for beef and lamb)—
Cauliflower coated with Mornay
sauce and glazed; tomatoes tuffed
with peas; serve with duche se potatoes. *Sauce:* Demi-glace.

Montmorency (for beef)—Artichoke hearts filled with tiny carrot balls; serve with noisette potatoes. (Tartlets may be used instead of artichokes.) *Sauce:* Demi-glace.

Montreuil (for beef)—Artichoke hearts or tartlets, some filled with peas and others filled with diced carrots. *Sauce:* Demi-glace.

Nantaise (for roast lamb or pork)—Glazed turnips; peas; served with mashed potatoes. *Sauce:* Diluted pan juices.

Niçoise (for lamb and chicken)—Small tomatoes sprinkled with garlic and baked; french beans; serve with château potatoes. *Sauce:* Thickened stock flavored with tomato or extended pan juices flavored with tomato paste.

Nivernaise no. 1 (for roast or braised beef, veal, and roast pork)—Carrots and turnips shaped with a parisienne cutter, cooked in butter and glazed; braised lettuce; served with plain, boiled potatoes. *Sauce:* Demi-glace or, if meat is braised, reduced stock.

Nivernaise no. 2 (for lamb and chicken)—Artichoke hearts or tartlets filled with glazed button onions; parisienne carrots and potatoes. *Sauce:* Extended pan juices.

Oriental (for beef, lamb, pork, and chicken)—Tomatoes stuffed with rice and chopped, sautéed almonds, colored with saffron; served with croquettes of sweet potato. *Sauce:* Demi-glace with tomato paste.

Orléanaise (for lamb, chicken, and pork)—Braised celery and mâitre d'hôtel potatoes served separately. *Sauce:* Thickened gravy.

Orloff (for lamb and chicken)—Dariole molds lined with braised celery, filled with mousseline of celery; stuffed tomatoes; served with château potatoes. *Sauce:* Demi-glace or pan gravy extended if necessary.

Paloise (for lamb and chicken)—New vegetables in a bouquet. *Sauce:* Demi-glace and béarnaise; half and half.

Panaches (for roast lamb, chicken, and braised veal)—Wax beans mixed with french beans and butter; served with croquette potatoes. *Sauce:* Thickened gravy.

Parisienne (for beef)—Braised lettuce and parisienne potatoes. *Sauce:* Demi-glace.

Paysanne (for lamb and veal)—Similar to fermière garnish; add cocotte potatoes and diced bacon. *Sauce:* Demi-glace flavored with mint (if served with lamb).

Petit-Duc (for chicken)—Tartlets filled with chicken purée mixed with cream; asparagus tips as extra garnish. *Sauce:* Demi-glace and a little butter.

Portuguese (for lamb, pork, veal, and beef)—Tomatoes stuffed with duxelles; cocotte potatoes. *Sauce:* Veal stock or extended pan gravy flavored with tomato paste.

Printanière (for chicken and lamb)—Similar to bouquetière garnish. *Sauce:* Reduced stock or demi-glace.

Provençale (for lamb, veal, and beef)—Tomatoes, eggplant, and mushrooms sautéed in butter with garlic; add stoned black olives. *Sauce:* Demi-glace with tomato paste.

Richelieu (for beef, lamb, and chicken)—Stuffed tomatoes; mushroom caps; braised lettuce, and château potatoes. *Sauce:* Thinned demi-glace or thickened veal stock.

Rochambeau (for pork, chicken, and veal)—Nests of duchesse potatoes filled with diced carrots; cauliflower *à la polonaise* and Anna potatoes. *Sauce:* Pan gravy or reduced braising stock.

Variety Meats

AMOURETTES

This is the culinary name for the marrow from beef and veal bones. It is generally used for filling patties, vol-au-vents, and hot timbales, etc., but is also used as an ingredient in croquettes. Many of the recipes given for calves' and lambs' brains may be made with amourettes. However, in every case they should be cooked first in stock or court bouillon, as brains are.

ANDOUILLES AND ANDOUILLETTES

Both types of sausages are sold already cooked. All that is required is that they be skinned and grilled. The preferred accompaniments are creamed potatoes, creamed celery, stewed onions, lentil purée, red beans, or raw red cabbage. A strong mustard is an essential condiment.

BRAINS

All recipes are for 1 lb. (450 g) brains. Lamb or calf brains are most commonly used.

Basic Preparation: Soak in cold water for 1 hour; remove skin and any remaining blood. Poach in court bouillon for 20 minutes; drain, and plunge in ice-cold water. Allow to cool, drain, and dry. Brains are now ready for further treatment.

Court bouillon:
36 fl. oz. (1 L) cold water
1½ tsp. (7½ g) salt
1 fl. oz. (¼ dcL) vinegar

Allemande—Poach as in basic preparation. Cut each set of brains into uniform slices. Dip in flour, and sauté until brown. Arrange on croûtons fried in butter; cover with allemande sauce.

4 croûtons
7 fl. oz. (2 dcL) allemande sauce

Anglaise—Poach and slice. Marinate as for fritters. Dip in beaten egg and breadcrumbs; sauté in very hot butter. Serve with tomato sauce.

Browned Butter—Poach, slice, and season. Arrange on a dish. Heat butter in pan until nut-brown, add vinegar, sprinkle with parsley, and pour over brains.

salt and pepper to taste
3 oz. (90 g) butter
1 tsp. (5 mL) vinegar
parsley to taste

Coquilles au Gratin—Line scallop shells with Mornay sauce; place poached, sliced brains on top. Make a border around shells with duchesse potatoes; cover brains with more sauce. Sprinkle with breadcrumbs, and bake in oven to brown.

    10 fl. oz. (3 dcL) Mornay sauce
    potatoes and breadcrumbs as
       needed

Croûtes—Poach and slice brains. Place in hollowed, fried croûtons. Sprinkle with grated cheese; brown in hot oven.

Fritters—Poach brains, and cut into squares. Marinate in oil, lemon juice, salt, pepper, and pinch of curry for 20 minutes. Dip in light batter; deep-fry. Arrange on a dish in pyramid shape. Sprinkle with parsley; serve with tomato sauce.

Italian—Poach and slice brains. Sprinkle with flour, and fry lightly in oil and butter. Arrange on a dish in a circle. Fill center with Italian sauce.

Matelote—Poach brains in court bouillon with red wine. Cut into thick slices, and put in pan with glazed onions and sautéed mushrooms. Reduce cooking liquid by half. Thicken with beurre manié, and pour over slices in pan. Simmer a few minutes; do not boil. Serve with fleurons.

    14 fl. oz. (4 dcL) each court bouil-
       lon and wine
    16 onions
    16 mushrooms
    2 oz. (60 g) beurre manié
    12 fleurons

Montrouge—Poach and slice brains. Arrange in tartlets, cover with Mornay sauce, and garnish with minced, sautéed mushrooms mixed with cream.

Parisienne—Poach and slice brains. Arrange on a dish. Cover with suprême sauce mixed with minced mushrooms. Garnish with mushroom caps and sliced truffles.

    7 fl. oz. (2 dcL) suprême sauce
    1 oz. (30 g) mushrooms
    mushroom caps and sliced truffles
       as needed

Vol-au-Vent—Dice and cook calf brains. Add sautéed mushrooms and bind with Madeira sauce. Serve in puff pastry cases.

CALVES' LIVER

All recipes are for 2¼ lb. (1 kg) of liver.

Anglaise—Cut liver into slices weighing about 3 oz. (85 g) each. Season, and dredge in flour; grill. Arrange on a dish, alternating slices of brain with grilled rashers of bacon.

Bercy—Slice liver. Season, and dredge in flour; grill. Cover with Bercy sauce.

Espagnole—Slice, season, and dredge; grill. Grill tomato halves; deep-fry onion rings and fry parsley. Arrange liver in center of dish. Place tomato half on each slice; set onions on one side of dish, parsley on the other.

    12 tomato halves
    8 oz. (225 g) onions
    5 Tbs. (75 g) parsley

Fines Herbes—Slice, dredge, and fry in butter. Arrange liver in a circle on a dish. Mix parsley and thyme into suprême sauce; pour over slices.

    7 fl. oz. (2 dcL) suprême sauce
    1 Tbs. (15 g) each parsley and
       thyme

Italian—Slice, season, and dredge. Fry in butter. Serve with Italian sauce.

Lyonnaise—Slice, season, and dredge. Fry in butter and oil. Fry onions rings in butter. Arrange liver in a circle on a dish. Put onions in the center; sprinkle with a little vinegar heated in the same pan.

Provençale—Proceed as for Italian recipe. Serve with provençale sauce.

Quenelles Viennoise—Chop the livers very fine. Mix well with cooked onion, chopped parsley, and beaten eggs. Add white breadcrumbs, salt, pepper, and nutmeg. Shape with tablespoon into quenelles. Poach; serve with maître d'hôtel butter in a side dish.

    1 lb. (450 g) each calves' liver and
       chicken livers
    4 oz. (115 g) onions
    2 Tbs. (30 g) parsley
    8 eggs
    breadcrumbs as needed to bind
    salt and pepper to taste
    nutmeg to taste
    maître d'hôtel butter as needed

Raisins—Slice liver. Fry in butter; deglaze pan with vinegar. Add brown sugar and demi-glace. Arrange liver on a dish. Sprinkle with currants and raisins plumped in warm water; cover slices with sauce.

    6 fl. oz. (1¾ dcL) vinegar
    2 oz. (60 g) brown sugar
    7 fl. oz. (2 dcL) demi-glace
    4 oz. (115 g) currants and raisins

Soufflé—Pound cooked liver in mortar, or purée in blender, with butter and béchamel sauce. Bind with egg yolks, add heavy cream, and season to taste. Rub through a sieve. Fold in stiffly beaten whites. Spoon into soufflé dish; bake.

    2¼ lb. (1 kg) liver
    6 oz. (170 g) butter
    12 fl. oz. (3½ dcL) béchamel
       sauce
    6 egg yolks
    3 fl. oz. (¾ dcL) heavy cream
    salt and pepper to taste
    3 egg whites

FEET (MUTTON, PORK, AND VEAL)

Basic Preparation: Mutton and veal feet are cooked *en blanc;* pigs' feet are cooked in an aromatic stock.

Fritters—Blanch, cook in stock, and bone. Roll in beaten eggs and breadcrumbs; deep-fry. Serve with tomato sauce.

Grilled—Blanch, cook, and bone. Roll in butter and breadcrumbs; grill. Serve with diable sauce.

Poulette—Blanch, cook, and bone. Mold in a timbale. Coat with poulette sauce; sprinkle with parsley.

Tyrolian—Cook chopped onion in butter with diced tomatoes. Season; add garlic, parsley, and poivrade sauce. Add cooked, boned, and chopped calves' feet; simmer for 30 minutes.

4 oz. (115 g) onions
2 oz. (60 g) butter
12 oz. (340 g) tomatoes
salt and pepper to taste
garlic to taste
parsley to taste
7 fl. oz. (2 dcL) poivrade sauce
3 calves' feet

Vinaigrette—Blanch and cook. Serve very hot with a vinaigrette.

KIDNEYS

Lamb, veal, beef, and pork kidneys are most commonly used. Lamb kidneys are either grilled or sautéed; others may be grilled, braised, or stewed. All recipes for 12 kidneys, unless otherwise noted.

Américaine—Grill. Place each lamb kidney on a grilled tomato half. Surround with rashers of grilled bacon. Serve with noisette potatoes.

Bonne Femme—Slice veal kidneys. Cook in a casserole with diced bacon, white onions, sliced potatoes, herbs, and white wine. Remove slices to a plate. Surround with garnish. Reduce cooking liquid by one-fourth, strain, and pour over kidneys.

2 veal kidneys
4 oz. (115 g) bacon
16 onions
1 lb. (450 g) potatoes
thyme and parsley to taste
12 fl. oz. (3½ dcL) white wine

Bouchère—Dice fillet of beef, kidney, and chipolata sausages. Sauté in butter. Remove, and arrange in a timbale or on a platter. Cover with Madeira sauce.

8 oz. (225 g) fillet of beef
2 veal kidneys
12 chipolata sausages
7 fl. oz. (2 dcL) Madeira sauce

Croûte aux Rognons—Prepare croûtons 2½ inches (1 cm) in diameter and about 1¼ inches (50 mm) thick; alllow one for each portion. Hollow out the center, leaving a thin base. Butter, and dry in oven. Set a spoonful of tomato at bottom of croûton. Then place the sliced, sautéed kidneys and sliced, sautéed mushrooms inside.

Henri IV—Split and grill lamb kidneys. Cover with béarnaise sauce; garnish with french-fried potatoes and watercress.

Liègeoise—Open veal kidneys; remove hard core. Sauté in butter. Just before serving, ignite gin in a ladle, and pour into casserole.

2 veal kidneys
2 oz. (90 g) butter
4 fl. oz. (1 dcL) gin

Louis XIV—Cook skewered kidneys. Arrange on slices of grilled ham. Cover with thickened gravy flavored with tarragon. Garnish with watercress.

Rognons Clémentine—Open veal kidneys, and remove hard core. Season, and sauté in butter for 20 minutes. Add button onions previously sautéed in butter and port wine. Cover dish, and cook 10 minutes more. Remove kidney and onions. Add cream and French mustard to pan, mixing quickly; heat through. Pour over kidneys.

2 veal kidneys
salt and pepper to taste
3 oz. (90 g) butter
6 oz. (170 g) onions
2 oz. (60 g) butter
4 fl. oz. (1 dcL) port wine
1 fl. oz. (¼ dcL) cream
1 tsp. (5 mL) mustard

Sautés Bercy—Slice and season kidneys. Sauté in butter with chopped shallots; remove kidneys. Deglaze pan with white wine; reduce cooking liquid by one-half. Add meat glaze and lemon juice. Return kidneys to pan; reheat, and add butter. Arrange in a timbale; sprinkle with parsley.

3 oz. (90 g) butter
1 oz. (30 g) shallots
7 fl. oz. (2 dcL) white wine
2 fl. oz. (½ dcL) meat glaze
squeeze of lemon juice
2 oz. (60 g) butter

Sautés à la Bordelaise—Slice, season, and sauté as for Sautés Bercy. Remove kidneys from pan. Slice mushrooms, and sauté them in the same pan. Remove and drain. Put mushrooms and kidney into a pan with bordelaise sauce and chopped parsley; heat. Arrange in a timbale.

4 oz. (115 g) butter
6 oz. (170 g) mushrooms
7 fl. oz. (2 dcL) bordelaise sauce
parsley to taste

Sautés Chasseur—Slice, season, and sauté kidneys. Remove kidneys. Deglaze pan with white wine;

reduce cooking liquid by three-quarters. Add chasseur sauce. Return kidneys to pan; heat through. Arrange in a timbale, and sprinkle with parsley.

3 oz. (90 g) butter
3 fl. oz. (¾ dcL) white wine
12 fl. oz. (3½ dcL) chasseur
   sauce
parsley to taste

Sautés Hongroise—Slice, season, and pan-fry kidneys; remove and drain. In the same pan, sauté onion. Add paprika, moisten with cream, and add velouté. Pass sauce through a sieve. Return kidneys to pan; heat through. Arrange in timbale.

3 oz. (90 g) butter
4 oz. (115 g) onion
pinch of paprika
1 fl. oz. (¼ dcL) cream
7 fl. oz. (2 dcL) velouté

Sautés à l'Indienne—Slice and season kidneys. Sauté in pan with butter; remove kidneys. Sauté onions in same pan with a pinch of curry powder. Moisten with velouté; cook for 5 minutes. Pass through a tammy. Return the kidneys to the pan; heat through. Arrange in a timbale. Serve rice separately.

4 oz. (115 g) butter
2 onions
curry powder to taste
7 fl. oz. (2 dcL) velouté

Sautés Turbigo—Slice lamb kidneys in half; sauté in butter. Arrange in a circle in a timbale; garnish with small, cooked mushrooms and grilled chipolata sausages. Pour a highly seasoned tomato glaze over.

Sautés au Vin—Slice, season, and sauté the kidneys in 3 oz. of butter. Arrange on plate. Deglaze the pan with an appropriate wine; reduce the cooking liquid by half. Add meat glaze, then 2 oz. of butter to enrich the sauce. Heat through, and pour over the kidneys. The dish should be named after the type of wine used.

3 oz. (90 g) butter
12 fl. oz. (3½ dcL) wine
2 fl. oz. (½ dcL) meat glaze
2 oz. (60 g) butter

OXTAILS

All recipes are for 4 lb. of oxtails.

Auvergnate—Section oxtails, and braise in white wine with aromatics. Garnish with squares of lean bacon, chestnuts cooked in consommé and glazed, and baby white onions sautéed in butter. Serve with slightly reduced braising stock.

white wine to cover
6 oz. (170 g) bacon
12 chestnuts
12 onions

Cavour—Cut oxtails into sections. Braise in white wine with brown sugar and aromatics to taste. Arrange in ramekins. Strain braising stock, thicken slightly; pour over pieces. Serve with chestnut purée.

Charolaise—Proceed as for Cavour recipe. Arrange oxtails on a dish, and surround with plain, boiled carrots and turnips; make a border of duchesse potatoes.

Moisten platter with a little stock, and sprinkle with parsley.

Chipolata—Proceed as for Charolaise recipe. Garnish with chipolata sausages; replace turnips with onions.

Daube—Proceed as for Cavour recipe. Garnish with small white onions, diced bacon, and julienne of cooked calf's foot.

Grilled—Cut oxtails into sections twice the usual length. Cook in stock for 4 hours; cool. Spread each section with French mustard; sprinkle with butter and breadcrumbs. Grill, and serve with diable sauce.

In addition, the following garnishes for braised meats are suitable for oxtail: *Berrichonne, bourgeoise, bourguignonne, fermière, flamande, maraîchère, nivernaise, piémontaise.*

SWEETBREADS (LAMB AND VEAL)

All recipes are for 3 pairs, which weigh about 2½ to 3 lb. (1.125 to 1.35 kg)

Basic Preparation:—Soak sweetbreads in cold water for 3 hours until white. Cover with salted water; bring slowly to a boil, and cook for 5 minutes. Remove, and cool under running water. Drain and trim. Lard with fat bacon, then press sweetbreads lightly between two plates to flatten. Proceed with recipe.

There are two types of sweetbreads, the elongated "throat" varieties and the rounder "heart" varieties; the latter are superior.

Bonne Maman—Slice onions, carrots, and celery in fine julienne, and put them in bottom of a buttered casserole. Arrange sweetbreads on top, then add chopped ham and bouquet garni. Pour white stock over all; cover pan, and bring to a boil. Set in a moderate oven; cook for 35 minutes. Arrange sweetbreads on platter, and surround with vegetables. Reduce cooking liquid by half; add butter. Pour over sweetbreads; sprinkle with parsley.

  8 oz. (225 g) assorted vegetables
  3 oz. (90 g) ham
  bouquet garni
  16 fl. oz. (4½ dcL) white stock
  1 oz. (30 g) butter
  parsley as needed

Bravo—Braise, slice, and pan-fry sweetbreads in butter. Arrange on bed of leaf spinach. Cover with cream sauce, sprinkle with cheese, and glaze.

Bristol—Braise, slice, and pan-fry sweetbreads. Place a poached egg on each portion. Garnish with stewed tomatoes, and serve with straw potatoes.

Broche—Wrap prepared sweetbreads in oiled paper. Bake in moderate oven for 35 minutes. Garnish with suitable sauce.

Caisse—Cover thin slices of prepared sweetbreads with suprême sauce. Arrange in large vol-au-vent cases. Garnish with sautéed mushroom caps.

Carmago—Brush sliced sweetbreads with melted butter, season, and grill slices under moderate flame. Place slices on scooped-out, baked jacket potatoes lined with mushroom purée. Garnish with grilled tomato halves.

Cévenole—Braise sweetbreads in brown stock with small whole onions. Arrange on a dish with the onions. Add glazed chestnuts and brown bread croûtons. Reduce cooking liquid by half; coat dish with sauce.

  16 fl. oz. (4½ dcL) stock
  24 onions
  24 chestnuts
  24 croûtons

Chestnut Purée—Braise and slice sweetbreads. Cover with Madeira sauce. Serve chestnut purée separately.

Dolphin Bay—Braise and slice sweetbreads. Place on a slice of foie gras. Cover with Colbert sauce; garnish with stewed tomatoes.

Don Carlos—Braise and slice sweetbreads. Cover with Madeira sauce mixed with sliced, sautéed mushrooms and julienned red peppers.

Gourmands—Braise and slice sweetbreads. Arrange slices of foie gras between sweetbread slices. Garnish with asparagus tips. Reduce cooking liquid by half; coat dish with sauce.

Au Gratin—Braise prepared sweetbreads in brown stock; then slice. Arrange on a dish surrounded with sliced, sautéed mushrooms. Cover with duxelles sauce, sprinkle with breadcrumbs, and brown in oven. Sprinkle lemon juice and parsley before serving.

  8 oz. (225 g) mushrooms
  10 fl. oz. (3 dcL) duxelles sauce

breadcrumbs, lemon juice, and
parsley as needed

Neselrode—Braise and slice
sweetbreads. Set slices in pastry
shells lined with chestnut purée; use
concentrated braising liquid to coat.
Spinach—Braise sweetbreads
in brown stock; slice. Arrange
on spinach purée; coat with well-
reduced braising liquid.
Vol-au-Vent no. 1—Thin slices of
poached or braised sweetbreads and
asparagus tips served with suprême
sauce in puff pastry cases.
Vol-au-Vent no. 2—Thin slices of
poached or braised sweetbreads and
mushrooms served with Madeira
sauce in puff pastry cases.

TONGUE

If the tongue is salted or pickled, it
should be poached in water. If
fresh, it should be braised. The skin
is removed in all cases after cooking. Suitable methods of garnishing
include *alsacienne, bourgeoise, flamande, italienne,* and *milanaise.*
Suitable purées for serving with
tongue are celery, cauliflower,
chestnut, pea, potato, and spinach.

TRIPE

Tripe is sold uncooked or cooked.
If bought uncooked, it will need to
be simmered for 3½ hours in a
court bouillon before proceeding.
Recipes are for 2¼ lb. (1 kg) of
tripe.
Fermière—Brown chopped onions and diced carrots in butter;
sprinkle with flour, and allow to

color. Add stock; cook for 5 minutes. Add diced, cooked tripe; season. Cover, and cook for 1½ hours.
Just before serving, add sliced, sautéed mushrooms.
2 oz. (60 g) onions
2 oz. (60 g) carrots
2 oz. (60 g) butter
1 oz. (30 g) flour
20 fl. oz. (6 dcL) stock
salt and pepper to taste
4 oz. (115 g) mushrooms

Gras-double en Blanquette—
Brown chopped onions in 2 oz. of
butter. Sprinkle with flour, add
stock, and simmer for 5 minutes.
Add diced, cooked tripe; season.
Add garlic and bouquet garni; cook
uncovered for 1½ hours. Mix egg
yolks and water, and add to pan.
Add 1 oz. butter, chopped parsley,
and lemon juice. Serve in a deep
tureen.
2 oz. (60 g) onions
2 oz. (60 g) butter
1 Tbs. (15 g) flour
20 fl. oz. (6 dcL) stock
salt and pepper to taste
1 clove garlic
bouquet garni
2 egg yolks
1 oz. (30 g) butter
parsley and lemon juice to taste

Portuguese—Sauté sliced onions
in butter, and add them to the diced
tripe. Simmer with tomato fondue
for 20 minutes in a covered pan. Arrange on a dish; sprinkle with parsley.
1 oz. (30 g) butter
2 oz. (60 g) onions

10 fl. oz. (3 dcL) tomato fondue
parsley as needed

WHITE AND BLACK PUDDINGS

White puddings are fat sausages
made from white meat, the best of
which are made with chicken and
pork. They are seasoned with onions. The poorer qualities contain
veal and breadcrumbs. Black pudding is made from a mixture of pig's
blood, chopped suet, and herbs.
Both varieties are served grilled or
pan-fried.

Beef

GROUND BEEF

Andalouse—Mix lean beef with finely minced onion and garlic that have been sautéed in butter; season, and shape into patties. Dredge in flour; fry in oil. Set on a bed of stewed tomatoes. Deglaze pan with sherry; reduce liquid by one-quarter. Pour sauce over patties; serve with rice pilaf.

    4 oz. (115 g) onions
    1 clove garlic
    butter as needed
    flour as needed
    oil as needed
    2 lb. (900 g) tomatoes
    4 fl. oz. (1 dcL) sherry

Cheval—Proceed as for Andalouse. Sauté flour-dredged patties quickly in butter. Arrange on a hot plate. Top each patty with two fried eggs.

    eggs as needed

Meat Loaf—Combine ground beef, egg yolks, parsley, 1 Tbs. of the butter, breadcrumbs, salt, and pepper. Form into a loaf. Bake until done to taste; baste with the remaining 3 Tbs. butter mixed with vegetable stock.

    2 egg yolks
    4 Tbs. (60 g) each chopped pars-
      ley and butter
    2 Tbs. (30 g) breadcrumbs
    16 fl. oz. (4½ dcL) vegetable
      stock

Porcupines—Combine ground beef, breadcrumbs, egg, salt, paprika, and chopped green peppers. Form mixture into patties, and roll in raw rice. Heat tomato sauce; add chili powder. Add patties, and cook for 45 minutes.

    16 oz. (450 g) breadcrumbs
    2 eggs
    salt and paprika to taste
    4 Tbs. (60 g) chopped green pep-
      pers
    raw rice as needed
    24 fl. oz. (7 dcL) tomato sauce
    chili powder to taste

Russe—Mince lean meat and add 3 oz. of the butter. Season with salt, pepper, and nutmeg. Shape into patties, dip in flour, and fry in remaining 5 oz. butter. Remove to a hot platter. Add sour cream and demi-glace to pan; deglaze. Pour sauce over patties; garnish with sautéed onions. Serve with sautéed potatoes.

3 oz. (90 g) butter
salt and pepper to taste
nutmeg to taste
flour as needed
5 oz. (140 g) butter
7 fl. oz. (2 dcL) sour cream
4 fl. oz. (1 dcL) demi-glace
6 oz. (170 g) onions

Tartare—Mince fillets of beef, and shape into flat cakes. Make a depression in the center of each, and slide a raw egg yolk into it. Arrange each steak on a dish, and surround with small heaps of chopped onion, capers, hard-boiled egg, and parsley. This dish should be mixed at the table by the waiter, who moistens it with Worcestershire sauce and seasons to taste. Chopped, desalted anchovy is also often added.

POT ROASTS

All recipes are for 2¼ lb. (1 kg) of beef.

Bourguignonne—Braise meat slices on mirepoix in red wine and veal stock, with mushroom parings and a bouquet garni. When almost cooked, remove meat to service casserole. Add fried bacon pieces, button onions, and sautéed mushrooms. Strain sauce over, cover, and finish cooking in oven.
12 oz. (340 g) mirepoix
7 fl. oz. (2 dcL) each red wine
     and veal stock
mushroom parings as needed
bouquet garni
7 oz. (200 g) bacon
24 onions
24 mushroom caps

Bülow—Marinate meat in brandy and Madeira for 1 hour; drain and dry. Brown meat; braise on mirepoix. Add white wine and brown stock, then the marinade. Remove meat to a hot platter. Strain cooking liquid, and thicken slightly. Pour over meat. Garnish with potato nests filled with green peas and with baked cherry tomatoes.
3 fl. oz. (1 dcL) brandy
5 fl. oz. (1½ dcL) Madeira
12 oz. (340 g) mirepoix
5 fl. oz. (1½ dcL) each white
     wine and brown stock
cornstarch or arrowroot as
     needed
potato nests, green peas, and
     cherry tomatoes as needed

Champagne—Set meat on bed of mirepoix; add veal stock and dry champagne. Braise. Remove meat to hot platter. Strain cooking liquid and thicken. Serve separately.
12 oz. (340 g) mirepoix
10 fl. oz. (3 dcL) stock
7 fl. oz. (2 dcL) champagne
arrowroot or cornstarch as
     needed

Dauphinoise—Braise meat on mirepoix in white wine and light demi-glace. Serve with strained sauce and potatoes dauphine.
12 oz. (340 g) mirepoix
10 fl. oz. (3 dcL) white wine
7 fl. oz. (2 dcL) demi-glace
potatoes as needed

Grecque—Braise meat on mirepoix in brown stock and tomato purée. Arrange on a bed of rice.

Strain stock, and add macédoine of vegetables. Pour sauce over meat.

12 oz. (340 g) mirepoix
16 fl. oz. (4½ dcL) brown stock
2 oz. (60 g) tomato purée
rice as needed
8 oz. (225 g) macédoine of
    vegetables

Italian—Braise meat in red wine, brown stock, and tomato purée. Add chopped anchovies and powdered cloves. Remove meat to a platter. Reduce cooking liquid by one-quarter; strain, and thicken slightly. Serve meat on a bed of buttered macaroni. Sprinkle with grated Parmesan. Serve sauce separately.

10 fl. oz. (3 dcL) red wine
16 fl. oz. (4½ dcL) brown stock
4 oz. (115 g) tomato purée
4 anchovies
pinch of cloves
macaroni as needed
Parmesan cheese as needed

Lyonnaise—Marinate meat in white wine, tarragon vinegar, and chopped onions for 1 hour. Set meat on mirepoix, and braise in veal stock and half the volume of marinade. Remove meat to a platter. Reduce cooking liquid by one-fourth; strain. Pour over meat. Garnish with fried onion rings mixed with meat glaze.

10 fl. oz. (3 dcL) white wine
2 fl. oz. (½ dcL) tarragon vinegar
1 onion
12 oz. (340 g) mirepoix
10 fl. oz. (3 dcL) veal stock
onions as needed

Providence—Braise meat in white wine with mirepoix and demi-glace; remove to a hot platter. Strain cooking liquid and serve with the meat. Garnish with florets of cauliflower mixed with hollandaise sauce, glazed carrots, and wax beans.

10 fl. oz. (3 dcL) white wine
12 oz. (340 g) mirepoix
7 fl. oz. (2 dcL) demi-glace
cauliflower, carrots, and wax
    beans as needed

STEAK

Américaine—Grill. Arrange a fried egg on top. Serve with tomato sauce.

Bercy—Grill. Serve with Bercy sauce.

Cecelia—Pan-fry. Garnish with large, grilled mushroom caps filled with asparagus tips. Surround with soufflé potatoes.

Georgette—Brown in very hot pan; allow to go cold. Spread with anchovy butter, and wrap in puff pastry, and glaze. Bake in oven.

Maître d'Hôtel—Grill; serve with maître d'hôtel butter.

Marchand de Vin—Grill; coat with red wine sauce.

Marseillaise—Grill; serve with a piece of herb butter on top. Surround with ribbon potatoes and halves of grilled tomatoes; sprinkle with thyme.

Mirabeau—Grill. Garnish the steak with blanched tarragon leaves, anchovy fillets, and pitted olives. Serve with anchovy butter.

Planked—Pan-fry or grill. Place on a wooden plank; border with duchesse potatoes and assortment of young vegetables.

TOURNEDOS, FILLETS OF BEEF, AND FILETS MIGNONS

In this section, quantities of the garnish are not given, because this generally depends on the policy of the kitchen. The average weight of a tournedos is 4 oz. (125 g); fillet steaks usually weigh about 7 oz. (200 g) and therefore require extra sauce and garnish.

The meats in this category are often accompanied by a sauce. If the meat is not served with a sauce, moisten with a buttered meat glaze, using 2½ oz. (75 g) butter to 20 fl. oz. (dcL) glaze. Pan juices deglazed with wine and extended with stock may also be used. Alternatively, thickened gravy may be used. In some preparations, the garnish will be sufficiently moist so that a sauce or gravy will not be required.

Algerian—Season fillet, and cook in butter. Set each fillet on a galette of mashed sweet potato; surround with grilled tomato halves. Serve with demi-glace mixed with a touch of tomato purée.

Alsacienne—Prepare tartlets for each portion, and fill with braised, drained sauerkraut. Cover with a shaped piece of ham, stamped out with a round cutter. Set each grilled tournedos in a tartlet; moisten with buttered demi-glace.

Andalouse—Cook fillet in butter. Garnish with stuffed, baby green peppers; chipolata sausages; and whole, baked tomatoes stuffed with diced ham.

Arlésienne—Cook fillet in butter and oil. Surround with a garnish of rounds of fried eggplant and slices of tomato. Serve with Chateaubriand sauce.

Baltimore—Cook fillet in butter. Arrange on a tartlet filled with creamed corn. Garnish with slices of sautéed tomato and smaller slices of sautéed green pepper.

Barthole—Grill fillet. Arrange on a croûton spread with anchovy paste. Garnish with black and green pitted olives and diced tomatoes. Serve with meat glaze mixed with tomato purée.

Béarnaise—Grill tournedos. Place each on a croûton. Coat with meat glaze. Serve with buttered new potatoes and béarnaise sauce.

Bercy—Grill fillet. Brush with meat glaze. Serve with Bercy sauce.

Bonnard—Grill fillet. Place on a croûton spread with liver pâté. Garnish with chopped, sautéed mushrooms and quartered artichokes; serve with Madeira sauce.

Bonneville—Grill fillet. Arrange on half of a large, grilled tomato. Garnish with grilled mushroom caps filled with diced red and green peppers sautéed in butter. Serve with parisian potatoes and Madeira sauce.

Bouscaut—Grill fillet. Arrange on a croûton spread with cream cheese. Serve bordelaise sauce separately.

Brabançonne—Pan-fry fillet in butter. Arrange on a tartlet lined with baby brussels sprouts sautéed in butter. Cover with Mornay sauce, and glaze. Serve with croquette potatoes and Madeira sauce.

Brebant—Grill fillet. Arrange on a croûton. Garnish with watercress and straw potatoes; serve with béarnaise sauce.

Castillian—Grill fillet. Arrange on a croûton. Surround with tiny tartlets or puff bouchées filled with diced tomatoes, peas, and diced carrots, all moistened with cream.

Chasseur—Pan-fry tournedoes in butter. Arrange on a dish. Deglaze pan with white wine; add chasseur sauce. Heat, and pour over tournedos.

Choron—Grill tournedos. Set on a croûton. Place an artichoke heart filled with asparagus tips on the tournedos; surround meat with fried rounds of eggplant and noisette potatoes. Serve with Choron sauce.

Clamart—Cook fillet in butter. Arrange on a croûton. Garnish with artichoke hearts filled with peas. Serve with thickened gravy mixed with a touch of Madeira wine.

Colbert—Pan-fry fillet in butter. Arrange on a base of minced, cooked chicken and creamed potatoes; cover with a fried egg. Serve with Colbert sauce.

Cussy—Pan-fry tournedos in butter. Garnish with artichoke hearts filled with diced, sautéed kidney. Deglaze the pan with port wine, and add veal stock. Reduce by one-quarter; pour over tournedos.

Dubarry—Pan-fry fillet in butter. Arrange on a large, grilled tomato half; surround with balls of mashed cauliflower covered with Mornay

sauce and glazed. Serve with demi-glace mixed with Madeira.

Dugléré—Pan-fry fillet in butter. Arrange on a croûton. Garnish with whole, peeled tomatoes, braised chicory, and mushroom caps. Serve with demi-glace.

Duroc—Similar to Chasseur recipe. Garnish with diced tomatoes; serve with noisette potatoes.

Florentine—Grill fillet. Arrange on a bed of chopped spinach. Cover tournedos with Chateaubriand sauce. Serve with croquette potatoes.

Forestière—Pan-fry fillet in butter. Arrange on a croûton. Garnish with button mushrooms and diced bacon. Serve with Parmentier potatoes and demi-glace.

Hauser—Grill fillet. Arrange on a croûton. Garnish with deep-fried onion rings and fresh watercress. Serve with straw potatoes and Colbert sauce.

Henri IV—Grill fillet. Arrange on a croûton. Garnish with artichoke hearts filled with tiny parisian potatoes and tiny baked cherry tomatoes. Serve with béarnaise sauce.

Ismaîl Bayaldi—Pan-fry tournedos in butter. Arrange each on a thick slice of cooked zucchini. Set a grilled tomato half on each tournedos. Surround with pilaf mixed with diced red and green peppers. Serve with thickened gravy mixed with tomato purée.

Italian—Pan-fry fillet in butter. Garnish with cooked, quartered artichoke hearts. Serve with Italian sauce.

Japanese—Pan-fry fillet. Arrange on a croûton or galette of mashed potato. Cover with demi-glace; garnish with croustades filled with diced, sautéed Japanese artichokes.

Lakmé—Pan-fry fillet. Set a grilled mushroom on top. Arrange on a tartlet filled with purée of green beans. Serve with thickened gravy.

Lesdiguières—Grill fillet. Arrange on a large, almost cooked Spanish onion filled with chopped spinach and Mornay sauce. Cover with extra sauce, and glaze.

Lili—Pan-fry tournedos. Arrange on a bed of hashed brown or Anna potatoes. Set artichoke hearts filled with foie gras on top of the tournedos. Serve with Périgueux sauce.

Lola Montez—Pan-fry fillet. Arrange in a tartlet filled with chopped, stewed tomatoes. Garnish with mushroom caps filled with diced green peppers simmered in butter. Serve with Madeira sauce mixed with tomato purée.

Marseillaise—Pan-fry tournedos. Arrange each on a croûton. Coat with provençale sauce. Set a pitted green olive wrapped with an anchovy fillet on each tournedos; Garnish with tomatoes and ribbon potatoes.

Mikado—Pan-fry fillet. Coat with provençale sauce. Garnish with Japanese artichokes sliced and tossed in butter.

Mirabeau—Grill tournedos. Arrange each on a croûton. Garnish with anchovy fillets crossed on top of the tournedos. Serve with béarnaise sauce.

Opéra—Pan-fry fillet. Arrange on a croûton. Cover with demi-glace and finely chopped and sautéed chicken livers. Serve with croquette potatoes.

Paloise—Grill fillet. Cover with béarnaise sauce with chopped, fresh mint added. Garnish with grilled tomatoes. Serve with noisette potatoes.

Regina—Grill fillet. Arrange on a croûton. Garnish with scooped-out tomatoes filled with rice and sweet pickles. Serve with Madeira sauce.

Rossini—Pan-fry tournedos. Arrange each on a croûton. Set a thin slice of foie gras, then a slice of truffle on top of tournedos. Coat with Madeira demi-glace.

Sarah Bernhardt—Pan-fry tournedos. Arrange each on a croûton. Deglaze pan with port wine and meat glaze. Pour sauce over tournedos. Garnish with grilled tomatoes and buttered french beans.

Lamb

CHOPS AND CUTLETS

Arlésienne—Pan-fry chops. Garnish with deep-fried onion rings, sliced, sautéed eggplant, and stewed tomatoes.

Bardoux—Dip chops in beaten eggs and breadcrumbs; pan-fry. Garnish with green peas in butter mixed with chopped, cooked ham.

Bergère—Trim chops; dip in beaten eggs and breadcrumbs. Pan-fry in butter. Arrange on a dish with slices of grilled ham. Garnish with straw potatoes, grilled button mushrooms, and glazed baby onions.

Bressanne—Pan-fry chops. Garnish with chipped, sautéed chicken livers bound with demi-glace. Serve with sautéed mushrooms.

Chemise—Brown chops on both sides; allow to cool. Wrap in puff pastry, and bake. Serve with mushroom sauce.

Dauphine—Grill chops. Garnish with dauphine potatoes, and serve with Madeira sauce.

Jeanne d'Arc—Pound meat into thin cutlets. Dip in light batter, and deep-fry. Garnish with noisette potatoes. Serve with Madeira sauce.

Malmaison—Dip meat in beaten eggs and breadcrumbs; pan-fry. Serve with nests of duchesse potatoes filled with an assortment of vegetables.

Maréchale—Dip meat in beaten eggs and breadcrumbs; pan-fry. Garnish with asparagus tips and grilled mushrooms. Serve with demi-glace.

Minute—Cut meat thin; pan-fry. Add chopped parsley and lemon juice to cooking butter.

Moreland—Dip meat in beaten egg. Roll in crushed hazelnuts, then in breadcrumbs; pan-fry. Garnish with grilled mushrooms and green peas. Serve with buttered meat glaze.

Orsay—Grill meat. Garnish with chopped mushrooms and salted ox-tongue mixed with a velouté.

Réforme—Dip meat in beaten egg, then in breadcrumbs mixed with minced, cooked ham; pan-fry. Serve with Réforme sauce.

Sandringham—Dip meat in beaten eggs and breadcrumbs; pan-fry. Garnish with green peas in butter mixed with minced ham.

LEG OF LAMB

All recipes are for a 4½ lb. (2 kg) leg, boned.

Anglaise—Season the lamb with salt and pepper. Wrap in muslin, and cover with a little butter and flour. Put in a pot with enough water to cover; bring to a boil. Add carrots, onions, garlic, and bouquet garni. Simmer until cooked. Remove to a hot platter with carrots and onions. Heat maître d'hôtel butter and capers, and add up to half the cooking liquid. Serve sauce and turnip purée with lamb.

    salt and pepper to taste
    butter as needed
    flour as needed
    4 carrots, quartered
    4 onions, quartered
    1 clove garlic
    bouquet garni
    6 oz. (170 g) maître d'hôtel butter
    3 tsp. (15 g) capers
    1½ lb. (675 g) white turnips

Ham and Mushroom Stuffing—Sauté the onions and mushrooms; add the remaining ingredients, and mix. Stuff the boned lamb with the mixture. Roll into a cylindrical shape, sew up, and roast until cooked.

    4 oz. (115 g) minced onions
    8 oz. (225 g) minced mushrooms
    2 Tbs. (30 g) butter
    8 oz. (225 g) minced ham
    2 oz. (60 g) pork fat
    salt, pepper, and herbs to taste

Au Jus—Insert the garlic and basil into slits made in the leg of lamb. Brush joint with brandy; season. Brown in the oven. Mix wine with water and baste with wine mixture while cooking. Remove lamb to a hot platter; pour off fat. Add veal stock; reduce. Add chives.

    2 cloves garlic, slivered
    1 Tbs. (15 g) basil
    2 fl. oz. (½ dcL) brandy
    salt and pepper to taste
    8 fl. oz. (2¼ dcL) each red wine,
        water, and veal stock
    chives to taste

Périgourdine—Mix the sausage meat, goose liver, truffles, and beaten egg; coat lamb with this mixture. Wrap lamb in pie crust; remove a small circle from the top of the pastry. Brush pastry with beaten egg; bake in the oven. Warm périgueux sauce; pour into pastry hole just before serving.

    1 lb. (450 g) pork sausage meat
    4 oz. (115 g) minced goose liver
    2 truffles, minced
    1 egg
    1 12-inch pie crust
    1 egg, beaten
    16 fl. oz. (4½ dcL) périgueux
        sauce

LOIN

All recipes are for a 3½ lb. (1.6 kg) loin.

Bonne Femme—Season lamb; brown in a casserole. Add potatoes, stock, and bouquet garni. Cover, and bake for 30 minutes. Add the onions and bacon; bake for another 30 minutes or until cooked. Sprinkle with parsley and chives.

    salt and pepper to taste
    butter as needed
    32 oz. (900 g) potatoes, blanched
        and cut into ovals

4 fl. oz. (1 dcL) beef stock
1 bouquet garni
24 small onions
8 oz. (225 g) lean bacon
parsley and chives to taste

Bordelaise—Brown the mushrooms in olive oil. Simmer the espagnole sauce with tomato paste and garlic. Put 1 Tbs. (15 g) each of butter and oil into a casserole, add meat, and season with salt and red pepper. Add mushrooms and potatoes, and bake in the oven. Pour espagnole sauce/tomato paste mixture over meat just before finishing. Remove from oven. Sprinkle with parsley.

    8 oz. (225 g) mushroom caps
    olive oil as needed
    16 fl. oz. (4½ dcL) espagnole
      sauce
    2 Tbs. (30 g) tomato paste
    1 clove garlic
    salt and red pepper to taste
    24 oz. (675 g) potato balls
    parsley as needed

Niçoise—Brown the lamb in a casserole. Sauté zucchini in butter; sauté tomatoes lightly in oil. Put the zucchini, tomatoes, and potatoes in the casserole; season. Cook until done, and sprinkle with parsley and chives.

    butter as needed
    1 zucchini, diced
    2 tomatoes, peeled, seeded, and
      diced
    oil as needed
    20 small new potatoes, peeled
    salt and pepper to taste
    parsley and chives as needed

Viennoise—Bone and halve lamb loin. Rub salt and pepper into the lamb, and marinate it in the oil, lemon juice, and parsley. Drain the lamb, and dry. Dredge in flour; coat with beaten egg and breadcrumbs. Bake until cooked. Serve with lemon wedges.

    salt and pepper to taste
    8 fl. oz. (2 dcL) olive oil
    4 fl. oz. (1 dcL) lemon juice
    1 Tbs. (15 g) parsley
    flour as needed
    3 eggs, beaten
    breadcrumbs as needed
    2 lemons, quartered

STEW

Anglaise—Place potatoes, onions, stock, and bouquet garni in a pot; season with salt and pepper. Add lamb; simmer until meat is tender. Garnish with parsley.

    4 medium potatoes, sliced thick
    3 medium onions, sliced thick
    beef or veal stock to cover
    bouquet garni
    salt and pepper to taste
    2 lb. (900 g) lamb chunks
    parsley as needed

Catalane—Cut bacon into thin strips and sauté in oil until crisp. Add lamb chunks and sear until brown. Remove lamb. Add onions and rice to pan and sauté so rice absorbs some of the frying liquid. Remove onions and rice. Deglaze pan with a little of the wine. Pour pan liquid into a casserole, adding the lamb, beef stock, remaining wine, salt, pepper, thyme, saffron, garlic, and bay leaf. Cook for 1 hour. Stir in tomatoes, rice, and onions. Cook until lamb is tender and rice is ready.

2 oz. (60 g) slab bacon
3½ fl. oz. (1 dcL) olive oil
3 lb. (1.35 kg) lamb chunks
12 oz. (340 g) sliced onions
8 oz. (225 g) uncooked rice
8 fl. oz. (2¼ dcL) dry white wine
24 fl. oz. (7 dcL) beef stock
salt, pepper, thyme, and saffron
    to taste
2 cloves garlic, minced
1 bay leaf
16 oz. (450 g) tomatoes, peeled,
    seeded, and chopped

Navarin Printanière—Dredge lamb chunks in seasoned flour and brown in oil. Transfer to casserole with stock, tomato paste, garlic, thyme, rosemary, and bay leaf. Add potatoes, carrots, turnips, and onions. Cook in oven until the lamb is tender; add blanched green peas during last 10 minutes of cooking time.

3 lb. (1.35 kg) lamb chunks
salt and pepper to taste
3 Tbs. (45 g) flour
oil as needed
24 fl. oz. (7 dcL) beef stock
1 Tbs. (15 g) tomato paste
2 cloves garlic, minced
thyme and rosemary to taste
1 bay leaf
8 boiling potatoes, peeled and
    quartered
6 carrots, peeled and chopped
6 turnips, peeled and chopped
12 white onions, peeled and
    chopped
8 oz. (225 g) green peas

Pork

CHOPS AND CUTLETS

Bretonne—Trim chops. Dip in beaten eggs and breadcrumbs; pan-fry. Garnish with beans *à la Bretonne*. Serve with thickened gravy.

Charcutière—Pan-fry chops. Cover with charcutière sauce, and serve with mashed potatoes.

Chatillon—Make incision in edge of chop to form a pocket; insert a thin slice of foie gras. Dip chop in beaten egg and breadcrumbs; pan-fry. Garnish with green beans or peas. Serve with mashed potatoes and gravy mixed with tomato purée.

Courlandaise—Dip chops in butter and breadcrumbs; grill. Serve with sliced red cabbage, glazed chestnuts, and Madeira sauce.

Eszterhazy—Brown chops quickly in butter; sprinkle with paprika. Simmer in sour cream. Serve with julienne of carrots and peas.

Flamande—Partially pan-fry chops. Finish cooking with sliced apple. Serve as is.

Grand-Mère—Chop meat fine with minced onion. Add egg, butter, and seasonings. Reshape into cutlets. Dip in beaten egg and breadcrumbs; pan-fry. Insert a piece of macaroni at the end to represent the bone.

Milanaise—Dip chops in beaten eggs and breadcrumbs mixed with grated cheese; pan-fry. Serve on a bed of buttered macaroni mixed with chopped, cooked ham.

Westmorland—Pan-fry chops. Cover with demi-glace mixed with minced pickles.

LOIN

Bonne Femme—Season pork loin with salt and pepper; brown in butter in a casserole. Add potatoes, stock, and bouquet garni; cook, covered, for 30 minutes. Add onions and bacon, and cook until tender. Serve with parsley and chives.

4–5-lb. (1.80–2.25 kg) pork loin
salt and pepper to taste
butter as needed
2 lb. (900 g) potatoes, cut into
    ovals and blanched
4 fl. oz. (1 dcL) chicken stock
bouquet garni
24 small onions
8 oz. (225 g) lean bacon, diced
    and sautéed
parsley and chives as needed

Languedocienne—Insert garlic slivers in the pork. Season with salt and pepper; sprinkle with basil, oregano, and olive oil. Brown roast on top of oven. Cover, and roast. Remove to a hot platter. Remove excess fat from the pan. Add wine; boil down. Add tomato paste, orange rind, and demi-glace.

4–5-lb. (1.80–2.25 kg) pork loin
2 cloves garlic, slivered
salt and pepper to taste
basil and oregano to taste
olive oil as needed
3 fl. oz. (¾ dcL) dry white wine
2 Tbs. (30 g) tomato paste
2 tsp. (10 g) grated orange rind
12 fl. oz. (3½ dcL) demi-glace

Mustard Sauce—Dry meat thoroughly. Place fat side up in a casserole; brown pork. Roast. Remove roast to a hot platter. Strain the meat juices into a bowl, and degrease. Add vinegar and peppercorns to juices; boil down. Add cream and mustard, and simmer. Serve sauce with roast.

3-lb. (1.35 kg) pork loin or roast
3 fl. oz. (¾ dcL) cider vinegar
12 fl. oz. (3½ dcL) whipping
  cream
10 peppercorns, crushed
2 tsp. (10 g) dry mustard

Veal

BREAST

Allemande—Cut a pocket into the veal breast. Stuff the pocket with the pork sausage, and sew the breast closed. Put veal in a pan with the stock, and cook for one hour. Add vegetables; cook until tender. Remove veal to a hot platter. Surround with baked vegetables.

    6-lb. (2.7 kg) veal breast
    2 lb. (900 g) pork sausage
    16 fl. oz. (4½ dcL) chicken stock
    1½ lb. (675 g) carrots, sliced
    1 lb. (450 g) leeks, sliced
    1½ lb. (675 g) potatoes, sliced

Alsacienne—Brown veal in butter in a casserole; season with salt and pepper. Add stock, and cook. One hour before the meat is done, add blanched sauerkraut and caraway seed.

    5-lb. (2.5 kg) veal breast
    butter as needed
    white pepper and salt to taste
    8 fl. oz. (2¼ dcL) chicken stock
    16 oz. (450 g) sauerkraut,
        blanched
    ½ tsp. (1 g) caraway seed

CHOPS AND CUTLETS

Basilic—Pan-fry chops. Deglaze pan with white wine; add meat glaze and basil butter.

Casserole—Trim chops. Cook in buttered casserole on mirepoix. Serve with thickened gravy.

Champvalon—Trim chops. Partially cook both sides in butter. Lay chops in casserole on a bed of sliced, raw potatoes, onions, garlic, and bouquet garni. Season, and cover cutlets with another layer of vegetables. Moisten with stock. Cook, covered, in oven. Serve from dish.

Fines Herbes—Pan-fry chops. Deglaze pan with white wine. Add thickened gravy and herbs. Cover and serve.

Marigny—Pan-fry chops. Garnish with tartlets filled with green beans and peas. Serve with thickened gravy.

Printanière—Braise chops in oven. Garnish *à la printanière,* and serve with strained braising liquor.

Vert-Pré—Grill chops. Cover with slightly melted maître d'hôtel butter. Garnish with watercress. Serve with straw potatoes.

ROAST

Dijonnaise—Season the roast with salt and pepper. Brown in a casserole. Add the mushrooms. Combine the cream, mustard, onion, parsley, chives, lemon juice, salt, and red pepper; pour over the veal. Roast until done.

6-lb. (2.70 kg) veal roast
salt and pepper to taste
3 oz. (90 g) butter
1 lb. (450 g) mushrooms, sliced
10 fl. oz. (3 dcL) heavy cream
2 Tbs. (30 g) each Dijon mustard
    and minced onion
2 Tbs. (30 mL) lemon juice
1 Tbs. (15 g) each parsley and
    chives
salt and red pepper to taste

SCALLOPS AND MEDALLIONS

Anglaise—Dip meat in beaten eggs and breadcrumbs; pan-fry in butter. Garnish with slice of grilled ham; pour beurre noisette over ham.

Crème—Pan-fry meat in butter. Deglaze pan with cream; add lemon juice. Pour sauce over meat.

Grenadins—Pan-fry meat in butter. Serve with any of the following garnishes: Japanese artichokes, spinach, *jardinière,* peas, asparagus, *Vichy* carrots, or vegetable purée.

Holstein—Dip meat in beaten eggs and breadcrumbs; pan-fry. Garnish with fried egg and anchovy fillets.

Paprika—Sprinkle meat with paprika; pan-fry in butter. Deglaze pan with cream. Pour sauce over meat.

Viennoise—Dip meat in beaten eggs and breadcrumbs; pan-fry. Place a slice of lemon on the meat; top this with an anchovy fillet rolled around a pitted green olive. Sprinkle with chopped, hard-boiled egg and chopped parsley. Serve with thickened gravy.

Yorkshire—Proceed as for Scallops *à l'Anglaise,* but serve with caper sauce.

Poultry

Chicken

BREASTS, DEBONED

All recipes are for 8 deboned chicken breasts or suprêmes. Chicken breasts may be cooked *à blanc* or *à brun* according to the recipe used, but both styles are cooked without liquid. Only butter and a few drops of lemon juice are used.

Basic Preparation for **à Blanc:** Season breasts, and place in pan containing melted butter and a few drops of lemon juice. Roll fillets in this mixture. Remove to pan or casserole. Cover, and cook in a hot oven for 6 minutes.

Basic Preparation for **à Brun:** Season breasts, and roll in flour. Place in a pan containing very hot clarified butter, and quickly brown on both sides. Cover, and cook in a hot oven for 6 minutes.

To Stuff Fillets: Make an opening in the thickest part of the fillet; insert stuffing using a piping bag. Pipe enough stuffing to give the fillet a nicely puffed look. Proceed with recipe.

Archiduc—Cook *à blanc*. Set each suprême on a croûton coated with archiduc sauce. For the sauce, add champagne to suprême sauce, and reduce by one-fourth; strain.

croûtons as needed
Sauce:
4 fl. oz. (1 dcL) suprême sauce
4 fl. oz. (1 dcL) champagne

Arlésienne—Season suprêmes, roll in flour, and brown. Meanwhile, fry rounds of eggplant and dredged onion rings in oil; remove and keep warm. Sauté roughly chopped, peeled, and seeded tomatoes until soft. Arrange eggplant on the base of a serving dish. Set the suprêmes on this base. Surround with alternating mounds of fried onions and tomatoes. Serve tomato-flavored demi-glace separately.

flour and butter as needed
12 oz. (340 g) eggplant
12 oz. (350 g) onion
4 fl. oz. (1 dcL) oil
1 lb. (450 g) tomatoes
demi-glace as needed

Belleview—Chop mushrooms; julienne red and green peppers. Blanch; simmer in butter. Add mixture to suprême sauce; add a pinch of curry. Cook fillets *à blanc*. Arrange on a dish; pour sauce over fillets.

8 oz. (225 g) mushrooms
½ each red and green pepper
2 oz. (60 g) butter
5 fl. oz. (1½ dcL) suprême sauce
pinch of curry powder

Boitelle—Stuff fillets with mousseline forcemeat mixed with 2 oz. minced, raw mushroms. Cook *à blanc* in a moderate oven with 12 oz. seasoned, sliced mushrooms. Arrange fillets in a circle; put mushrooms in the center. Deglaze pan with white wine; add butter. Blend, and heat through; drizzle over fillets.

6 oz. (170 g) mousseline force-
     meat
2 oz. (60 g) minced mushrooms
12 oz. (340 g) sliced mushrooms
2 fl. oz. (½ dcL) white wine
2 oz. (60 g) butter

Chimay—Cook fillets *à brun*. Arrange on a dish, and surround with button mushrooms and asparagus tips tossed in butter. Drizzle thickened gravy over entire dish.

8 oz. (225 g) mushrooms
24 asparagus tips
butter as needed
3 fl. oz. (1 dcL) gravy

Crème—Cook *à brun*. Deglaze pan with brandy. Add cream; reduce by one-quarter. Add cream sauce; remove fillets. Pour sauce over fillets.

1 fl. oz. (¼ dcL) brandy
2 fl. oz. (½ dcL) cream
4 fl. oz. (1 dcL) cream sauce

Henri IV—Slice suprèmes into thin slices. Slightly flatten each. Season and dredge; sauté *à brun*. Set each slice on a cooked artichoke heart. Serve béarnaise sauce separately.

Hungarian—Season fillets with paprika, and cook *à brun*. Set fillets on a base of rice pilaf combined with stewed tomato flesh. Deglaze pan with brandy and cream; add Hungarian sauce. Blend; coat fillets.

6 oz. (170 g) raw rice
8 oz. (225 g) tomatoes
1 Tbs. (15 mL) brandy
2 fl. oz. (½ dcL) cream
3½ fl. oz. (1 dcL) Hungarian sauce

Jardinière—Sauté fillets *à brun*. Remove to a dish. Garnish with small mounds of assorted vegetables of your choice. Sprinkle fillets with a little beurre noisette just before serving.

Maréchale—Dip fillets in beaten egg and breadcrumbs; sauté in butter. Garnish with green asparagus and truffles. Pour thickened gravy over fillets.

Marie-Louise—Cut suprèmes into thick slices. Dip in beaten egg and breadcrumbs; cook in butter. Set each slice in a prebaked, short-crust tartlet lined with a purée of mushrooms and onions. Sprinkle each tartlet with beurre noisette just before serving.

tartlets as needed
mushroom and onion purée, pre-
     pared with 2 parts mushroom
     to 1 part onion, as needed

Marie-Thérèse—Slice fillets lengthwise. Cook *à blanc*. Place slices around a mound of pilaf of rice. Coat entirely with suprême sauce; sprinkle with blanched, diced, and sautéed red peppers.

  7 oz. (200 g) raw rice
  10 fl. oz. (3 dcL) suprême sauce
  1 red pepper

Parmesan—Season fillets. Dip in beaten egg and grated cheese; sauté in butter. Place on croûtons spread with foie gras. Sprinkle with beurre noisette just before serving.

Pojarski—Chop fillets fine. Combine with breadcrumbs steeped in milk and squeezed dry. Add butter, then cream mixture. Season, and add nutmeg to taste. Shape mixture into ovals; dredge in flour, and cook in butter. Sprinkle with beurre noisette just before serving.

Port—Sauté *à brun*. Deglaze pan with port wine. Add espagnole sauce, and blend. Coat fillets.

  2 fl. oz. (½ dcL) port
  5 fl. oz. (1½ dcL) espagnole
    sauce

Valois—Flatten fillets slightly. Dip in beaten egg and breadcrumbs; cook in butter. Arrange in a circle. Garnish with stuffed olives, and coat with Valois sauce.

BROILERS

Broilers are young, tender chickens weighing from 1½ lb. (675 g) to 2¼ lb. (1 kg). They can be prepared *en casserole,* roasted, or grilled. All recipes are for 1 bird. The amount of stuffing will depend on the size of the bird. If the bird is roasted and is to be served whole, the breast meat should be sliced and reshaped before being brought to the table.

Américaine—Stuff bird with chicken forcemeat; cook in casserole. Serve with slices of grilled bacon and slightly thickened chicken or veal gravy.

Belle Meunière—Stuff chicken with chopped livers and 6 oz. of mushrooms sautéed in butter and extended with a little cooked rice. Brown chicken. Place in cocotte with butter; cover with lid, and set in oven. Toward the end of cooking time, add chopped, lean bacon and 4 oz. quartered mushrooms. When serving, pour a little veal gravy over the bird.

  6 oz. (170 g) each livers and
    mushrooms
  rice as needed
  4 oz. (115 g) butter
  4 oz. (115 g) bacon
  4 oz. (115 g) mushrooms
  veal gravy as needed

Bonne Femme—Cook chicken in a cocotte in butter with parisienne potatoes. When half-cooked, add diced, fried bacon and glazed onions. Pour veal gravy over each serving.

  3 oz. (90 g) butter
  8 oz. (225 g) potatoes
  3 oz. (90 g) bacon
  4 oz. (115 g) onions
  veal gravy as needed

Champeaux—Cook chicken in a cocotte. Remove, and drain excess butter. Deglaze pan with white wine; add demi-glace. Garnish with small glazed onions and parisienne potatoes; cover with sauce.

3 oz. (90 g) butter
3 fl. oz. (¾ dcL) white wine
2 fl. oz. (½ dcL) demi-glace
5 oz. (140 g) onions
6 oz. (170 g) potatoes

Crapaudine—Split bird; flatten slightly. Dip in butter and bread-crumbs; set under broiler. Serve with diable sauce.

Fermière—Cook chicken in cas-serole. Surround with paysanne of carrots, white turnip, onions, and celery previously braised in butter.

4 oz. (115 g) each vegetable

Grand-Mère—Cook chicken in cocotte. Garnish with small croû-tons and diced, sautéed mush-rooms.

Jacques—Stuff bird with force-meat; cook in covered casserole. Remove, and deglaze pan with red wine. Add veal stock; reduce by one-quarter. Add butter; strain, and coat bird.

1 lb. (450 g) forcemeat
3 oz. (90 g) butter
5 fl. oz. (1½ dcL) red wine
2 oz. (½ dcL) veal stock
1 oz. (30 g) butter

Katoff—Split as for grilled chicken. Partially cook in oven, and finish off under broiler. Place bird on a galette of duchesse potatoes. Serve with veal gravy.

Limousin—Stuff chicken with pork sausage meat mixed with chopped onions; cook in a cocotte. Garnish with chopped bacon and glazed chestnuts; serve with veal gravy.

12 oz. (340 g) sausage meat
6 oz. (170 g) onions
4 oz. (115 g) bacon
5 oz. (140 g) chestnuts
veal gravy as needed

Palace—Split as for grilled chicken. Cook in oven. Remove bird; deglaze pan with brandy. Add meat glaze and tarragon; enrich with butter. Blend, heat, and pour over bird.

2 fl. oz. (½ dcL) brandy
3½ fl. oz. (1 dcL) meat glaze
pinch of tarragon
1½ oz. (46 g) butter

Parmentier—Cook chicken in a cocotte. Remove bird; deglaze pan with white wine and demi-glace. Garnish with Parmentier potatoes.

4 fl. oz. (1 dcL) white wine
2 fl. oz. (½ dcL) demi-glace
potatoes as needed

Paysanne—Proceed as for Par-mentier recipe. Garnish with pay-sanne potatoes.

CUTLETS

All recipes are for 8 cutlets. When speaking of raw chicken, the differ-ence between a *côtelette* and a *su-prême* is that the latter is a breast of chicken with the wing-tip (humerus bone) attached. The *côtelette* is usually a slice of the breast. It can be treated just like a *suprême,* and the cuts are interchangeable in these recipes.

Amphytrion—Flatten, trim, and sauté the cutlets in butter. Arrange on a bed of mushroom purée. Cover with Madeira sauce.

6 oz. (170 g) mushroom purée
6 fl. oz. (1½ dcL) Madeira sauce

Béarnaise—Open cutlets lengthwise and stuff with chopped, mixed
herbs sautéed in butter and
squeezed dry. Serve béarnaise
sauce separately.
    equal quantities of chives, thyme,
        and savory
    double quantity of parsley
    béarnaise as necessary

Berchoux—Open cutlets lengthwise, and stuff with chicken forcemeat. Sauté. Place on prebaked
barquettes lined with mushroom
purée. Serve Madeira sauce separately.
    Chartres—Open cutlets length-
wise, and stuff with chicken forcemeat mixed with chopped tarragon.
Sauté. Cover with suprême sauce
flavored with tarragon, and minced
mushrooms sautéed in butter.
    2 Tbs. (30 g) tarragon per 1 lb.
        (450 g) forcemeat
    1 Tbs. (15 g) tarragon per 16 fl.
        oz. (4½ dcL) suprême sauce
    6 oz. (170 g) minced mushrooms

Colbert—Dip cutlets in beaten
egg and breadcrumbs; fry in butter.
Place on artichoke purée. Serve
Colbert sauce separately.
    Gauloise—Sauté cutlets. Place on
a slice of fried ham; sprinkle diced,
fried chicken livers on top. Serve
Madeira sauce separately.
    Kiev—Open cutlets lengthwise,
flatten and stuff with a slice of
chilled garlic butter mixed with
chopped parsley. Roll and skewer
with a toothpick. Chill for 1 hour.

Remove toothpick. Dip in beaten
egg and breadcrumbs; chill again.
Deep-fry. Place on bed of egg noodles mixed with a macédoine of
vegetables.
    Lyonnaise—Sauté cutlets. Place
on a platter, and cover with thick
gravy mixed with fried onions.
    Mushrooms—Sauté cutlets in but-
ter and lemon juice. Place on a dish,
and cover with suprême sauce
mixed with sliced, sautéed mushrooms.
    Oriental—Pan-fry cutlets in oil.
Place on a bed of saffron rice.
Cover with suprême sauce tinted
with tomato purée and saffron.
    Purée de Marrons—Open breast
lengthwise, and stuff with chestnut
purée. Sauté. Serve Madeira sauce
separately.

FRICASSÉES

All recipes are for a 2¼-lb. chicken.
    Basic Preparation: Cut the chicken
as for sauté, but separate the legs
from the thighs. Brown in butter;
remove pieces. Add flour and
moisten with stock. (Pay attention
as you add the flour to the butter
that remains after browning the
chicken pieces; you may need to
add more butter to make enough
roux.) Season, and set to boil, stirring constantly. Return chicken to
pan; add vegetables and bouquet
garni. Cook until tender. Remove
chicken to another dish. Strain
cooking liquid. Thicken with egg
yolks and cream; add lemon juice.
    4 oz. (115 g) butter
    2 oz. (60 g) flour
    24 fl. oz. (7 dcL) chicken stock

salt and pepper to taste
1 carrot
1 onion with clove
bouquet garni
3 egg yolks
2 fl. oz. (½ dcL) cream
lemon juice to taste

Ancienne—Proceed as for basic preparation. Cover with sauce, and garnish with boiled button onions and sautéed mushrooms. Finish sauce with chopped parsley and chives.
12 button onions
12 small mushrooms
1 Tbs. (15 g) each parsley and
   chives

Archiduc—Cook the chicken, and cover with sauce. Garnish with mushrooms, peas, and small, boiled new potatoes.

Bretonne—Cook the chicken, and cover with sauce. Garnish with julienne of mushrooms, leeks, and celery sautéed in butter.

Duchesse—Cook the chicken, and cover with sauce. Garnish with white asparagus tips; sprinkle with finely chopped, well-blanched red peppers.

Française—Cook the chicken, and cover with sauce. Garnish with potatoes and carrots cut with a parisienne cutter and boiled. Add cooked peas at the end of the cooking time.

Radizcy—Cook the chicken. Finish sauce with a little paprika, and cover chicken pieces. Garnish with rounds of eggplant sautéed in butter.

ROASTERS

Roasters are chickens of 4 lb. (1.8 kg) and heavier. The amount of stuffing will depend on the size of the bird. The following recipes are for a small, 4-lb. (1.8 kg) roaster. If the bird is to be brought to the table and served whole from a trolley, the joints should be severed and reassembled and the breast sliced and reshaped prior to coming to the table.

American—Stuff the chicken with a mixture of thyme, onion, parsley, and breadcrumbs. Roast. Garnish with slices of lean, fried bacon. Deglaze pan with white wine; thicken slightly with arrowroot if necessary. Pour sauce over bird.
pinch of thyme
1 Tbs. (15 g) each onion and parsley
6 oz. (170 g) breadcrumbs
6 slices of bacon
7 fl. oz. (2 dcL) white wine
arrowroot as needed

Anglaise—Poach bird in chicken stock to which pieces of bacon fat have been added. Serve surrounded by pieces of lean, boiled bacon, with parsley sauce on the side.

Argenteuil—Poach chicken in stock. Coat with suprême sauce to which asparagus purée has been added. Garnish with green asparagus.
7 fl. oz. (2 dcL) suprême sauce
2 fl. oz. (½ dcL) asparagus purée
green asparagus as needed

Aurore—Stuff the bird with chicken forcemeat flavored with tomato purée; poach in stock. Coat with Aurore sauce.

Bouquetière—Roast chicken in butter on a bed of matignon in a covered pan; remove bird. Deglaze pan with Madeira and demi-glace; reduce by one-quarter. Garnish *à la bouquetière*.

3 oz. (90 g) butter
6 oz. (170 g) matignon
4 fl. oz. (1 dcL) Madeira
7 fl. oz. (2 dcL) demi-glace

Cavour—Lard breast with bacon fat; braise bird without coloring. Serve with buttered noodles mixed with grated Parmesan.

Châtelaine—Roast the chicken. Deglaze pan with white wine and veal stock. Garnish with artichoke hearts lined with Soubise and topped with cooked chestnuts. Serve with noisette potatoes.

7 fl. oz. (2 dcL) white wine
5 fl. oz. (2½ dcL) veal stock
6 artichoke hearts
3 oz. (90 g) Soubise
6 chestnuts
potatoes as needed

Chimay—Stuff chicken with chopped, cooked noodles mixed with diced foie gras. Roast, and serve with thickened gravy made from chicken stock.

7 oz. (200 g) uncooked noodles
6 oz. (170 g) foie gras
gravy as needed

Chipolata—Roast the chicken. Garnish with glazed onions, chipolata sausages, chestnuts, and diced bacon.

6 oz. (170 g) white onions
1 chipolata sausage per portion
6 oz. (170 g) chestnuts
4 oz. (115 g) bacon

Chivry—Poach the chicken in white stock; remove to a platter. Cover with Chivry sauce. Garnish with prepared, short-crust tartlets filled with peas and asparagus tips, or surround with macédoine of vegetables.

Diva—Stuff the chicken with pilaf mixed with diced foie gras; poach. Cover with Hungarian sauce. Surround with small mounds of diced, raw cucumbers mixed with cream.

Stuffing:
1 lb. (450 g) cooked rice
5 oz. (140 g) foie gras

Hungarian sauce as needed
cucumbers and cream as needed

Ecossaise—Stuff bird with chicken forcemeat mixed with large brunoise; poach. Cover with écossaise sauce. Serve with french beans moistened with cream.

Stuffing:
two-thirds chicken forcemeat
one-third brunoise
8 fl. oz. (2¼ dcL) écossaise sauce
french beans and cream as
needed

Edouard VII—Stuff as for Diva recipe. Poach in white stock. Remove, and coat with suprême sauce flavored with curry and mixed with finely diced, blanched red peppers. Serve with diced, raw cucumbers mixed with cream.

Sauce:
4 oz. (115 g) peppers per 16 fl. oz.
     (4½ dcL) suprême sauce
curry powder to taste

cucumbers and cream as needed

Espagnole—Stuff chicken with pilaf mixed with finely diced bell peppers and cooked whole chickpeas (garbanzos). Roast; remove. Cover with thickened veal gravy. Garnish with small, grilled tomatoes and deep-fried onion rings.
Stuffing:
4 oz. (115 g) each bell peppers
     and chick-peas per lb. (450 g)
     cooked rice
gravy, tomatoes, and onions as
     needed

Fermière—Roast chicken until half-done; transfer into cocotte on a bed of sliced carrots, onions, celery, and diced ham sautéed in butter. Deglaze pan with strong veal stock; pour into cocotte. Cover, and cook in oven for about 45 minutes.
4 oz. (115 g) of each vegetable
     and ham
butter as needed
7 fl. oz. (2 dcL) veal stock

Fruits—Roast the chicken. Garnish with grilled tomatoes, fried bananas, and peach halves. Deglaze pan with brandy, and flame. Add veal gravy, and cover chicken with sauce.
tomatoes, bananas, and peaches
     as needed
2 fl. oz. (½ dcL) brandy
7 fl. oz. (2 dcL) veal gravy

Indian—Poach the chicken. Cover with curry sauce. Serve rice à l'indienne separately.

Infante—Poach the chicken. Remove, and cover with suprême sauce mixed with mushroom purée. Garnish with small, grilled tomatoes.
2 fl. oz. (½ dcL) mushroom purée
     to each 16 fl. oz. (4½ dcL)
     suprême sauce

Ivoire—Poach the chicken, keeping it very white; remove. Serve with a garnish of noodles or macaroni mixed with creamed mushrooms. Serve greatly reduced cooking liquid separately.

Languedocienne—Roast the chicken; remove. Serve with thickened chicken stock flavored with Madeira; enrich with cream. Garnish with a mixture of rounds of eggplant sautéed in oil; chopped, sautéed tomatoes; minced, raw mushrooms; and chopped parsley.
12 fl. oz. (3½ dcL) chicken stock
arrowroot or cornstarch as
     needed
2 fl. oz. (½ dcL) Madeira
2 fl. oz. (½ dcL) cream
8 oz. (225 g) eggplant
8 oz. (225 g) tomatoes
2 oz. (60 g) mushrooms
parsley to taste

Lorraine—Stuff chicken with veal forcemeat mixed with chopped herbs; poach. Cover with suprême sauce flavored with the same herbs.
12 oz. (340 g) veal forcemeat
5 tsp. (75 g) each parsley, thyme,
     chervil, and tarragon

10 fl. oz. (3 dcL) suprême sauce
1 tsp. (5 g) extra herbs

Louisiana—Stuff chicken with corn kernels and diced, blanched red peppers moistened with cream; roast. Garnish with rice pilaf, fried bananas, and prebaked tartlets filled with corn. Serve Madeira sauce separately.

1 lb. (450 g) corn kernels
3 oz. (90 g) red peppers
2 fl. oz. (½ dcL) cream
12 oz. (340 g) cooked rice
4 bananas
8 tartlets
Madeira sauce as needed

Ménagère—Poach chicken in stock; remove. Cook sliced carrots, onions, and new potatoes in poaching liquid. Surround chicken with this garnish. Reduce cooking liquid to 8 fl. oz. (2¼ dcL), and pour over dish.

Monglas—Roast the chicken. Cover with Madeira demi-glace combined with julienne of ham, ox tongue, and mushrooms.

9 fl. oz. (2½ dcL) Madeira demi-glace
1 oz. (30 g) each ham, ox tongue, and mushrooms

Niçoise—Roast the chicken. Deglaze pan with Madeira. Add tomato-flavored veal stock. Garnish with small baked tomatoes, french beans, and black olives. Surround chicken with garnish, and cover with sauce.

3 fl. oz. (¾ dcL) Madeira
5 fl. oz. (1½ dcL) veal stock
12 tomatoes

8 oz. (225 g) french beans
12 black olives

Normande—Poach the chicken in white stock. Cover with suprême sauce. Garnish with small boiled potatoes, turnips, carrots, and leeks.

Oysters—Poach the chicken in white stock; remove. Prepare suprême sauce to which has been added the poaching liquid from 24 oysters. Reduce by one-third; add cream and oysters. Cover chicken with sauce.

10 fl. oz. (3 dcL) suprême sauce
white stock to cover
10 fl. oz. (3 dcL) cream
24 poached oysters

Paysanne—Brown the chicken in pan; transfer to casserole. Surround chicken with finely chopped carrots, onions, and celery. Cover, and complete cooking in oven. Moisten with stock from time to time. Serve from casserole.

5 oz. (140 g) carrots
4 oz. (115 g) onions
3 oz. (90 g) celery
stock as required

Petite Mariée—Poach chicken in rich white chicken stock; remove. Cover with suprême sauce thinned with concentrated stock. Garnish with whole, young carrots, white onions, and baby new potatoes, all previously sautéed in butter.

Portuguese—Stuff chicken with 12 oz. of cooked rice mixed with 6 oz. of chopped, sautéed tomatoes. Roast; remove. Cover with Portuguese sauce, and garnish with tomatoes stuffed with a mixture of rice, red and green peppers, and chopped black olives.

  12 oz. (340 g) cooked rice
  6 oz. (170 g) tomatoes
  8 fl. oz. (2¼ dcL) Portuguese
    sauce
  8 whole tomatoes
  equal quantities of rice, red and
    green peppers, and black
    olives

Princesse—Poach the chicken. Cover with suprême sauce mixed with asparagus purée. Garnish with duchesse potato nests filled with green asparagus purée. Place a black olive on top of each potato nest.

  10 fl. oz. (3 dcL) suprême sauce
  3 oz. (90 g) asparagus purée
  8 potato nests
  extra asparagus purée as needed
  8 olives

Stanley—Stuff the chicken with cooked rice mixed with chopped mushrooms. Poach in stock with chopped onions and a little curry powder; remove. Pass liquid through a tammy. Add chicken velouté and cream; reduce to fairly thick consistency. Rub through a tammy again, and pour over chicken.

  10 oz. (280 g) cooked rice
  4 oz. (115 g) mushrooms
  1 lb. (450 g) onions
  pinch of curry powder
  7 fl. oz. (2 dcL) chicken velouté
  7 fl. oz. (2 dcL) cream

SAUTÉ

Young chickens, when dressed, have a weight of 2¼ lb. (1 kg) to 3½ lb. (1.6 kg) and are preferred for sauté work. Smaller chickens are better for grilling or casseroles rather than for sauté. All recipes are for 1 chicken weighing 2½ to 3 lb. (1.125 to 1.35 kg).

Basic Preparation: Cut chicken in pieces, and put in pan with heated butter or oil. Let pieces color quickly and evenly. Cover pan, and put in oven to complete cooking. Remove breasts and wings after 6 to 8 minutes; the legs and carcass need 10 to 12 minutes. Drain excess butter, and deglaze pan with stock or wine. Reduce pan liquid by half, then add the sauce or cream, as recipe demands. Arrange the pieces on a dish, and pour the sauce over them. Garnish as described.

Some recipes call for the chicken pieces to be quickly stiffened in the hot butter or oil. This is called *sauté à blanc.* The pieces should not be colored. The cooking is completed in the oven as described above. Other ingredients are sometimes added at this stage. In the case of chicken *sauté à blanc,* the liquid used to deglaze is usually white, as are the supplementary sauces.

Alexandra—Sauté *à blanc;* finish cooking in oven. Drain butter, and dilute pan juices with white stock; reduce by one-third. Add chicken velouté, onion purée, cream, and butter; strain. Garnish with asparagus tips.

  3 fl. oz. (¾ dcL) white stock
  3 fl. oz. (¾ dcL) chicken velouté
  2 Tbs. (30 ml) onion purée
  1 fl. oz. (¼ dcL) cream
  2 oz. (60 g) butter
  asparagus tips as needed

Algerian—Sauté *à brun;* finish cooking in oven with chopped onions, garlic, and stewed tomatoes. Remove chicken pieces and vegetables with slotted spoon; drain excess butter. Deglaze pan with white wine; reduce by one-third. Add demi-glace and cooked vegetables. Arrange chicken pieces on a dish; pour heated sauce over them. Garnish with diced eggplant sautéed in butter.

2 oz. (60 g) onions
1 clove garlic, minced
8 oz. (225 g) tomatoes
4 fl. oz. (1 dcL) white wine
4 fl. oz. (1 dcL) demi-glace
12 oz. (340 g) eggplant
2 oz. (60 g) butter

Ambassadrice—Sauté *à brun* with chopped mushrooms; remove chicken pieces. Drain pan, and deglaze with white wine; reduce by one-third. Add Madeira; reduce by one-quarter. Add tomato purée and thickened chicken gravy; coat chicken pieces. Garnish with green peas and parisienne potatoes.

3 oz. (90 g) mushrooms
5 fl. oz. (1½ dcL) white wine
3 fl. oz. (¾ dcL) Madeira
1 Tbs. (15 mL) tomato purée
peas and potatoes as required

Annette—Sauté *à brun;* finish cooking in oven. Deglaze pan with Madeira; add onion purée and slightly thickened chicken gravy. Sprinkle herbs and lemon juice into pan. Add butter, and mix thoroughly. Arrange pieces over potatoes Anna in a dish, and coat with sauce.

6 fl. oz. (1¾ dcL) Madeira
4 oz. (115 g) onion purée
3 fl. oz. (¾ dcL) chicken gravy
1 oz. (30 g) butter
potatoes Anna as needed

Archiduc—Sauté *à blanc;* when half-cooked in oven, add chopped onions and paprika. Remove pieces; drain butter. Deglaze pan with white wine; reduce by one-third. Add brandy, then cream, then chicken velouté; mix well. Add butter and lemon juice; strain sauce. Combine with cooked vegetables. Arrange pieces on dish, and coat with sauce.

4 oz. (115 g) onions
1 tsp. (5 g) paprika
6 fl. oz. (1¾ dcL) white wine
1 fl. oz. (¼ dcL) brandy
3½ fl. oz. (1 dcL) cream
3½ fl. oz. (1 dcL) chicken velouté
1 oz. (30 g) butter
squeeze of lemon juice
vegetables as needed

Arlésienne—Sauté *à brun* in oil; remove. Drain excess butter; deglaze pan with white wine. Add garlic and demi-glace mixed with tomato purée; reduce by one-third. Arrange chicken on platter, and cover with sauce. Surround with deep-fried onion rings, stewed tomatoes, and rounds of eggplant sautéed in butter.

5 fl. oz. (1½ dcL) white wine
1 clove garlic
5 fl. oz. (1½ dcL) demi-glace
onions, tomatoes, and eggplant as needed

Armagnac—Sauté *à blanc;* remove to oven, and add sliced mushrooms. Finish cooking. Remove pieces; deglaze pan with brandy. Add lemon juice and cream; heat, but do not boil. Finish with crayfish butter. Arrange pieces on a platter, and coat with sauce.

  4 oz. (115 g) mushrooms
  5 fl. oz. (1½ dcL) brandy
  squeeze of lemon juice
  4 fl. oz. (1 dcL) cream
  2 oz. (60 g) crayfish butter

Artois—Sauté *à brun;* remove pieces to a dish. Deglaze pan with Madeira. Add pale meat glaze; blend. Add thickly diced carrots and small white onions previously cooked in butter. Enrich with butter. Pour sauce over pieces. Garnish with quartered artichoke hearts, and sprinkle with chopped chives.

  2 fl. oz. (½ dcL) Madeira
  3½ fl. oz. (1 dcL) meat glaze
  8 carrots
  12 onions
  1½ oz. (45 g) butter
  4 artichokes
  chives as needed

Bagatelle—Sauté *à brun.* Deglaze pan with Madeira and thick cream. Arrange pieces on a dish. Sprinkle chopped chives over pieces, then cover with sauce. Garnish with asparagus tips.

  2 fl. oz. (½ dcL) Madeira
  3 fl. oz. (¾ dcL) cream
  chives to taste
  asparagus tips as needed

Basilic—Sauté *à brun.* Remove pieces, and arrange on a dish. Deglaze pan with white wine; add chopped, fresh basil. Reduce volume by half. Add butter; blend. Sprinkle sauce over pieces.

  7 fl. oz. (2 dcL) white wine
  1 Tbs. (15 g) chopped basil
  2 oz. (60 g) butter

Beaulieu—Sauté *à brun;* remove pieces to oven. When half-cooked, add parisienne potatoes and artichoke hearts previously cooked in butter. Finish cooking. Set pieces on platter with vegetables; add pitted black olives. Deglaze pan with white wine and veal stock with a touch of lemon juice. Blend, and simmer for 5 minutes; pour sauce over pieces.

  6 oz. (170 g) potatoes
  8 artichoke hearts
  12 olives
  3 fl. oz. (¾ dcL) white wine
  4 fl. oz. (1 dcL) veal stock
  lemon juice to taste

Bercy—Sauté *à brun.* Halfway through, add chopped shallots and sliced mushrooms. Arrange pieces on a hot platter. Deglaze pan with white wine and meat glaze; add lemon juice. Reduce by one-third. Add butter, blend, and heat through. Pour sauce over pieces. Garnish with fried chipolata sausages.

  2 oz. (60 g) shallots
  4 oz. (115 g) mushrooms
  6 fl. oz. (1¾ dcL) white wine
  3 fl. oz. (¾ dcL) meat glaze
  squeeze of lemon juice
  2 oz. (60 g) butter
  chipolata sausages as needed

Bergère—Sauté *à brun*. Deglaze pan with Madeira and veal stock; reduce by one-third. Add cream. Garnish with whole, sautéed mushrooms and straw potatoes.

    4 fl. oz. (1 dcL) Madeira
    7 fl. oz. (2 dcL) veal stock
    4 fl. oz. (1 dcL) cream
    mushrooms and potatoes as needed

Bohemian—Sauté *à brun* with a little paprika added. Remove to oven. When half-cooked, add blanched, chopped green peppers, chopped onions, and peeled sliced tomatoes. Toward the end, add minced garlic and a little chopped fennel. Arrange pieces on dish with vegetables. Deglaze pan with white wine and thickened veal gravy. Coat chicken with sauce. Serve on pilaf of rice.

    ½ tsp. (2½ mL) paprika
    4 green peppers
    1 onion
    4 tomatoes
    1 clove garlic
    pinch of fennel
    4 fl. oz. (1 dcL) white wine
    8 fl. oz. (2¼ dcL) veal gravy

Bourguignonne—Sauté *à brun* with small button onions. Halfway through, add sliced mushrooms and diced, lean bacon. Arrange pieces on a hot platter; surround with cooked vegetables. Deglaze pan with red wine. Add minced garlic. Reduce by half. Add espagnole sauce, and bring to boil; strain. Coat pieces with sauce. Serve on heart-shaped croûtons.

    12 onions
    12 mushrooms
    2 slices bacon
    8 fl. oz. (2¼ dcL) red wine
    1 clove garlic, minced
    6 fl. oz. (1¾ dcL) espagnole sauce

Bretonne—Sauté *à blanc*. Halfway through cooking, add sliced white of leeks and chopped onion previously sautéed in butter. Arrange chicken on a platter; leave vegetables in the pan. Add minced, raw mushrooms; sauté for 2 minutes. Deglaze pan with suprême sauce and cream; reduce by one-half. Pour sauce and vegetables over chicken.

    4 oz. (115 g) leeks
    2 oz. (60 g) onion
    3 oz. (30 g) mushrooms
    7 fl. oz. (2 dcL) each suprême sauce and cream

Catalane—Sauté *à brun* in oil with small onions. At end, add roughly chopped mushrooms, cooked chestnuts, and diced tomatoes. Arrange chicken pieces on a hot platter; surround the chicken with cooked vegetables. Deglaze pan with white wine; reduce by one-third. Add demi-glace; blend. Pour sauce over chicken. Garnish with slices of spiced sausage quickly tossed in butter.

    12 button onions
    6 oz. (170 g) mushrooms
    12 chestnuts
    6 tomatoes
    8 fl. oz. (2¼ dcL) white wine
    2 fl. oz. (½ dcL) demi-glace
    sausages as needed

Champeaux—Sauté *à brun*. Arrange chicken pieces on hot platter. Surround with parisienne potatoes and small onions previously cooked in butter. Deglaze pan with white wine. Add veal gravy, then meat glaze, and blend. Reduce by one-fourth; enrich with butter. Pour sauce over chicken pieces.

12 potatoes
12 onions
5 fl. oz. (1½ dcL) white wine
5 fl. oz. (1½ dcL) veal gravy
1 fl. oz. (¼ dcL) meat glaze
1 oz. (30 g) butter

Chasseur—Sauté *à brun* in oil and butter with chopped shallots. When almost done, add sliced mushrooms. Arrange chicken pieces on a hot platter; leave vegetables in the pan. Deglaze pan with white wine; reduce by one-fourth. Add Chasseur sauce; heat through. Spoon mixture over pieces. Sprinkle with chopped parsley.

1 oz. (30 g) shallots
6 oz. (170 g) mushrooms
4 fl. oz. (1 dcL) white wine
5 fl. oz. (1½ dcL) Chasseur sauce
parsley as needed

Crécy—Sauté *à blanc*. Remove pieces to a hot platter. Deglaze pan with light cream; add suprême sauce, and blend. Add diced carrots. Pour sauce over pieces.

5 fl. oz. (1½ dcL) half-and-half
    (light cream)
5 fl. oz. (1½ dcL) suprême sauce
diced, cooked carrots to taste

Cynthia—Sauté *à brun*. Remove chicken pieces. Deglaze pan with dry champagne; reduce by half.

Add poultry glaze, and enrich with butter. Add lemon juice and Curaçao. Blend and heat. Coat chicken-pieces. Surround with skinned, seedless grapes and sections of skinned tangerines.

7 fl. oz. (2 dcL) dry champagne
1 fl. oz. (¼ dcL) poultry glaze
2 oz. (60 g) butter
juice of ½ lemon
1 fl. oz. (¼ dcL) Curaçao
4 oz. (115 g) seedless grapes
2 tangerines

Duroc—Proceed as for Chasseur recipe. Deglaze pan with white wine; reduce by half. Add thickened chicken gravy and tomato sauce; blend. Finish with brandy. Add chopped parsley, chervil, and tarragon.

4 fl. oz. (1 dcL) white wine
5 fl. oz. (1½ dcL) chicken gravy
1 fl. oz. (¼ dcL) tomato sauce
2 Tbs. (30 mL) brandy
1 Tbs. (15 mL) each parsley,
    chervil, and tarragon

Egyptian—Brown chicken pieces. Add to the pan diced onions, mushrooms, and diced ham that have been sautéed in butter. Set chicken in a casserole; cover with drained vegetables. Add raw tomato slices. Finish cooking in oven for 20 minutes. Remove chicken and vegetables to a hot platter. Pour veal stock over each serving.

3 oz. (90 g) onions
3 oz. (90 g) mushrooms
6 oz. (170 g) ham
butter as needed
3 whole tomatoes
veal stock as needed

Espagnole—Sauté *à brun* in oil. Drain excess oil, but keep enough to moisten cooked pilaf rice, mixed with diced red peppers, cooked peas, and sliced, cooked pork sausage. Set chicken and accompaniments in terrine. Cook in oven for 10 minutes; remove to a hot platter. Cover with garnish; surround with small, grilled tomatoes.

    8 oz. (225 g) uncooked rice
    2 oz. (60 g) red peppers
    3 oz. (90 g) peas
    2 sausages
    tomatoes as needed

Fermière—Brown chicken pieces in a pan; place in a casserole. Deglaze pan with white wine. Add vegetable fondue; blend, then add to chicken. Add diced, lean ham. Finish cooking in oven. Serve from dish.

    5 fl. oz. (1½ dcL) white wine
    5 oz. (140 g) vegetable fondue
    2 oz. (60 g) ham

Fines Herbes—Sauté *à brun* with chopped shallots. Deglaze pan with white wine; reduce by one-third. Add thickened veal or chicken gravy; blend, and heat through. Add chopped parsley, chervil, and tarragon. Finish with lemon juice; enrich with butter. Remove to a hot platter, and pour sauce over pieces.

    1 oz. (30 g) shallots
    5 fl. oz. (1½ dcL) white wine
    7 fl. oz. (2 dcL) veal or chicken
        gravy
    ½ tsp. (2½ mL) each parsley,
        chervil, and tarragon
    squeeze of lemon juice
    2 oz. (60 g) butter

Forestière—Sauté *à brun* with chopped shallots. When almost cooked, add sliced mushrooms. Remove pieces to a hot platter. Deglaze pan with white wine and veal stock; reduce by one-third. Coat pieces. Garnish with Parmentier potatoes and sliced, grilled bacon.

    1 oz. (30 g) shallots
    3 oz. (90 g) mushrooms
    5 fl. oz. (1½ dcL) each wine and
        veal stock
    6 oz. (170 g) potatoes
    6 slices bacon

Indian—Sauté *à blanc*. Sear chicken pieces and remove from pan. Add curry powder and flour; make roux. Extend with chicken stock to make sauce. Add bouquet garni and minced onion. Return pieces to pan, and cook till tender. Remove to a hot platter. Reduce sauce by one-quarter; strain. Coat pieces. Serve with rice.

    1 Tbs. (15 g) curry powder
    1 Tbs. (15 g) flour
    8 fl. oz. (2¼ dcL) chicken stock
    bouquet garni
    1 small onion

Japanese—Brown chicken pieces in pan. Add peeled Jerusalem artichokes. Finish cooking in oven. Remove pieces to a hot platter. Deglaze pan with white wine and slightly thickened chicken stock; enrich with butter. Pour sauce over chicken.

    1 lb. (450 g) Jerusalem artichokes
    2 fl. oz. (½ dcL) white wine
    5 fl. oz. (1½ dcL) chicken stock
    1½ oz. (45 g) butter

Lyonnaise—Sauté *à brun*. When half-cooked, add sliced onions sautéed in butter and slightly browned. Finish cooking together. Remove chicken; leave onions. Deglaze pan with veal gravy; reduce by one-fourth. Pour sauce over pieces. Sprinkle with chopped parsley.

6 oz. (170 g) onions
6 fl. oz. (1¾ dcL) veal gravy
parsley as needed

Marengo—Sauté *à brun*. Deglaze pan with white wine; reduce by one-quarter. Add tomato purée, garlic, and thickened brown veal gravy; strain. Pour sauce over pieces. Garnish with sautéed mushrooms, fried egg yolks, crayfish tails, and truffle slices sautéed in butter. Finish with chopped parsley.

5 fl. oz. (1½ dcL) white wine
1 Tbs. (15 mL) tomato purée
1 clove garlic
5 fl. oz. (1½ dcL) veal gravy
8 mushrooms
4 egg yolks
4 crayfish tails
2 truffles
parsley as needed

Marseillaise—Sauté *à brun*. When half-cooked, add minced garlic, chopped green peppers, and quartered tomatoes, all previously sautéed in oil. Remove chicken; leave vegetables. Drain excess oil. Deglaze pan with white wine and lemon juice; reduce by one-quarter. Cover pieces with vegetable garnish. Sprinkle with parsley.

2 cloves garlic
4 oz. (115 g) green peppers
3 tomatoes
7 fl. oz. (2 dcL) white wine
squeeze of lemon juice
parsley as needed

Mireille—Sauté *à brun*. When three-quarters cooked, add crushed garlic, chopped onion, tomatoes, and diced green pepper. Remove the chicken. Add tomato juice to pan; reduce by one-half. Strain, and pour over pieces. Serve with saffron rice.

1 clove garlic
1 onion
4 tomatoes
1 green pepper
10 fl. oz. (3 dcL) tomato juice
saffron rice as needed

Normande—Sauté *à brun*. When half-cooked, add peeled and sliced cooking apples. Remove chicken and apples to casserole serving dish. Deglaze pan with Calvados, and flame. Pour sauce into casserole, and serve from dish.

1 lb. (450 g) apples
2 fl. oz. (½ dcL) Calvados

Oysters—Sauté *à blanc*. Remove chicken pieces to a platter. Deglaze pan with white wine and oyster liquor; reduce by one-quarter. Add chicken velouté; blend and heat through. Add lemon juice; enrich with butter. Strain sauce, and pour over pieces. Garnish with poached oysters.

3 fl. oz. (¾ dcL) white wine
liquor from 12 oysters
5 fl. oz. (1½ dcL) chicken velouté
squeeze of lemon juice

2 oz. (60 g) butter
12 oysters, poached

Panetière—Sauté *à blanc*. Deglaze pan with cream and chicken velouté; reduce by one-half. Add butter. Arrange pieces on fried croûtons spread with foie gras. Coat pieces with sauce.
   10 fl. oz. (3 dcL) cream
   5 fl. oz. (1½ dcL) chicken velouté
   croûtons and foie gras as needed

Stanley—Sauté *à blanc*. When half-cooked, add finely chopped onions. Remove chicken pieces, and garnish with mushroom caps cooked in butter. Deglaze pan with cream; cook for few minutes, and strain. Reduce sauce by one-quarter. Add curry powder and cayenne pepper; enrich with butter. Coat pieces with sauce.
   2 onions
   12 mushroom caps
   7 fl. oz. (2 dcL) cream
   pinch of curry powder
   pinch of cayenne pepper
   2 oz. (60 g) butter

Vins Divers—Sauté *à brun*. Deglaze pan with wine; reduce by one-third. Add thickened brown gravy; finish with butter. Pour sauce over pieces. These preparations are designated by the name of the wine used: Chablis, Champagne, Graves, Medeira, Pouilly, sherry, etc.

MISCELLANEOUS CHICKEN DISHES

Chicken Pie—Cut chicken as for fricassée. Remove skin and excess bone, season, and sprinkle with finely chopped onions and mushrooms sautéed in butter. Line bottom of pie dish with thin slices of veal, and set chicken pieces on top, putting the legs in first. Add chopped bacon and hard-boiled egg yolks cut in half. Moisten with enough chicken consommé to cover three-quarters of the chicken. Place a necklace of puff pastry around the edge of the dish, then cover the whole with puff pastry and gild with beaten egg. Make a slit in the pastry, and bake in moderate oven.
   2¼ lb. (1 kg) cooked chicken
      meat
   salt and pepper to taste
   3 onions
   3 oz. (90 g) mushrooms
   6 oz. (170 g) veal
   3 oz. (90 g) bacon
   3 egg yolks
   chicken consommé as needed
   puff pastry as needed
   beaten egg as needed

Chicken Tetrazzini—Slice mushrooms thin, and sauté in butter; reserve. Cook spaghetti in boiling, salted water. Finely shred chicken meat. Add sherry to suprême sauce. Mix half the volume of sauce with the spaghetti and mushrooms; mix the other half with the chicken. Put the spaghetti mixture in a casserole, and make a well in the center. Put the chicken in the well; sprinkle with grated Parmesan cheese. Bake in a moderate oven; serve from the casserole.
   8 oz. (225 g) mushrooms
   1 oz. (30 g) butter
   8 oz. (225 g) spaghetti

2 lb. (900 g) cooked chicken meat
2 fl. oz. (½ dcL) sherry
16 fl. oz. (4½ dcL) suprême sauce
Parmesan cheese as needed

Coq au Vin—Fry pieces of chopped bacon. Sauté chicken pieces in the same pan with chopped onions until chicken is lightly colored. Warm brandy, and flame. Pour brandy over chicken in pan. Add white stock, and season. Add garlic and bouquet garni. Cover, and simmer until tender. Remove bouquet garni and garlic. Sauté mushrooms in butter; add to casserole. Thicken sauce to desired consistency with beurre manié.

8 oz. (225 g) bacon
2¼ lb. (1 kg) chicken
8 oz. (225 g) small onions
1 fl. oz. (¼ dcL) brandy
16 fl. oz. (4½ dcL) white stock
salt and pepper to taste
2 cloves garlic
bouquet garni
8 oz. (225 g) mushrooms
1 oz. (30 g) butter
beurre manié as needed

Croquettes—Mince the cooked chicken and ham. Toss minced mushrooms in butter for 1 minute, and add to mixture. Blend and season. Make a roux with the butter and flour; moisten with stock. Allow to cook thoroughly. Add chicken mixture and cream; chill. Shape as desired into croquettes weighing 2 to 3 oz. (60 to 90 g); chill again to harden. Dip in beaten egg and breadcrumbs; deep-fry. Drain well.

8 oz. (225 g) chicken
2 oz. (60 g) ham
4 oz. (115 g) mushrooms
1 oz. (30 g) butter
1 oz. (30 g) flour
4 fl. oz. (1 dcL) stock, or as needed
1 Tbs. (15 mL) thick cream
beaten egg as needed
breadcrumbs as needed

Vol-au-Vent no. 1—Dice cooked chicken. Add sauced mushrooms and bind with Nantua sauce. Serve in puff pastry cases.
Vol-au-Vent no. 2—Dice cooked chicken. Add cooked asparagus tips and cover with thickened veal gravy. Serve in puff pastry cases.

Duck

All recipes are for 1 duck weighing about 5½ lb. (2 kg).
Béarnaise—Brown duck in butter. Simmer in white stock with bacon and vegetables; remove duck. Carve and reassemble. Set in serving casserole. Strain stock, and reduce by one-third. Arrange vegetables around duck. Garnish with slices of French bread sprinkled with grated Parmesan and glazed. Serve the reduced stock separately.

3 oz. (90 g) butter
12 fl. oz. (3½ dcL) white stock
3 oz. (90 g) bacon
6 oz. (170 g) each carrots, turnips, and french beans
French bread as needed

Parmesan and beaten egg as
needed

Beaulieu—Roast the duck. Carve,
and reassemble in ovenproof dish.
Garnish with pitted black olives,
quartered artichoke hearts, and
parisienne potatoes. Deglaze pan
with Madeira; add demi-glace.
Strain, and pour over duck.
> olives, artichokes, and potatoes
> as needed
> 2 fl. oz. (½ dcL) Madeira
> 7 fl. oz. (2 dcL) demi-glace

Bordelaise—Stuff duck with pork
forcemeat mixed with duck liver,
shallots, garlic, parsley, chives,
oregano, and chopped onions. Bind
with egg. Truss, and brown bird in
butter in ovenproof dish. Add
mushrooms, cover, and cook in hot
oven. Serve with thickened brown
gravy.
> 12 oz. (340 g) pork forcemeat
> duck liver
> 1 oz. (30 g) shallots
> 1 clove garlic
> 1 Tbs. (15 g) parsley
> 1 Tbs. (15 g) chives
> 1 tsp. (5 g) oregano
> 2 oz. (60 g) onions
> 1 egg
> 4 oz. (115 g) butter
> 1 lb. (450 g) mushrooms
> brown gravy as needed

Cherries—Roast the duck. Carve
and reassemble. Deglaze pan with
Madeira; extend with thickened
veal gravy. Strain, and add pitted
red cherries. Pour sauce over
bird.

> 2 fl. oz. (½ dcL) Madeira
> 7 fl. oz. (2 dcL) veal gravy
> 6 oz. (170 g) cherries

Chipolata—Brown the duck in
butter with mirepoix; remove. Deglaze pan with white wine; add
chicken stock. Braise the duck in
the oven. When it is almost cooked,
add garnish of small white onions,
glazed chestnuts, lightly fried
bacon, and carrot rounds. Finish
cooking. Remove the bird, carve,
and reassemble. Place in a serving
casserole; surround with garnish.
Add small chipolata sausages.
Strain cooking liquid, reduce by
half, and serve separately.
> 3 oz. (90 g) butter
> 6 oz. (170 g) mirepoix
> 3 fl. oz. (¾ dcL) white wine
> 12 fl. oz. (3½ dcL) chicken stock
> 10 onions
> 10 chestnuts
> 4 rashers of bacon
> 5 carrots
> 2 chipolata sausages per portion

Duclaire—Stuff the duck with
forcemeat, and roast. Carve and
reassemble; arrange on a dish. Deglaze pan with red wine and orange
juice; strain. Add demi-glace; reduce by one-quarter. Pour over
duck.
> 3 fl. oz. (¾ dcL) each red wine
> and orange juice
> 10 fl. oz. (3 dcL) demi-glace

Fermière—Braise the duck in
white wine and light demi-glace
with sliced carrots, turnips, celery,
and onions. Carve and reassemble;
place in casserole. Add diamonds of

french beans and green peas to cooking mixture; pour over bird. Serve from casserole.

  10 fl. oz. (3 dcL) each white wine
    and demi-glace
  4 oz. (115 g) each carrots, tur-
    nips, celery, onions, french
    beans, and green peas

Grapes—Brown the duck in butter with mirepoix; remove. Deglaze pan with red wine and thick veal gravy. Return the duck. Add julienned, blanched orange peel; braise. Remove the duck, carve, and reassemble. Strain sauce, and reduce slightly. Add peeled grapes. Pour sauce over bird. Serve with pilaf.

  3 oz. (90 g) butter
  6 oz. (170 g) mirepoix
  3 fl. oz. (¾ dcL) red wine
  10 fl. oz. (3 dcL) veal gravy
  2 Tbs. (30 g) orange peel
  8 oz. (225 g) grapes
  rice as needed

Mint—Place a little butter combined with chopped fresh mint into the cavity; roast. Remove the duck. Deglaze pan with clear veal gravy and a little lemon juice. Add chopped mint, and pour over bird.

  1½ oz. (45 g) butter
  1 tsp. (5 g) fresh mint
  7 fl. oz. (2 dcL) veal gravy
  squeeze of lemon juice
  additional chopped mint as
    needed

Moderne—Cut the duck into pieces as for fricassée; brown in butter. Remove pieces. Deglaze pan with port; add demi-glaze. Return pieces; add minced onion and chopped anchovies. Braise in oven. Strain sauce, and pour over chicken.

Montmorency—Roast the duck, and arrange on platter. Deglaze pan with white wine; strain into saucepan. Flame with brandy. Add port wine; boil. Strain again. Add pitted black cherries. Thicken as desired with beurre manié. Pour sauce over carved duck.

Normande—Brown the duck in butter; remove. Deglaze pan with Calvados, then flame. Add brown stock and cider. Return duck to pan; cover and braise. Carve and reassemble; arrange on a dish. Reduce liquid by one-third; add cream. Garnish with apple slices tossed in butter.

  3 oz. (90 g) butter
  2 fl. oz. (½ dcL) Calvados
  12 fl. oz. (3½ dcL) brown stock
  4 fl. oz. (1 dcL) cider
  2 fl. oz. (½ dcL) cream
  apple slices as needed

Olives—Brown the duck in butter; remove to a deep saucepan. Drain excess butter. Deglaze pan with white wine; add chicken stock. Strain; pour over duck. Add bouquet garni and seasoning. Braise in moderate heat; arrange bird on platter. Strain sauce; skim, and reduce by one-quarter. Add pitted green olives. Carve duck, and reassemble. Pour half the sauce over the duck; serve remainder separately. Serve with chilled applesauce.

  4 oz. (115 g) butter
  8 fl. oz. (2¼ dcL) white wine
  12 fl. oz. (3½ dcL) chicken stock
  bouquet garni

salt and pepper to taste
24 green olives
applesauce as needed

Petits Pois—Brown onions and diced bacon in butter; remove. Brown the duck on all sides in same butter; drain any excess. Deglaze pan with white wine; add chicken stock. Replace duckling, bacon, and onions. Add peas, sugar, bouquet garni, and seasoning. Cover; simmer gently until tender. Carve bird, and reassemble on platter; surround with cooked peas. Reduce liquid by one-third; pour over bird.

3 oz. (90 g) onions
3 oz. (90 g) bacon
4 oz. (115 g) butter
8 fl. oz. (2¼ dcL) white wine
5 fl. oz. (1½ dcL) chicken stock
2 oz. (60 g) peas
pinch of sugar
bouquet garni
salt and pepper to taste
1 lb. (450 g) young peas

Pineapple—Roast the duck; carve and reassemble. Deglaze pan with brandy, and flame; add pineapple juice and thick gravy. Garnish with pineapple slices lightly sautéed in butter.

2 fl. oz. (½ dcL) brandy
4 fl. oz. (1 dcL) pineapple juice
8 fl. oz. (2¼ dcL) gravy
pineapple slices as needed

Provençale—Cut up the duck as for fricassée. Brown in oil; drain. Simmer in white wine with diced tomatoes, garlic, basil, chopped anchovies, and pitted black olives. Serve from dish.

2 fl. oz. (½ dcL) oil
12 fl. oz. (3½ dcL) white wine
8 oz. (225 g) peeled tomatoes
1 clove garlic
pinch of basil
3 anchovies
15 black olives

Villageoise—Cut duck into pieces as for fricassée. Brown in butter in saucepan; cover with vegetables. Sprinkle with rosemary and sugar; season. Add white wine; cover, and simmer for 1½ hours. Thicken cooking liquid, if necessary, just before serving. Garnish with chopped parsley.

3 oz. (90 g) butter
8 oz. (225 g) quartered carrots
1 leek, sliced
8 oz. (225 g) baby white onions
8 pieces of celery, cut in 2-inch
    lengths
¼ tsp. (2½ g) rosemary
1 Tbs. (15 g) sugar
salt and pepper to taste
12 fl. oz. (3½ dcL) white wine
parsley as needed

Squab

Anglaise—Stuff hens with breadcrumbs and livers that have been chopped and tossed in butter with chopped onion. Lard with bacon; roast in butter. Serve with grilled rashers of bacon.

Bonne Femme—Truss and roast hens. Garnish with glazed onions, mushrooms, parisienne potatoes, and thickened gravy.

Bressane—Stuff hens with risotto containing diced chicken livers; roast. Deglaze pan with Madeira and demi-glace. Arrange on risotto; coat with reduced pan juices.

Casanova—Split bird along back, separate halves, and flatten. Season with salt, pepper, and a little mustard. Sprinkle with breadcrumbs mixed with minced ham and chopped parsley; grill. Arrange on potatoes Anna; coat with Chateaubriand sauce.

Casserole—Truss hens. Cook in casserole with baby white onions and assorted vegetables. Serve whole with gravy.

Diable—Split hens along the back. Open, season, and dip in butter and breadcrumbs. Grill, and serve with diable sauce.

Gourmet—Split as for grilled hens. Season, and arrange on potatoes Anna. Garnish with sliced gherkins. Serve Chateaubriand sauce with sliced mushrooms added.

potatoes as needed
gherkins as needed
4 fl. oz. (1 dcL) Chateaubriand
    sauce
1½ oz. (45 g) mushrooms

Minute—Cut hens into four pieces. Toss in butter with chopped onions. Sauté gently until tender. Deglaze pan with brandy, meat glaze, and lemon juice; add butter. Arrange pieces on a dish, and coat with pan gravy. Garnish with mushrooms cooked in butter.

Paysanne—Cook as for casserole. When nearly done, add blanched, diced bacon and slices of plain, boiled potato.

Tartare—Split hens in half, and flatten slightly. Brush with made mustard, then with melted butter. Roll in breadcrumbs; grill. Serve tartare sauce separately.

Viennoise—Cut hens into four pieces; season. Dip pieces in beaten egg and breadcrumbs; deep-fry. Arrange on a dish with lemon slices and chopped parsley.

Turkey

All recipes given for roasters are suitable for turkey. However, those given below are especially suitable.

Bismarck—Stuff the turkey with sliced apples and raisins steeped in brandy. Bard breast with fat bacon, and roast. Serve with pan gravy extended with cider.

2¼ lb. (1 kg) apples
6 oz. (170 g) raisins
brandy to cover
gravy as needed

Blanc des Gourmets—Roast the young turkey; remove and skin breasts. Cut them in fairly thick slices, and arrange on a dish in a circle. Sauté slices of foie gras in butter. Place a slice of foie gras between slices of turkey. Sprinkle with a thread of demi-glace. Garnish with whole chestnuts cooked in consommé, peas, and young whole carrots. Serve cranberry jelly separately.

Bourgeoise—Braise the turkey. Garnish *à la bourgeoise*.

Catalane—Cut a young turkey into pieces as for fricassée. Sauté in butter; remove. Deglaze pan with white wine; add garlic. Reduce by three-quarters; moisten with espagnole sauce and brown stock mixed with tomato purée. Cook in oven until tender. Arrange pieces on a dish; garnish with sautéed, quartered mushrooms, chestnuts cooked in consommé, small glazed onions, quartered tomatoes, and chipolata sausages.

3 oz. (90 g) butter
8 fl. oz. (2¼ dcL) white wine
1 clove garlic
equal quantities of espagnole
    sauce and brown stock to
    cover
1 Tbs. (15 mL) tomato purée
8 oz. (225 g) mushrooms
24 chestnuts
consommé as needed
20 onions
5 tomatoes
10 chipolata sausages

Chestnuts—Cook chestnuts in beef stock, pass through a tammy, and mix with sausage meat. Stuff the turkey with this mixture; roast. Serve gravy separately.

equal quantities of chestnuts and
    sausage meat, (depending on
    the size of the bird)
beef stock as needed

Mode du Chef—Remove turkey breasts, and poach gently. Slice thin, and reassemble. Cover with suprême sauce; garnish with poached oysters, stuffed olives, and julienned, blanched red peppers.

20 fl. oz. (6 dcL) suprême sauce
20 oysters
30 olives
5 oz. (140 g) red peppers

Game _____

CORNISH GAME HENS

All recipes are for 2 birds weighing 16 to 22 oz. (450 to 620 g) each.

Blane—Bard breast and roast. Deglaze pan with white wine; add poivrade sauce. Garnish with poached apple rings. Serve cranberry jelly separately.

7 fl. oz. (2 dcL) white wine
2 fl. oz. (½ dcL) poivrade sauce
apple rings and cranberry jelly as
    needed

Castillian—Rub the hens with butter; sprinkle with flour. Put in pan with chicken broth, onion, parsley, and bay leaf, and cook in oven for 20 minutes. Add more broth if necessary. Cover, and continue cooking. Meanwhile, sauté chopped onions, tomatoes, sliced green peppers, and mushrooms in oil. Add this mixture to cream sauce; heat through. Carve the hens, reassemble, and place on serving dish. Pour sauce over them.

butter and flour as needed
5 fl. oz. (1½ dcL) chicken broth
1 small onion
parsley sprigs to taste
1 bay leaf
additional broth as needed

3 Tbs. (45 mL) oil
1 large onion
3 tomatoes
1 green pepper
4 oz. (115 g) mushrooms
10 fl. oz. (3 dcL) cream sauce

Chez Moi—Bard breast after filling cavity with peeled and chopped apples, powdered bay leaf, and clove. Baste with a little chicken stock. Roast for 35 to 40 minutes. Serve with pan gravy mixed with red currant jelly and applesauce.

3 or 4 apples
pinch of ground bay leaf
pinch of clove
chicken stock as needed
equal quantities of red currant
    jelly and applesauce

Creole—Cut the hens as for fricassée. Brown in butter. Add demi-glace and stock. Braise with chopped onions, tomatoes, mushrooms, green pepper, and diced ham.

3 oz. (90 g) butter
4 fl. oz. (1 dcL) demi-glace
4 fl. oz. (1 dcL) brown stock
2 onions
2 tomatoes
4 oz. (115 g) mushrooms

½ green pepper
3 oz. (90 g) ham

Maltaise—Bard and roast the
hen. Deglaze pan with brandy; add
tangerine juice. Add thick veal
gravy. Disjoint the hen, and remove
to a hot platter. Pour sauce over
hen.
  2 fl. oz. (½ dcL) brandy
  juice of 5 tangerines
  8 fl. oz. (2¼ dcL) veal gravy

Nesselrode—Cut the hen into
pieces as for fricassée. Coat with
flour, and sauté in butter. Deglaze
pan with red wine; add demi-glace,
tomato purée, and cooked, chopped
chestnuts. Pour sauce over pieces.
  flour as needed
  3 oz. (90 g) butter
  5 fl. oz. (1½ dcL) red wine
  5 fl. oz. (1½ dcL) demi-glace
  1 Tbs. (15 mL) tomato purée
  8 chestnuts

PARTRIDGE

Partridge can be substituted for
pheasant in any of the pheasant
recipes. The recipes given below
are best suited to partridge. All
recipes given are for 1 bird.
  Anchovy Butter—Roast the partridge. Cut in half, and reassemble.
Set on a bed of rice. Garnish with
watercress, and pour melted anchovy butter over bird.
  Béarnaise—Brown partridge in
oven. Place in casserole, and braise
in white wine, brown stock, garlic,
and tomato purée.
  7 fl. oz. (2 dcL) white wine
  7 fl. oz. (2 dcL) brown stock

1 clove garlic
1 Tbs. (15 mL) tomato purée

Bourguignonne—Roast partridge
until three-quarters done; transfer
to casserole with glazed onions and
chopped, cooked mushrooms. Deglaze pan with red wine; reduce by
one-quarter. Add game demi-glace;
strain. Pour sauce over bird, cover,
and finish cooking in oven for about
15 minutes.
  8 onions
  8 mushrooms
  7 fl. oz. (2 dcL) red wine
  2 fl. oz. (½ dcL) game demi-glace

Estouffade—Brown partridge in
oven; set in casserole over matignon moistened with gin. Pour
melted butter over partridge. Flame
brandy in ladle, pour over partridge. Add game fumet. Cover, and
bake in oven. Serve from dish.
  2 oz. (60 g) matignon
  1 fl. oz. (¼ dcL) gin
  1 oz. (30 g) butter
  2 fl. oz. (½ dcL) brandy
  7 fl. oz. (2 dcL) game fumet

Forestière—Roast the partridge.
Deglaze pan with white wine; add
demi-glace. Enrich with mashed
liver pâté. Add chopped parsley,
and pour over partridge.
  7 fl. oz. (2 dcL) white wine
  7 fl. oz. (2 dcL) demi-glace
  3 oz. (90 g) liver pâté
  chopped parsley to taste

Fried—Cut partridge into four
pieces. Dip in beaten egg and breadcrumbs; deep-fry. Garnish with
lemon and parsley sprigs.

Grenobloise—Cut partridge into pieces as for fricassée. Sauté in butter with minced garlic, diced bacon, and tiny croûtons; remove. Deglaze pan with Madeira; add demi-glace. Arrange on a hot platter, and cover with sauce.

2 oz. (60 g) butter
3 cloves garlic, minced
6 oz. (170 g) lean bacon
croûtons as needed
4 fl. oz. (1 dcL) Madeira
4 fl. oz. (1 dcL) demi-glace

Grillé au Diable—Split partridge down back; open, and flatten slightly. Brush with butter, and grill under moderate heat for 5 minutes on each side. Brush with more butter, and dip in breadcrumbs; finish grilling. Place on a dish. Garnish with watercress and sliced lemon; serve with diable sauce.

Lautrec—Split and grill young bird. Brush with herb butter and lemon juice. Garnish with large, grilled mushroom caps. Sprinkle with liquid meat glaze.

Provencale—Cut partridge into pieces. Brown in oil. Cook in casserole with stewed tomatoes, peas, garlic, black olives, and slices of eggplant sautéed in oil.

8 oz. (225 g) tomatoes
4 oz. (115 g) peas
1 clove garlic, minced
12 black olives
1 medium eggplant

PHEASANT

Airelles—Roast the pheasant, and remove. Deglaze pan with white wine and demi-glace. Add orange juice. Boil and strain. Pour sauce over pheasant. Garnish with tartlets filled with cranberries cooked with brown sugar and cinnamon to taste.

2 fl. oz. (½ dcL) white wine
4 fl. oz. (1 dcL) demi-glace
2 fl. oz. (½ dcL) orange juice
8 tartlets
cranberry mixture as needed

Allemande—Roast the pheasant. Deglaze pan with white wine; add sour cream. Boil up and strain. Serve with braised red cabbage.

3 fl. oz. (¾ dcL) white wine
4 fl. oz. (1 dcL) sour cream
red cabbage as needed

Alsacienne—Stuff pheasant with pork sausage meat and mushrooms; brown in pan. Braise on a bed of sauerkraut and cubes of cooked, lean ham; moisten with game stock. Carve and reassemble. Place on the sauerkraut and ham. Serve cooking liquid separately.

10 oz. (280 g) pork sausage meat
4 oz. (115 g) mushrooms
1 lb. (450 g) sauerkraut
6 oz. (170 g) ham
7 fl. oz. (2 dcL) game stock

Angoulême—Stuff the pheasant with minced mushrooms, minced chestnuts, and sieved pork fat. Bard with bacon. Roast, carve, and reassemble on serving dish. Drain pan. Deglaze with white wine; add veal gravy and red currant jelly. Reduce by one-third; strain. Pour sauce over pheasant.

6 oz. (170 g) raw, minced mushrooms

4 chestnuts cooked in consommé,
then minced
10 oz. (280 g) pork fat rubbed
through a sieve
bacon for barding
3 fl. oz. (¾ dcL) white wine
12 fl. oz. (3½ dcL) veal gravy
3 Tbs. (45 mL) red currant jelly

Bonne Femme—Brown the pheasant in pan with butter. Add sliced
onions, chutney, mushrooms, and
stock. Cover, and roast. Remove
pheasant; carve and reassemble.
Reduce liquid by one-third; pour
sauce over pheasant.
3 oz. (90 g) butter
1 onion
2 oz. (60 g) chutney
3 oz. (90 g) mushrooms
12 fl. oz. (3½ dcL) game stock

Casserole—Roast the pheasant in
butter; carve, and arrange on a hot
platter. Deglaze pan with brandy;
add rich game gravy. Pour over
pheasant.
2 fl. oz. (½ dcL) brandy
6 fl. oz. (1¾ dcL) game gravy

Chestnuts—Roast the pheasant;
Remove, carve, and reassemble.
Deglaze pan with brandy; strain,
and mix with cream. Set pheasant
on bed of chestnut purée. Sprinkle
sauce over it.
1 fl. oz. (¼ dcL) brandy
2 fl. oz. (½ dcL) cream
8 oz. (225 g) chestnut purée

Comte de Brabant—Roast the
pheasant with diced, lean ham.
Serve with prebaked tartlets filled
with tiny brussels sprouts

moistened with meat glaze. Serve
with pan gravy extended with a little game stock.
8 oz. (225 g) ham
8 tartlets
brussels sprouts as needed

Connaught—Stuff pheasant with
forcemeat of choice, but containing
about one-quarter chestnuts,
cooked and minced. Roast the
pheasant; carve and reassemble.
Deglaze pan with brandy and game
stock; reduce by one-quarter. Pour
sauce over bird. Garnish with fresh
watercress.
12 oz. (340 g) forcemeat
2 fl. oz. (½ dcL) brandy
10 fl. oz. (3 dcL) game stock

Crème—Roast pheasant in butter
with minced onion. When three-quarters done, add sour cream. Finish cooking, basting often. Serve
from pan.
3 oz. (90 g) butter
1 onion
5 fl. oz. (1½ dcL) sour cream

Flamande—Brown the pheasant
in butter. Place in casserole, and
braise with turnips, carrots, onions,
and cabbage.
3 oz. (90 g) butter
6 oz. (170 g) each turnip, carrot,
and onion
1 cabbage cut into 8 wedges

Georgienne—Poach the pheasant
covered in a mixture of grape and
orange juice, Madeira wine, butter,
and chopped walnuts. Carve, reassemble, and arrange on a hot platter. Surround with walnut halves.

Strain poaching liquid. Add espagnole sauce based on game stock; reduce by one-third. Coat the pheasant, and garnish. Serve remaining sauce separately.

10 fl. oz. (3 dcL) grape juice
6 fl. oz. (1¾ dcL) orange juice
5 fl. oz. (1½ dcL) Madeira
2 oz. (60 g) butter
24 walnuts, chopped
24 walnuts for garnish
7 fl. oz. (2 dcL) espagnole sauce

Languedocienne—Cut the pheasant into 8 pieces as for fricassée. Brown in 3 oz. butter; set pieces on bed of mirepoix. Sprinkle with flour; moisten with red wine and clear stock. Add bouquet garni. Cover, and cook for about 30 minutes. Drain pieces; remove to ovenproof dish. Add mushrooms and julienned, blanched red peppers. Moisten with brandy and strained cooking liquid; enrich with 1½ oz. butter. Cover, seal, and set in bainmarie in oven to cook for 40 minutes more.

3 oz. (90 g) butter
12 oz. (340 g) mirepoix
1 oz. (30 g) flour
10 fl. oz. (3 dcL) red wine
3 fl. oz. (¾ dcL) clear stock
bouquet garni
8 oz. (225 g) mushrooms
½ red pepper
1 fl. oz. (¼ dcL) brandy
1½ oz. (45 g) butter

Normande—Brown young bird in 2 oz. butter. Peel, core, and mince apples; toss them in 3 oz. hot butter. Line bottom of casserole with apples; place pheasant on top.

Sprinkle with fresh cream and Calvados; cover and cook. Carve and reassemble; serve from casserole.

2 oz. (60 g) butter
6 large apples
3 oz. (90 g) butter
3 fl. oz. (¾ dcL) cream
1 fl. oz. (¼ dcL) Calvados

Strasbourgeoise—Proceed as for Alsacienne recipe, adding small, fried pork sausages as an extra garnish.

QUAIL

All recipes are for 2 birds. In addition to those shown below, recipes for partridge may also be used. Spit-roasting is preferred over ovenroasting.

Cendre—Bard, and roast quail until almost cooked; remove. Wrap in thin puff pastry spread inside with cold meat glaze, leaving feet of bird outside pastry shell. Make a small hole in top to allow chasseur sauce to be poured inside when cooked. Brown pastry, and bake.

Cherries—Proceed as for Quail en Cocottes. When half-cooked, add 12 cherries for each bird.

En Cocottes—Place a knob of butter inside the cavity of each quail; truss. Bard breasts. Put quail in casserole with a little heated butter; season. Cover, and cook in oven for 15 minutes, basting frequently. Add a little game stock and a small glass of sherry toward the end of the cooking time.

Gourmandise—Stuff the quail with a mixture of butter, chopped ham, and 8-oz. minced mushrooms;

roast. Deglaze pan with champagne; add chicken stock. Arrange quail on a dish over a bed of coarsely chopped mushrooms sautéed in butter. Garnish with tartlets lined with foie gras and topped with a green stuffed olive. Heat sauce, and pour over quail.

> 4 oz. (115 g) butter
> 6 oz. (170 g) ham
> 8 oz. (225 g) minced mushrooms
> 10 fl. oz. (3 dcL) champagne
> 12 fl. oz. (3½ dcL) chicken stock
> 8 oz. (225 g) coarsely chopped
>   mushrooms
> 3 oz. (90 g) butter
> 4 tartlets
> 3 oz. (90 g) foie gras
> 4 green olives

Grand-Duc—Split the quail along the back; season. Brush with melted butter, roll in breadcrumbs, and grill. Arrange on a dish over a bed of browned duchesse potatoes. Garnish with large, grilled mushroom caps filled with horseradish cream. Make a sauce with game fumet, Madeira, and butter; pour over quail.

> salt and pepper to taste
> butter and breadcrumbs as
>   needed
> potatoes as needed
> 8 mushroom caps
> 8 Tbs. (120 mL) horseradish
>   cream
> *Sauce:*
> 3 fl. oz. (¾ dcL) game fumet
> 3 fl. oz. (¾ dcL) Madeira
> 2 oz. (60 g) butter

Grape Leaves—Wrap the quail in buttered grape leaves; roast. De-glaze pan with Cognac and brown stock. Serve sauce separately.

> 2 fl. oz. (½ dcL) brandy
> 6 fl. oz. (1¾ dcL) brown stock

Grapes—Roast the quail; drain excess butter. Deglaze pan with white wine and brandy; add strong game fumet. Arrange quail in serving casserole with peeled grapes as garnish. Pour sauce over quail.

> 3 oz. (90 g) butter
> 2 fl. oz. (½ dcL) white wine
> 1 fl. oz. (¼ dcL) brandy
> 2 fl. oz. (½ dcL) game fumet
> 6 oz. (170 g) grapes

Lucullus—Split the quail lengthwise. Remove breasts, leaving bone in place. Lard with bacon fat, and bake in oven for 20 minutes, basting frequently with brown stock to glaze. Serve with espagnole sauce separately.

Minute—Open quail down the back, and remove small rib-bone and backbone. Flatten slightly; season inside. Sauté the halves quickly in butter; arrange on dish. Add chopped onions, chopped parsley, and sliced mushrooms to pan; cook quickly. Add brandy and game stock. Deglaze; reduce by one-quarter. Pour sauce over bird.

> salt and pepper to taste
> 4 oz. (115 g) butter
> 2 oz. (60 g) chopped onions
> chopped parsley to taste
> 3 oz. (90 g) sliced mushrooms
> 1 fl. oz. (¼ dcL) brandy
> 8 fl. oz. (2¼ dcL) game stock

Mouquin—Sauté minced shallot, bay leaf, garlic, and cloves in butter. Brown quail in saucepan; remove. Deglaze pan with white wine. Return quail; cover, and simmer for 30 minutes. Remove quail again; strain liquid into serving casserole. Add cream; season. Return quail, cover, and place in oven to heat through. Serve.

3 oz. (90 g) butter
1 shallot, minced
½ bay leaf
1 clove garlic
pinch of ground cloves
5 fl. oz. (1½ dcL) white wine
5 fl. oz. (1½ dcL) cream
salt and pepper to taste

Oriental—Bard and roast the quail. Deglaze pan with tomato juice; add veal gravy. Arrange quail on a bed of rice. Serve sauce separately.

Portuguese—Roast quail in butter; drain excess. Deglaze pan with Madeira; add veal gravy. Serve on risotto mixed with blanched red and green peppers in large dice. Pour sauce over quail.

butter as needed
2 fl. oz. (½ dcL) Madeira
8 fl. oz. (2¼ dcL) veal gravy
risotto and diced red and green
    peppers as needed

Red Cabbage—Bard and roast the quail. Deglaze pan with sherry; add veal stock. Serve on bed of braised red cabbage mixed with stewed apple and chestnut purée. Pour sauce over quail.

2 fl. oz. (½ dcL) sherry
8 fl. oz. (2¼ dcL) veal stock
10 oz. (280 g) cabbage and purée
    mixture

Romaine—Sauté chopped scallion and diced ham in butter. Place bird in the same pan, and brown. Add shelled peas; season. Add sugar; cover, and cook in oven for 40 minutes.

4 oz. (115 g) butter
1 scallion
1 oz. (30 g) ham
4 oz. (115 g) shelled peas
salt and pepper to taste
pinch of sugar

Singapore—Proceed as for Quail with Grapes, using diced pineapple instead of grapes.

RABBIT

A choice young rabbit will weigh between 3 lb. (1.35 kg) and 4½ lb. (2 kg). All recipes are for 1 rabbit.

Curry—Cut rabbit into pieces. Sweat onions in butter until tender; brown rabbit in same pan. Add curry powder; sprinkle with flour. Mix and brown. Add white wine and clear stock; add cream and sliced mushrooms to pan. Cover, and cook for about 35 minutes. Transfer to serving casserole, and serve.

3 oz. (90 g) butter
5 oz. (140 g) onions
2 tsp. (10 g) curry powder
2 Tbs. (30 g) flour
4 fl. oz. (1 dcL) white wine
clear stock to cover
2 fl. oz. (½ dcL) cream
6 oz. (170 g) mushrooms

Espagnole—Cut rabbit into pieces; brown in oil. Add chopped onions, diced bacon, paprika, peeled and chopped tomatoes, and julienne of red and green peppers. Add game stock to cover; simmer until tender. Transfer rabbit pieces to serving casserole; leave vegetables in cooking liquid, and reduce volume. Pour sauce over pieces, and serve.

2 fl. oz. (½ dcL) olive oil
1 large onion
3 oz. (90 g) bacon
paprika to taste
8 oz. (225 g) tomatoes
½ each red and green pepper
game stock to cover

Au Four—Cut rabbit into pieces; sauté in butter. When half-cooked, brush with Dijon mustard, and roll in breadcrumbs mixed with chopped thyme. Finish cooking in oven. Serve with red currant jelly.

Grand-Mère—Cut rabbit into 8 pieces; marinate for 2 hours, and drain. Brown gently in butter; add chopped onions and lean bacon. Sauté all together. Sprinkle with flour; mix. Add white wine, strong, clear stock, and bouquet garni; simmer for 20 minutes. Add small new potatoes, and cook for about 25 minutes more. Transfer to serving casserole, sprinkle with chopped parsley, and serve.

raw marinade as needed
3 oz. (90 g) butter
12 oz. (340 g) onions
6 oz. (170 g) bacon
1 Tbs. (15 g) flour
7 fl. oz. (2 dcL) white wine
4 fl. oz. (1 dcL) clear stock
bouquet garni
10 oz. (280 g) potatoes
chopped parsley

Minute—Cut rabbit into pieces; brown quickly in 3 oz. butter to a good color. Reduce heat, and sauté until tender. Place in serving casserole. Deglaze pan with white wine, add chopped shallots, and reduce by one-third. Add thickened veal stock; heat. Enrich with 1 oz. butter; add lemon juice. Pour sauce over pieces.

3 oz. (90 g) butter
5 fl. oz. (1½ dcL) white wine
1 shallot
6 fl. oz. (1¾ dcL) veal stock
1 oz. (30 g) butter
squeeze of lemon juice

Paprika—Cut rabbit into pieces, and marinate for 1 hour. Sweat onions in butter until tender; brown rabbit in same pan. Add paprika; sprinkle with flour. Mix and brown. Add white wine and clear stock; add cream and sliced mushrooms to pan. Cover, and cook for 35 minutes. Transfer to serving casserole, and serve.

raw marinade as needed
3 oz. (90 g) butter
5 oz. (140 g) onions
2 tsp. (10 g) paprika
2 Tbs. (30 g) flour
4 fl. oz. (1 dcL) white wine
clear stock to cover
2 fl. oz. (½ dcL) cream
6 oz. (170 g) mushrooms

Prunes—Cut rabbit into pieces, and marinate for 1 hour; brown in butter. Add marinade, water, and soaked prunes; simmer until tender. Place pieces in a serving casserole, and surround with prunes. Thicken

stock with beurre manié, and flavor
with red currant jelly.

raw marinade as needed
2 oz. (60 g) butter
equal quantities of marinade and
    water to cover
16 prunes
1½ oz. (45 g) beurre manié
2 Tbs. (30 mL) red currant jelly

VENISON

Meat derived from the red deer
and fallow deer is superior to that of
the roebuck. Fallow deer is now
raised on private commercial es-
tates and should be readily available. Both red and fallow deer need
to be hung in a cool place or mari-
nated for 2 to 3 days for the meat to
mature. Roebuck should be cooked
fresh. All venison should be cleaned
of sinew and the large joints larded
with fat bacon or lardons.

The saddle of venison consists of
the entire back. When roasting the
saddle, the ribs are cut short so that
the joint can stand steady in the
oven. Should a smaller saddle be required, only the lumbar portions are
used and the ribs are prepared as
cutlets. The saddle and legs should
be given 2 to 3 days of marinating
or hanging; cutlets will do with marinating for 3 hours. The following
recipes apply to either saddle or
cutlets, but are suitable for other
cuts, including the loin and leg. All
recipes are for approximately 6½
lb. (3 kg) saddle or cutlets.

Basic Marinade: Heat oil in large
pan; add carrots and onions, and
cook until onions begin to brown.
Add shallots, garlic, herbs, wine

vinegar, white wine, and water;
cook for 20 minutes. Add salt, peppercorns, and brown sugar; cook
for 10 minutes more. Strain, and let
cool before using. Marinade needs
to be boiled up every 2 days for it to
remain sweet. This recipes makes
96 fl. oz. (6 quarts).

3 fl. oz. (¾ dcL) oil
8 oz. (225 g) minced carrots
8 oz. (225 g) minced onions
4 oz. (115 g) shallots
4 cloves garlic, minced
parsley sprigs, rosemary, thyme,
    and bay leaf to taste
20 fl. oz. (6 dcL) wine vinegar
2 bottles white wine
60 fl. oz. (8 dcL) cold water
2 oz. (60 g) salt
1 Tbs. (15 g) peppercorns
4 oz. (115 g) brown sugar

Allemande—Chop vegetables,
place on bottom of roasting pan,
and moisten with marinade. Place
saddle on vegetables; roast. Drain
excess fat, and deglaze pan with a
little meat stock; reduce by one-
quarter. Add cream and gin, then
meat glaze. Strain through a metal
sieve, pressing vegetables to purée.
Set saddle on platter or carve in
kitchen; accompany with sauce.

8 oz. (225 g) each carrots and on-
    ions
4 fl. oz. (1 dcL) marinade
10 fl. oz. (3 dcL) meat stock
16 fl. oz. (4½ dcL) cream
1 fl. oz. (¼ dcL) gin
2 fl. oz. (½ dcL) meat glaze

Baden-Baden—Chop vegetables,
place on bottom of roasting pan,
and moisten with marinade. Set

saddle on vegetables; roast. Arrange saddle on a long serving dish with a garnish of poached unsweetened pear halves flavored with cinnamon and lemon rind. Drain excess grease from pan; deglaze with game stock, and cook for a few minutes. Strain; thicken with arrowroot or cornstarch. The cooked saddle may be presented whole or may be carved in the kitchen and presented as sliced meat in the restaurant.

2¼ lb. (1 kg) mixed carrots, onions, and celery
marinade as needed
pear halves as needed
cinnamon and lemon rind as needed
10 fl. oz. (3 dcL) game stock
arrowroot or cornstarch as needed

Cherries—Marinate saddle for 12 hours only. Roast, basting with marinade. Set on serving dish; accompany with cherry sauce.

10 fl. oz. (3 dcL) each poivrade sauce and red currant jelly
4 oz. (115 g) pitted, chopped cherries

Chestnuts—Trim cutlets as you would lamb cutlets; flatten. Season, and sauté in butter for 5 minutes on each side. Arrange on a pyramid of chestnut purée. Drain excess butter from pan; deglaze with sherry. Add red currant jelly and tomato sauce; pour over cutlets.

6 cutlets
salt and pepper to taste
5 oz. (140 g) butter
8 oz. (225 g) chestnut purée
1 fl. oz. (¼ dcL) sherry
3 Tbs. (45 mL) red currant jelly
8 fl. oz. (2¼ dcL) tomato sauce

Creole—Roast saddle, basting with marinade. Set on platter, and surround with halved bananas tossed in butter. Serve sauce separately.

6 bananas
10 fl. oz. (3 fl. oz.) each chasseur sauce and poivrade sauce
2 oz. (60 g) butter

Genièvre—Lard, and roast saddle without marinating. Drain excess fat. Deglaze dish with gin. Add cream, and reduce by one-quarter. Add poivrade sauce and lemon juice. Garnish saddle with stewed, quartered apples. Serve sauce separately.

4 fl. oz. (1 dcL) gin
6 fl. oz. (1¾ dcL) cream
4 fl. oz. (1 dcL) poivrade sauce
squeeze of lemon juice
apples as needed

Hungarian—Cook cutlets in butter. Arrange in the form of a crown on dish. Drain excess butter. Deglaze pan with sour cream. Add Hungarian sauce, and coat cutlets.

6 cutlets
5 oz. (140 g) butter
2 fl. oz. (½ dcL) sour cream
7 fl. oz. (2 dcL) Hungarian sauce

Vegetables

ARTICHOKES

The major edible part of the globe artichoke is the base, which is called the heart. It is obtained by removing the thistlelike "choke" from the center of the vegetable after it has been cooked. The base of the outer leaves also provides a small but delicious morsel, which is bitten off by the guest. In a recipe, "quartered artichokes" refers to very young artichokes whose outer leaves have been removed, leaving the yellow-green inner leaves and the heart. In this case, the "choke" is not removed, and the vegetable is simply quartered. All recipes are for 12 artichokes.

Argenteuil—Fill artichoke hearts with purée of white asparagus; serve as a garnish.

Barigoule—Trim and blanch artichokes; remove chokes. Fill center of the artichokes with duxelles combined with chopped ham. Wrap artichokes in bacon slices, and tie. Braise in white wine; untie, discard bacon. Strain liquid, and combine with demi-glace to make a coating sauce.

 6 oz. (170 g) duxelles and ham
  mixture

bacon as needed
12 fl. oz. (3½ dcL) white wine
cooking liquid and demi-glace as
 needed

Béarnaise—Parboil; remove choke. Braise in lightly seasoned chicken stock with lemon juice. Serve béarnaise sauce separately.

Beignets Colbert—Fill hearts with duxelles and forcemeat. Skewer two by two, dip in light batter, and deep-fry.

 1 Tbs. (15 mL) filling per artichoke heart
 equal quantities of duxelles and
  forcemeat

Boulangère—Parboil artichokes, and remove choke. Fill hearts with sausage meat. Wrap in short crust, and bake for 1 hour.

Bretonne—Fill artichoke hearts with purée of kidney beans; serve as a garnish.

Brunoise—Fill artichoke hearts with carrots, celery, onions, and french beans cut *brunoise;* serve as a garnish.

Butter—Strip leaves; blanch. Remove choke; cut hearts into quarters, and put in buttered pan.

Moisten with water; sprinkle with melted butter, and season. Cook covered; pour pan juices over hearts when serving.

Conté—Fill artichoke hearts with purée of lentils; serve as a garnish.

Dietrich—Strip heavy leaves; blanch hearts, and remove choke. Cook in light velouté with chopped onions previously sautéed in butter. Serve on a bed of rice.

    4 oz. (115 g) onions
    1½ oz. (45 g) butter
    16 fl. oz. (4½ dcL) velouté

Dubarry—Cook artichoke hearts. Fill with mashed cauliflower, and cover with Mornay sauce. Sprinkle with grated Parmesan cheese; glaze.

Favorite—Cook the hearts in lightly seasoned chicken stock. Garnish with asparagus tips; cover with Mornay sauce. Top with a sautéed button mushroom.

Florentine—Chop onions; sauté in butter with leaf spinach until all moisture is evaporated. Season; add anchovy paste and velouté. Cook together 10 minutes. Cook hearts in stock; stuff with mixture. Arrange on buttered tray; coat with Mornay sauce. Sprinkle with Gruyère; glaze.

    3 oz. (90 g) onion
    butter as needed
    8 oz. (225 g) spinach
    2 oz. (60 g) butter
    salt and pepper to taste
    1 Tbs. (15 mL) anchovy paste
    1 fl. oz. (¼ dcL) velouté
    16 fl. oz. (4½ dcL) chicken stock
    3 fl. oz. (¾ dcL) Mornay sauce
    2 oz. (60 g) Gruyère cheese

Fonds Farcis—Cook artichokes; remove leaves and choke. Fill hearts with duxelles; arrange on buttered tray. Sprinkle with breadcrumbs and melted butter; set in oven to form a gratin. Serve with Madeira sauce.

Hollandaise—Strip all heavy outer leaves. Cut artichokes in half; cook in salted water. Remove choke. Serve with hollandaise sauce.

Juive—Trim small artichokes, parboil, and remove the choke. Stuff with a mixture of breadcrumbs moistened with white wine, chopped fresh mint, and garlic; season. Pan-fry in oil until crisp.

Macédoine—Fill artichoke hearts with diced root vegetables and peas sautéed in butter; serve as a garnish.

Paysanne—Strip heavy leaves; blanch, and remove choke. Cut in quarters, then quickly sauté in pan with chopped bacon, onions, and diced potatoes. Cover with white consommé; add bouquet garni. Cook quickly in oven until nearly dry.

    6 oz. (170 g) bacon
    4 oz. (115 g) onions
    12 oz. (340 g) potatoes
    8 fl. oz. (2¼ dcL) white
        consommé
    bouquet garni

Princess—Fill artichoke hearts with asparagus tips and diced truffles; serve as a garnish.

Purée—Remove leaves, and cook. Remove choke; pass hearts through a sieve. Thicken with cream to correct consistency; season. Use as garnish.

Saint-Germain—Fill artichoke hearts with purée of fresh garden peas; serve as a garnish.

ASPARAGUS

All recipes are for 2¼ lb. (1 kg) of asparagus.

Asparagus Tips—cut stems to within 1½ inches (4 cms) of tips; tie tips in bundles. Cook, and drain; dip immediately in ice-water. Use for garnish.

Colbert—Boil green tips; arrange on toast. Cover with mousseline sauce; top with a poached egg.

Croûte Gratinée—Trim asparagus, and blanch in boiling water for 10 minutes; drain. Finish cooking in melted butter. Trim crusts from bread; cut bread to fit length of asparagus. Fry these croûtons in butter. Put 6 to 8 stems on each croûton. Sprinkle with grated Parmesan, drizzle with butter from pan, and brown lightly.

6 oz. (170 g) butter
bread as needed
3 oz. (90 g) Parmesan cheese

Flamande—Trim asparagus, and cook in boiling salted water. Serve with a sauce composed of mashed, hard-boiled eggs and melted butter.

4 eggs
6 oz. (170 g) butter

Glacées—Poach, drain, and chill the asparagus. Marinate in oil, vinegar, salt, pepper, chopped capers, sweet pickles, tarragon, and Worcestershire sauce. Serve with a little of the marinade.

6 fl. oz. (1¾ dcL) oil
2 fl. oz. (½ dcL) vinegar
salt and pepper to taste
1 oz. (30 g) capers
1 oz. (30 g) pickles
pinch of tarragon
1 tsp. (5 mL) Worcestershire
sauce

Au Gratin—Arrange cooked asparagus in rows. Cover heads with Mornay sauce; cover stems with butter paper. Sprinkle heads with grated cheese, and glaze. Remove paper, and serve.

4 fl. oz. (1 dcL) Mornay sauce
3 oz. (90 g) cheese

Ideal—Boil the asparagus. Serve with a vinaigrette sauce mixed with chopped, hard-boiled eggs.

Smoked Salmon—Cook asparagus tips. Moisten wtih cream sauce. Lay on thin slices of smoked salmon.

BEETS

Beets can be used as a garnish for salads, hors d'oeuvres, and in some game entrées.

Américaine—Boil, peel, and slice the beets. Moisten with bâtarde sauce sharpened with a touch of tarragon vinegar.

Béchamel—Bake and peel the beets. Cut into thick slices. Simmer gently in sauté pan with butter. Arrange on a dish, and cover with béchamel sauce to which the pan butter has been added.

Orange—Boil and peel the beets. Cut them into large dice; simmer in butter moistened with orange juice, orange zest, and a dash of sherry. Arrange beets on dish. Thicken sauce with cornstarch; pour over beets.

Paysanne—Boil, peel, and slice the beets. Mix with lightly sautéed onions; moisten with hollandaise sauce. Use equal quantities of beets and onions.

Russe—Boil, peel, and slice the beets. Simmer in butter, and garnish with chopped, fresh mint when serving.

BROAD BEANS

All recipes are for 2 lb. (900 g) of shelled beans.

Basic Preparation: Shell beans; remove the tough outer skin (unless the beans are very young) by blanching for 5 minutes, then cook in boiling salted water with a small bunch of savory. Drain, and proceed according to selected recipe.

Allemande—Cook beans. Mix with diced, cooked carrots; moisten with chicken stock. Add chopped parsley and savory. Thicken with beurre manié.

   1 lb. (450 g) carrots
   12 fl. oz. (3½ dcL) chicken stock
   parsley and savory to taste
   beurre manié as needed

Bacon—Fry chopped onions in butter; add blanched, diced bacon. Dredge mixture in flour, and brown lightly. Moisten with enough stock to make a sauce of the desired consistency. When sauce is made, add cooked beans, and heat through.

   6 oz. (170 g) onions
   3 oz. (90 g) butter

   6 oz. (170 g) bacon
   3 oz. (90 g) flour
   stock as needed

Butter—Cook and drain the beans. Toss in pan over a high flame to dry. Finish away from fire with added butter.

   3 oz. (90 g) butter

Purée—Proceed as for Purée of Peas. This style makes a particularly good accompaniment to boiled ham.

BROCCOLI

All recipes are for 2 lb. (900 g) of broccoli.

Basic Preparation: Cut florets from the heavy main stem. Trim and wash. Drop in boiling salted water and cook briefly (about 5 to 6 minutes). Drain well and serve plain or with the following sauces: Mousseline, butter, or cream. If desired, peel the heavy main stems to remove coarse outer fiber, cut in rings or julienne and use for salads.

Cardinal—Boil florets; drain. Cover with cardinal sauce. Sprinkle with grated Parmesan cheese. Put under broiler to gratin.

   9 fl. oz. (2½ dcL) cardinal sauce
   4 oz. (115 g) Parmesan cheese

French—Boil florets; drain. Sprinkle with diced, blanched red peppers and toasted, buttered breadcrumbs. Serve bâtarde sauce flavored with nutmeg separately.

   4 oz. (115 g) red peppers
   2 Tbs. (30 g) breadcrumbs
   7 fl. oz. (2 dcL) bâtarde sauce
   pinch of nutmeg

Au Gratin—Boil florets; drain. Cover with Mornay sauce. Sprinkle with grated cheese. Gratin in oven or under broiler.

Polish—Boil florets; drain. Cover with chopped hard-boiled eggs. Sprinkle parsley on top.

2 hard-boiled eggs
parsley as needed

Rebecca—Parboil florets. Dip in frying batter and deep-fry. Serve tomato sauce separately.

BRUSSELS SPROUTS

All recipes are for 2 lb. (900 g) of brussels sprouts.

Beauséjour—Cook brussels sprouts in salted water until crisp but tender. Meanwhile, fry diced bacon until crisp; stir in small, fried croûtons. Add tarragon vinegar and cream; heat through. Adjust seasoning, and pour sauce over drained sprouts. Sprinkle with parsley and paprika.

4 oz. (115 g) bacon
croûtons as needed
1 fl. oz. (¼ dcL) tarragon vinegar
7 fl. oz. (2 dcL) cream
salt and pepper to taste
parsley and paprika as needed

Butter—Cook and drain brussels sprouts. Toss in butter.

Crème—Cook brussels sprouts until almost soft in salted water; drain without cooling too much. Sauté in butter to finish; chop and season. Combine with as much fresh cream as desired.

Gourmet—Cook brussels sprouts in chicken stock for 8 minutes;

drain. Place in casserole with béchamel sauce and seedless grapes. Sprinkle with buttered breadcrumbs, and brown quickly in oven.

chicken stock as needed
16 fl. oz. (4½ dcL) béchamel
    sauce
6 oz. (170 g) grapes
breadcrumbs as needed

Limousin—Cook and drain the brussels sprouts. Mix with cooked, chopped chestnuts. Toss mixture in pan with butter; dish into a timbale.

8 oz. (225 g) chestnuts
1½ oz. (45 g) butter

Purée—Cook brussels sprouts in boiling salted water; chop up, and finish cooking in butter. Rub through a tammy, and add mashed potatoes; mix well. Enrich with butter, and dish into a timbale.

4 oz. (115 g) butter
10 oz. (180 g) potatoes

CABBAGE, GREEN

All recipes are for 2¼ lb. (1 kg) of cabbage, unless otherwise noted.

Basic Preparation: Wash and trim cabbage and remove coarse stalks.

Apples—Slice green and red cabbage; cook in salted water. Mix with sliced apples sautéed in butter; season lightly with sugar and vinegar.

16 oz. (450 g) red and green cabbage
16 oz. (450 g) apples
sugar and vinegar to taste

Chestnuts—Shred the cabbage, and gently sauté in pork drippings

or lard and chopped onions.
Moisten with white wine; season.
Cover, and cook until tender; drain.
Boil chestnuts in court bouillon;
shell, and chop roughly. Mix with
cabbage.

3 oz. (90 g) onions
5 oz. (140 g) lard
white wine as needed
12 chestnuts

Crème—Shred the cabbage. Boil
in white stock; drain. Mix with a little light cream.

Française—Chop the cabbage,
and braise in stock with diced fat
bacon, lean ham, and chopped onions. Drain and serve.

6 oz. (170 g) bacon
6 oz. (170 g) ham
2 oz. (60 g) onions

Stuffed—Blanch cabbage leaves;
cut out thick ribs. Use two overlapping leaves for each roll; form into a
rectangle. Spread with Madeira
sauce; place stuffing in the center of
the leaves, and wrap leaves around
stuffing. Lay stuffed leaves on piece
of waxed paper; roll and tie. Braise
in the usual manner.

CABBAGE, RED

All recipes are for 2 lb. (900 g) of
cabbage.

Flamande—Cut cabbage in quarters; remove stump. Slice in julienne. Cook slowly in ovenproof
dish with butter and vinegar. Toward the end, add diced apples and
brown sugar. Cook for a total of 2
hours.

3 oz. (90 g) butter
2 tsp. (10 mL) vinegar
1 lb. (450 g) apples
1 oz. (30 g) brown sugar

Limousin—Shred cabbage; place
in casserole. Add bouillon, lard,
and peeled, chopped chestnuts; season. Cover, and cook for 2 hours.

7 fl. oz. (2 dcL) bouillon
1 oz. (30 g) lard
12 chestnuts
salt and pepper to taste

Prunes—Slice cabbage, and simmer with pork fat and pitted prunes
in court bouillon. Season and strain.
Thicken stock with beurre manié;
serve with cabbage.

1 oz. (30 g) lard
12 prunes
10 fl. oz. (3 dcL) court bouillon
salt and pepper to taste

CARDOONS

Cardoons are similar to globe artichokes, but only the stalks are
eaten.

Basic Preparation: Strip the stalks
of leaves, then cut into 3-inch
(8 cm) lengths; rub with lemon. Remove fibrous part from center of
cardoon, and trim. Drop into boiling
water to which has been added 1 fl.
oz. (¼ dcL) oil to prevent vegetables from going black. Cook for
about 1½ hours. Drain, and proceed
with recipe.

Crème—Warm in butter; cover
with cream sauce.

Demi-glace—Warm in butter;
pour demi-glace over cardoons.

Fines Herbes—Warm in butter;

sprinkle with chopped thyme and parsley.

Au Gratin—Cover with Mornay sauce. Sprinkle with cheese; glaze.

Au Jus—Serve with well-flavored veal stock

CARROTS

All recipes are for 2¼ lb. (1 kg) of carrots.

Argenteuil—Blanch very young carrots. Simmer in butter, and mix with asparagus tips.

Crème—Proceed as for glazed carrots recipe; cover with almost boiling cream.

Flamande—Slice carrots and parsnips to same length. Cook in white stock; drain. Serve in a velouté sauce.

2 lb. (900 g) parsnips
32 fl. oz. (9 dcL) velouté sauce

Fondue—Sweat finely shredded carrots in butter in a covered pan. Season with salt and a pinch of sugar. Cook until pulp, adding drops of water as needed to keep carrots from frying.

Glazed—Trim young carrots; cook in as little salted water as possible mixed with a little sugar and butter. Cook until tender. Remove. Boil water until it has almost entirely evaporated (the remaining liquid will almost have the consistency of syrup). Sauté the carrots in this reduction to cover them with a brilliant glaze.

½ oz. (15 g) salt
1½ oz. (45 g) sugar and 2 oz.
(60 g) butter per 16 fl. oz.
(4½ dcL) water

Lyonnaise—Sauté thinly sliced carrots in butter with chopped onion and thyme. Season; sweeten with sugar. Cook all together until tender.

2 oz. (60 g) butter
4 oz. (115 g) onion
pinch of thyme
salt and pepper to taste
1 oz. (30 g) sugar

Marianne—Cut carrots in strips. Partially cook in water; drain. Finish cooking in sauté pan with butter and sliced mushrooms; add chopped herbs and meat glaze at end.

2½ oz. (45 g) butter
2 lb. (900 g) mushrooms
pinch of thyme
pinch of parsley
3 fl. oz. (¾ dcL) meat glaze

Paysanne—Cook carrots in water; drain. Simmer in butter with chopped, fried bacon and glazed, white button onions.

2 oz. (60 g) butter
6 oz. (170 g) bacon
6 oz. (170 g) onions

Peas—Cook thin carrot rounds in water; mix with cooked peas. Season; add sugar if desired. Toss in beurre noisette.

2¼ lb. (1 kg) peas
2 oz. (60 g) beurre noisette

Vichy—Slice carrots into rounds; cook in Vichy water and added butter. Remove carrots. Reduce cooking liquid until almost evaporated. Replace carrots, and coat in glaze.

water just to cover
2 oz. (60 g) butter per 16 fl. oz.
   (4½ dcL) water

CAULIFLOWER

All recipes are for 2 lb. (900 g) of
cauliflower.

Basic Preparation: Trim and wash
the cauliflower. Cook in salted
water, and serve with one of the following sauces: bâtarde, hollandaise,
mousseline, cream, or butter. If desired, serve cold with vinaigrette
sauce.

Dubarry—Cook florets. Sprinkle
with breadcrumbs and grated Parmesan; set under grill to glaze. Set
florets in cooked artichoke hearts.

Fritters—Break cauliflower into
small florets; cook partially. When
cold, dip in batter, and deep-fry.

Italian—Arrange florets on a gratin dish; cover with Italian sauce
combined with stewed tomatoes;
sprinkle with breadcrumbs and
cheese, and set under grill to
brown.
   12 fl. oz. (3½ dcL) Italian sauce
   4 oz. (115 g) stewed tomatoes
   breadcrumbs and cheese as
      needed

Purée—Cook florets; drain, and
dry in the oven for 2 minutes. Rub
through a sieve; mix with mashed
potatoes. Finish with butter and
cream.
   8 oz. (225 g) potatoes
   2 oz. (60 g) butter
   cream to obtain correct consis-
      tency

Ville—Proceed as for basic preparation. Separate florets, cook, and

drain. Heat butter with lemon juice
and chopped capers. Arrange cauliflower on dish, pour sauce over it.
Sprinkle with parsley and chives.
   3 oz. (90 g) butter
   1 fl. oz. (¼ dcL) lemon juice
   1 oz. (30 g) capers
   parsley and chives as needed

Villeroi—Coat cold, cooked florets with Villeroi sauce. Dip in egg
and breadcrumbs; deep-fry.

CELERIAC

Basic Preparation: Peel celeriac,
and divide into quarters; cut into
slices or pieces. Blanch in boiling
salted water for 5 minutes. Chill in
ice water, drain, and dry. All celery
recipes may be used for celeriac.

Française—Cook celeriac in court
bouillon; serve with a cream sauce
flavored with chervil.
   3 lb. (1.35 kg) celeriac
   12 fl. oz. (3½ dcL) cream sauce
   3 Tbs. (45 mL) chopped chervil

Italian Fritters—Cut celeriac in
small slices. Dip in beaten eggs and
breadcrumbs; deep-fry. Serve with
tomato sauce.

Purée—Boil celeriac; pass
through a sieve. Finish with butter
and cream to correct consistency.

CELERY

All recipes are for 4 trimmed heads.
Basic Preparation: Remove tough
outer stems, and trim root. Pare the
remaining stems if they appear too
fibrous; cut to a length of 6 inches

(15 cm). Parboil for 15 minutes; cool in ice water, and proceed.

Braised—Split heads lengthwise; blanch to soften. Fold in half; lay in buttered casserole on bed of chopped onions, carrots, and bacon rind. Cover with stock; add butter. Bring to boil on top of stove; transfer to oven. Cook for 1½ hours at low temperature.

   3 oz. (90 g) each onions and carrots
   2 oz. (60 g) bacon rind
   stock to cover
   1 oz. (30 g) butter

Espagnole—Braise as above, but add chopped tomatoes, shallots, and minced garlic to the base.

   8 oz. (225 g) tomatoes
   2 oz. (60 g) shallots
   garlic to taste

Fondue—Sweat finely shredded celery in butter in a covered pan. Season with salt and a pinch of sugar. Cook until pulp, adding drops of water as needed to keep celery from frying.

Génévoise—Braise as above. Arrange in buttered baking dish. Cover with cream sauce, breadcrumbs, and grated Gruyère cheese; dot with butter. Bake in hot oven to brown.

Madeira—Braise as above. Cover with Madeira sauce.

CHESTNUTS

All recipes are for 2¼ lb. (1 kg) of chestnuts.

Basic Preparation: Slit open the skins; put chestnuts in very hot oven for 10 to 12 minutes. Shell whole while still hot.

Boiled—Put chestnuts in pan; cover with cold water. Season with a dash of salt and a pinch of star anise; bring to boil. Simmer gently until tender (about 45 minutes). Drain and serve.

Braised—Put shelled chestnuts in sauté pan; moisten with veal stock. When tender, remove nuts. Strain stock, and reduce by three-quarters almost to a glaze. Return chestnuts, and coat. Arrange on a dish.

   7 fl. oz. (2 dcL) veal stock

Croquettes—Peel the chestnuts. Cook in a light syrup. Remove chestnuts; pass through a sieve. Dry purée over high flame; add egg yolks and butter. Allow to go cold. Shape into croquettes of about 2 oz. (60 g) each. Dip in beaten eggs and breadcrumbs; deep-fry.

   10 egg yolks
   4 oz. (115 g) butter
   eggs as needed
   breadcrumbs as needed

Etuvés—Put chestnuts to simmer in white consommé with a few stalks of celery; drain and serve.

Garnish—Lay peeled chestnuts flat in a buttered dish. Add bouquet garni and plenty of finely chopped celery; season. Pour concentrated veal stock just to cover bottom of pan. Cover pan, and bake in moderate oven without stirring for about 1¼ hours; remove bouquet garni. Use as garnish for various main dishes.

Purée—Proceed as for basic preparation. Pass through a sieve while still hot. Finish with butter, cream, and sugar if required for a dessert.

2 oz. (60 g) butter
cream as needed for desired consistency
1 oz. (30 g) confectioners' sugar, if required

CORN

Celery—Cook corn kernels. Mix with diced celery, chopped red peppers, and chopped black olives. Arrange in a greased baking dish. Cover with warmed, seasoned cream; sprinkle with buttered breadcrumbs. Bake in moderate oven.

equal quantities of corn, celery, and red peppers
half the quantity of black olives
cream as needed to cover surface only
breadcrumbs as needed

On the Cob—Remove husks and silk; cook in boiling, lightly salted water until tender. Drain and dry. Serve on the cob with butter, salt, and pepper on the side.

Maryland—Mix 1 part simmered tomatoes to 2 parts cooked corn kernels; season with a little salt and pepper. Add sugar and chopped mint.

Southern Style—Cook corn kernels. Simmer in cream with julienned and blanched red and green peppers.

equal quantities of corn, red peppers, and green peppers
cream as needed to cover

EGGPLANT

All recipes are for 2¼ lb. (1 kg) of eggplant. When eggplants are to be sautéed, baked, or fried, they should first be steeped in salt for 30 minutes to lessen the bitterness. They are then patted dry and cooked as required.

Andalouse—Cut eggplant in thick slices, and fry. Scoop out the center to make a trough. Fill with stewed tomatoes, pimentos, and chopped ham; border with demi-glace mixed with tomato purée.

12 oz. (340 g) tomatoes
6 oz. (170 g) pimentos
4 oz. (115 g) ham
7 fl. oz. (2 dcL) demi-glace
dash of tomato purée

Catalane—Halve eggplants; scoop out pulp. Chop the pulp, and mix it with finely chopped, hard-boiled egg; add lightly fried onion, 1 oz. breadcrumbs, minced garlic, and chopped parsley. Fill shells, and put in buttered dish. Sprinkle with more breadcrumbs, and drizzle a little melted butter over shells. Set in oven to brown. Arrange on a dish. Pipe a thread of demi-glace around border of each half.

1 egg
1 oz. (30 g) onion
1 oz. (30 g) breadcrumbs
1 clove garlic
parsley to taste
breadcrumbs to cover
melted butter as needed
4 fl. oz. (1 dcL) demi-glace

Châtelaine—Cut eggplant in half lengthwise, and sauté. Scoop out center; fill with a mixture of chopped chicken, tongue, and sautéed mushrooms moistened with allemande sauce. Pipe a thread of demi-glace across each half.

8 oz. (225 g) chicken
4 oz. (115 g) tongue
6 oz. (170 g) mushrooms
allemande sauce as needed to moisten
demi-glace as needed

Crème—Peel eggplant. Cut in ¼-inch (½ cm) slices; steep in salt. Drain and dry. Sauté in butter. When tender, carefully add cream sauce, and stir. Remove to a dish. Dilute pan juices with cream; reduce by half. Enrich with butter; pour over slices.

4 oz. (115 g) butter
5 fl. oz. (1½ dcL) cream sauce
10 fl. oz. (3 dcL) cream
1 oz. (30 g) butter

Fritter—Peel eggplant; Cut into thin rounds, dredge in flour, and deep-fry.

Garnish—(a) Dice eggplant, and fry in butter or oil; use as a garnish for eggs, lamb chops, lamb noisettes, chicken en cocotte, and fried chicken. (b) Peel eggplant, and cut in thick slices; fry or grill to be used as croûtons for tournedos or scallops. (c) Slice eggplant in half, and grill or fry; use as an accompaniment to fillets of fish.

Languedocienne—Proceed as for Eggplant à la Catalane, but fill shells with sausage meat.

Nîmes—Cut eggplant in half, fry in oil. Scoop out center; fill with chopped eggplant flesh, stewed tomatoes, and diced green peppers sautéed in oil. Add minced garlic and chopped parsley.

1 lb. (450 g) tomatoes
8 oz. (225 g) green peppers
1 clove garlic
parsley to taste

Reine—Proceed as for Eggplant à la Languedocienne, but fill halves with chopped pulp mixed with salpicon of chicken bound with thick velouté.

10 oz. (280 g) chicken
2 fl. oz. (½ dcL) velouté

Romaine—Peel eggplant, and cut in ½-inch (1½ cm) slices. Dip in beaten eggs and breadcrumbs; deep-fry. Top each slice with a portion of sliced cheese; cover with another slice of eggplant (sandwich fashion). Place in buttered dish and bake in moderate oven until cheese melts.

Soufflé—Boil eggplant until tender; peel. Mash pulp; add butter, beaten egg yolks, 4 fl. oz. milk, seasoning, and nutmeg. Soak soft breadcrumbs in milk, and squeeze very dry. Add eggplant mixture to breadcrumbs; add finely diced cooked ham. Fold in stiffly beaten egg whites, and turn into buttered soufflé mold. Sprinkle with blanched, toasted almonds mixed with toasted breadcrumbs and melted butter. Bake in hot oven for 30 minutes.

1 oz. (30 g) butter
3 egg yolks
4 fl. oz. (1 dcL) milk

salt and pepper to taste
nutmeg to taste
3 oz. (90 g) breadcrumbs
milk as needed
4 oz. (115 g) ham
4 egg whites
1½ oz. (45 g) each toasted,
    chopped almonds and
    toasted breadcrumbs
1 Tbs. (15 mL) melted butter

Toulousaine—Peel eggplant; cut in thick slices. Lightly sauté in oil. Arrange in layers in ovenproof dish, alternating with sautéed sliced tomatoes. Sprinkle with breadcrumbs mixed with minced garlic and chopped parsley. Drizzle a little oil over all, and brown in oven.
    equal quantities of eggplant and
        tomatoes
    breadcrumbs as needed
    garlic and parsley to taste
    oil as needed

Turkish Fritters—Peel eggplant; cut in slices, and fry in oil. Serve with plain yogurt flavored with garlic salt and powdered mace; pour sauce over slices.

ENDIVE

All recipes are for 2¼ lb. (1 kg) of endive.
Basic Preparation: Trim and wash endive; place in pan with butter, salt, and lemon juice. Cover, and stew for 45 minutes. Use in the following recipes as indicated.
    4 oz. (115 g) butter
    salt to taste
    juice of 1 lemon

Béchamel—Proceed as for basic preparation; cover with béchamel sauce.

Chiffonade—Remove center leaves; wash, dry, and shred finely. Cook as for basic preparation, adding a pinch of sugar instead of lemon juice.

Crème—Cook endive in boiling water for 10 minutes; drain and press out water. Chop fine. Moisten with cream sauce; season. Add a little vinegar, and braise in oven for 1 hour. Remove; arrange endives in another dish. Add cream and butter.
    21 fl. oz. (6 dcL) cream sauce
    salt and pepper to taste
    dash of vinegar
    5 fl. oz. (1½ dcL) cream
    1½ oz. (45 g) butter

Milanaise—Proceed as for basic preparation; drain. Arrange in baking dish in layers. Sprinkle with grated Parmesan; pour browned butter over. Cover, and bake in hot oven for 20 minutes.
    6 oz. (170 g) Parmesan cheese
    3 fl. oz. (¾ dcL) butter

Paysanne—Proceed as for basic preparation, but add chopped, sautéed onions and diced, fried bacon.
    4 oz. (115 g) onions
    5 oz. (140 g) bacon

Polonaise—Proceed as for basic preparation; drain. Arrange in baking dish, and cover with chopped, hard-boiled eggs and chopped parsley. Moisten breadcrumbs with butter and sprinkle them over eggs; bake in hot oven for 20 minutes.

4 eggs
parsley to taste
4 oz. (115 g) breadcrumbs with
    4 oz. (115 g) butter

Soufflé—Braise as in basic preparation, but cook only for 30 minutes. Rub through a sieve. Add egg yolks, Parmesan cheese, then stiffly beaten egg whites. Pour into soufflé dish; sprinkle with cheese. Cook as for any other soufflé.
12 egg yolks
8 oz. (225 g) Parmesan cheese
8 egg whites

GREEN BEANS

All recipes are for 2¼ lb. (1 kg) of green beans.
Basic Preparation: Trim ends; remove string around edges. Cook quickly in boiling salted water; strain; do not allow to cool before using.
Bacon—Cook and drain green beans. Toss in butter with diced, fried bacon.
4 oz. (115 g) butter
10 oz. (280 g) bacon

Beurre Noisette—Boil green beans; drain and dry. Brown butter in pan; add beans and seasoning. Toss until beans have absorbed butter.
2 oz. (60 g) butter
salt and pepper to taste

Bonne Femme—Cook beans until three-quarters cooked. Drain, and dry in cloth. Blanch diced bacon in the first 3 oz. butter; add beans. Moisten with brown veal stock;

cover, and simmer until cooked. Enrich with the second 3 oz. butter; garnish with chopped parsley.
12 oz. (340 g) bacon
3 oz. (90 g) butter
12 fl. oz. (3½ dcL) veal stock
3 oz. (90 g) butter
parsley as needed

Parmesan—Cook green beans, and drain. Mix with browned butter and grated Parmesan cheese.
4 oz. (115 g) each butter and Parmesan cheese

Poulette—Cook green beans, and drain. Moisten with poulette sauce.
12 fl. oz. (3½ dcL) poulette sauce

Purée—Cook as in basic preparation. Rub through a sieve. Mix with mashed potatoes and cream; heat. Add butter away from fire; dish into timbale.
Tourangelle—Blanch green beans for 5 minutes; drain. Finish cooking in a béchamel sauce extended with chicken stock and seasoned with garlic powder and chopped parsley.
14 fl. oz. (4 dcL) béchamel sauce
10 fl. oz. (3 dcL) chicken stock
garlic powder and parsley to taste

KOHLRABI

All recipes are for 2 lb. (900 g) of kohlrabi. Use young tubers only. Kohlrabi can be used in any turnip or celeriac recipe as well.
Artois—Peel and slice kohlrabi. Cook in lager beer with a little added sugar; drain. Use cooking liquid to make sauce; season to taste.

Fritters—Peel and cut kohlrabi as for french-fried potatoes. Cook in salted water until tender; drain and cool. Deep-fry.

Paysanne—Peel and slice kohlrabi. Brown in lard with minced onion. Add freshly sliced breast of pork; season. Moisten with white wine and chicken or veal stock; drain and serve.

2 oz. (60 g) lard
2 oz. (60 g) onion
4 oz. (115 g) pork
7 fl. oz. (2 dcL) each white wine and chicken or veal stock

Russe—Peel, slice, and parboil kohlrabi. Simmer in butter and sour cream. Remove to a dish; sprinkle with parsley. Serve with sliced, smoked sausage.

4 oz. (115 g) butter
5 fl. oz. (1½ dcL) sour cream
parsley as needed
smoked sausage as needed

LENTILS

All recipes are for 2¼ lb. (1 kg) of lentils.

Basic Preparation: Soak for no more than 1½ hours. Set to boil gently. Season when half-cooked.

½ oz. (15 g) salt to 5 pt. (2¼ L) water

Butter—Soak lentils. Change water; cook until tender. Drain, and dry over low flame. Mix with butter.

Française—Simmer lentils in red wine with diced, fried bacon; drain. Make brown roux with fat and flour; extend with cooking liquid to desired consistency. (Quantity of sauce is at chef's discretion.)

Meckelburg—Cook lentils until tender; drain and dry. Fry diced bacon, diced celery, and minced onion in butter until soft. Sprinkle with flour; stir together. Add vinegar and water; cook to make a sauce. Add lentils; serve with fowl or game.

12 oz. (340 g) fat bacon
8 oz. (225 g) each celery and onions
1 oz. (30 g) butter
2 oz. (60 g) flour
8 fl. oz. (2¼ dcL) each vinegar and water

Oil—Cook lentils; drain and dry. Mix with vinaigrette, minced raw onions, and minced garlic.

Russe—Cook lentils until almost tender; drain. Simmer in butter with minced onions. Add sour cream; finish with chopped chives.

6 oz. (170 g) butter
4 oz. (115 g) onions
10 fl. oz. (3 dcL) sour cream
3 Tbs. (45 mL) chives

LETTUCE

The three main types of lettuce—head lettuce (including butterhead, crisphead, and iceberg); leaf lettuce; and romaine (or cos)—are suitable for cooking. All recipes are for 10 good-sized lettuce of any type.

Basic Preparation: Blanch briefly; cool, and press between plates to remove water. Proceed as recipe indicates.

Chiffonade no. 1—Shred lettuce fine; put in pan with butter. Season with fine salt; moisten with bouillon. Cover, and simmer gently. Use as garnish for hot main courses.

3 oz. (90 g) butter
salt to taste
5 fl. oz. (1½ dcL) bouillon

Chiffonade no. 2—Shred lettuce fine; squeeze in towel to extract all moisture. Season with vinaigrette. Use to decorate salads and fish or poultry mayonnaise.

Au Gratin—Braise; arrange halved lettuce in gratin dish. Pour Mornay sauce over lettuce. Sprinkle with grated cheese and melted butter; brown in oven.

12 fl. oz. (3½ dcL) Mornay sauce
4 oz. (115 g) cheese
butter

Greek—Blanch, cool, and press small head of lettuce. Open leaves and stuff with rice à la grecque; tie with thread. Braise in white stock; remove thread. Cover with thickened veal gravy.

Au Jus—Blanch, cool, and press lettuce. Braise in pan with pork fat, sliced carrot, onion, and bouquet garni. Moisten to cover with white stock; simmer gently. Drain; cut lettuce in quarters, and set on dish or timbale. Reduce stock by two-thirds; mix with thickened veal gravy, and coat lettuce sections. Garnish with croûtons or fleurons.

2 oz. (60 g) pork fat
1 carrot
1 onion
bouquet garni
white stock to cover

equal quantities of reduced stock and veal gravy
croûtons or fleurons as needed

Stuffed—Blanch, cool, and press small lettuce. Open leaves, and coat inside with duxelles mixed with chicken forcemeat. Tie with thread; braise in white stock. Drain; remove thread.

16 oz. (450 g) combined duxelles and forcemeat

MUSHROOMS, CULTIVATED

All recipes are for 1½ lb. (675 g) of mushrooms.

Andalouse—Wipe and stem mushrooms; braise in butter. Sauté diced ham in olive oil; combine with mushrooms. Cook for 5 minutes; add sherry, seasoning, chopped pimento, and parsley. Cover pan, and bake in slow oven for 30 minutes. At end, add meat glaze and lemon juice.

4 oz. (115 g) butter
12 oz. (340 g) ham
1 fl. oz. (¼ dcL) olive oil
5 fl. oz. (1½ dcL) sherry
salt and pepper to taste
2 oz. (60 g) pimento
parsley to taste
1 fl. oz. (¼ dcL) meat glaze
lemon juice to taste

Cap Pelé—Sauté mushroom halves in equal parts of butter and oil. When half-cooked, add salt, pepper, and finely chopped tarragon. Continue cooking. Stir in cream, then butter; add lemon juice at end.

2 fl. oz. (½ dcL) oil
2 oz. (60 g) butter
salt and pepper to taste
pinch of tarragon
12 fl. oz. (3½ dcL) cream
1 oz. (30 g) butter
lemon juice to taste

Fondue—Mince mushrooms. Bind with cream and brown in slow oven.

3 Tbs. (45 mL) cream

Piémontaise—Thickly slice large caps, and sauté in olive oil with chopped shallots and herbs. Moisten with cream sauce, and fill greased baking dish. Top with breadcrumbs; sprinkle with Parmesan cheese. Dot with butter; brown in a hot oven.

3 Tbs. (45 mL) olive oil
1 oz. (30 g) shallots
parsley, thyme, and tarragon
3 fl. oz. (1¾ dcL) cream sauce
breadcrumbs, Parmesan cheese,
    and butter as needed

Port Wine—Sauté small, whole button mushrooms in butter until golden; arrange on a dish. Deglaze pan with port wine; add cream. Cook until thickened; pour over mushrooms.

Red Wine—Sauté crushed garlic in butter with finely chopped onions, green peppers, and shallots for 3 minutes. Sprinkle pan with flour; blend with mixture. When very hot, add red wine; stir until boiling. Cook for 5 minutes; season. Add nutmeg, then chopped chives and

halved mushrooms; mix well. Cover pan, and simmer for 20 minutes.

1 clove garlic
1½ oz. (45 g) butter
1½ oz. (45 g) onions
1 oz. (30 g) green peppers
1 oz. (30 g) shallots
1½ tsp. (7½ mL) flour
2 fl. oz. (½ dcL) red wine
salt and pepper to taste
nutmeg to taste
chives to taste

Saint-Germain—Sauté halved mushrooms in butter until golden. Sprinkle with lemon juice; season. Stir in meat jelly, and simmer 5 minutes. Just before serving, stir in egg yolks. Serve when mixture begins to thicken.

4 oz. (115 g) butter
4 fl. oz. (1 dcL) meat jelly
4 egg yolks

Stuffed—Use large, open caps. Dab garlic butter in each, then duxelles or any suitable filling. Top with breadcrumbs; drizzle with butter. Bake in oven for 15 minutes. Suitable fillings include duxelles; sweated onions; stewed tomatoes; minced, cooked peppers; chicken purée; game purée; and grated cheese.

garlic butter as needed
filling as needed
breadcrumbs as needed
butter as needed

MUSHROOMS, WILD

Cèpes are an excellent variety of mushroom with a large rounded cap and white stem. They are native to central and northern Europe and are marketed fresh, canned, or dried.

Morels are an edible fungus with a rounded, ridged cap. They must on no account be eaten raw. The recipes that follow are suitable for both types of wild mushroom and also for the cultivated mushroom. All recipes are for 16 oz. (450 g) of mushrooms.

Bordelaise—Slice mushrooms. Sauté in hot oil with chopped shallots and chopped green onions. At the end, add breadcrumbs and chopped parsley; mix with lemon juice.
  oil as needed
  2 oz. (60 g) shallots
  2 oz. (60 g) green onions
  2 Tbs. (30 mL) breadcrumbs
  parsley and lemon juice to taste

Crème—Slice mushrooms. Simmer in butter with chopped onions; add cream. Gently boil down to required consistency.
  3 oz. (90 g) butter
  2 oz. (60 g) onions
  7 fl. oz. (2 dcL) cream

Grilled—Marinate mushrooms in oil flavored with onion, garlic, and parsley. Dip mushrooms in butter; grill. Serve with herb butter.
  3 fl. oz. (1¾ dcL) oil
  2 oz. (60 g) chopped onion
  2 cloves garlic
  parsley to taste
  butter as needed

Moldavian—Slice mushrooms. Sauté in oil with chopped shallots. Drain mushrooms and shallots; mix

with heated sour cream. Flavor with chopped chives and fennel.
  oil as needed
  2 oz. (60 g) shallots
  10 fl. oz. (3 dcL) sour cream
  2 tsp. (10 mL) each chives and
    fennel

Toulousaine—Slice mushrooms. Sauté in butter and oil with minced onions, shallots, and garlic; drain. Mix with diced, fried ham and stewed tomatoes.
  1 oz. (30 g) butter
  1 fl. oz. (¼ dcL) oil
  1 oz. (30 g) onions
  2 oz. (60 g) shallots
  garlic to taste
  4 oz. (115 g) ham
  8 oz. (225 g) tomatoes

NAVY BEANS, OR DRIED HARICOTS

All recipes are for 1 lb. (450 g) of beans.

Basic Preparation: Soak beans in cold water for 4 hours. Boil gently with whole onions, carrots, cloves, and bouquet garni. Add salt halfway through cooking period. Remove aromatics; drain and serve.

Américaine—Cook the beans; drain. Add diced, fried bacon; mix with tomato sauce.
  6 oz. (170 g) bacon
  6 fl. oz. (1¾ dcL) tomato sauce

Bretonne—Cook the beans; drain. Mix with bretonne sauce and chopped parsley.
  7 fl. oz. (2 dcL) bretonne sauce
  parsley to taste

Butter—Cook the beans; drain. Season with a touch of nutmeg; add butter and chopped parsley.
Dash of nutmeg
3 oz. (90 g) butter
parsley to taste

Lyonnaise—Cook the beans; drain. Add sliced onions sautéed in butter.
5 oz. (140 g) onions
1 oz. (30 g) butter

Provençale—Cook the beans; drain. Simmer in oil with chopped tomatoes, chopped anchovies, and a sprinkling of garlic powder. Add chopped capers at end of cooking period.
1 fl. oz. (¼ dcL) oil
8 oz. (225 g) tomatoes
4 anchovy fillets
garlic powder to taste
capers to taste

Purée—Drain the beans. Rub through a sieve while hot. Add butter. Add milk if necessary to bring to desired consistency.
3 oz. (90 g) butter
milk as needed

Richard—Cook beans; drain. Mix with onion sauce in ratio of 4 parts beans to 1 part sauce.

OKRA

All recipes are for 2¼ lb. (1 kg) okra.
Basic Preparation: Cut off okra stems. Wash, then blanch in boiling salted water for 5 minutes. Proceed as indicated.

Beignets—Wash whole, young okra. Blanch, drain, and roll in seasoned cornmeal. Pan-fry in lard or bacon fat, or deep-fry until golden. Serve as a vegetable.

Creole—Proceed as for Okra with Tomato. Color with saffron. Arrange in a dish with a border of rice cooked in meat stock.

Fritters—Cook small, tender pods in salted water until tender; drain. Dip in beaten egg and seasoned breadcrumbs; deep-fry. Use as a garnish for steak.

Tomato—Blanch okra; drain. Brown in pan with a little sautéed onion. Cook together. Add peeled, seeded tomatoes and seasoning; add minced garlic. Cook, covered, for about 25 minutes.
4 oz. (115 g) onions
2 fl. oz. (½ dcL) oil
12 oz. (340 g) tomatoes
salt and pepper to taste
1 clove garlic

ONIONS

All recipes are for 2¼ lb. (1 kg) of onions.
Fondue—Sweat finely shredded onions in butter in a covered pan. Season with salt and a pinch of sugar. Cook until pulp, adding drops of water as needed to keep onions from frying.

Glazed no. 1 (white)—Peel button onions; put in pan with white stock just to cover. Add butter, and season; cover and simmer. Turn onions periodically. Remove onions. Reduce cooking liquid to glaze; pour glaze over onions.

4 oz. (115 g) butter to 36 fl. oz.
(1 L) white stock

Glazed no. 2 (brown)—Heat butter in shallow pan; put onions in one flat layer. Add pinch of superfine sugar. Cook in a moderate oven until tender and brown.
 butter as needed to cover base of pan
 2 tsp. (10 mL) superfine sugar per 16 oz. (450 g) onions

Lyonnaise—Slice onions. Fry until light brown in butter. Add meat glaze; season with tarragon vinegar.
 2¼ lb. (1 kg) onions
 4 oz. (115 g) butter
 2 fl. oz. (½ dcL) meat glaze
 1 tsp. (5 mL) tarragon vinegar

Reine—Cook large, whole onions stuck with a few cloves in salted water just to cover. Add thyme; cook uncovered until water has almost evaporated. Add Madeira to pan; onions will absorb it. Serve cream sauce separately.
 cloves as needed
 1 tsp. (5 mL) thyme
 4 fl. oz. (1 dcL) Madeira per onion
 cream sauce to taste

Stuffed—Peel whole onions; simmer in stock until tender. Remove center, leaving ⅓-inch (1 cm) wall. Stuff with chopped pulp, mushroom duxelles, and mirepoix bordelaise. Sprinkle with breadcrumbs; drizzle melted butter on top. Put in hot oven to brown.

PEAS

All recipes are for 36 fl. oz. (1 L) peas.

Anna—Proceed as for Peas à la Française. Add finely chopped mint at end.

Bonne Femme—Brown small, whole onions and fry diced lean bacon in butter; remove bacon and onions from pan. Add flour to butter to make roux; dilute with white stock. Cook for 5 minutes. Add shelled peas and bouquet garni. Return onions and bacon, Cover pan; simmer until tender.
 12 onions
 4 oz. (115 g) bacon
 1 oz. (30 g) butter
 1 oz. (30 g) flour
 7 fl. oz. (2 dcL) white stock
 bouquet garni

Fennel—Cook peas in lightly salted water together with a good bunch of fennel; drain. Toss peas in butter; add chopped fennel. Arrange in a timbale.
 12 oz. (340 g) fennel
 2 oz. (60 g) butter

Fermière—Cook new carrots with small white onions as for Glazed carrots recipe. When half-cooked, add shelled peas, julienne of lettuce, parsley, and chervil. Season with sugar and salt; moisten with water. Simmer, covered, until cooked. Remove herbs; drain vegetables. Replace in pan; toss with butter before serving.
 1¼ lb. (575 g) carrots
 15 onions
 1 head of lettuce

parsley and chervil to taste
sugar and salt to taste
3 fl. oz. (¾ dcL) water
2 oz. (60 g) butter

Florentine—Cook and drain peas. Mix with sliced, pan-fried onions, diced ham, chopped chervil, and parsley. Bind with tomato sauce.
    4 oz. (115 g) onions
    6 oz. (170 g) ham
    chervil and parsley to taste
    7 fl. oz. (2 dcL) tomato sauce

Française—Put peas in a saucepan with chiffonade of lettuce no. 1, small white onions, parsley, chervil, 4 oz. butter, salt, and sugar. Add water; bring to boil. Simmer, covered. When cooked, remove herbs, and drain. Add 2 oz. butter; mix, and arrange vegetables on dish.
    1 lettuce heart
    12 onions
    parsley and chervil to taste
    4 oz. (115 g) butter
    salt and sugar to taste
    2 oz. (60 g) butter

Hollandaise—Cook and drain peas. Bind with hollandaise sauce.
Parmentier—Cook and drain peas. Mix with diced, boiled new potatoes; bind with hollandaise sauce.

POTATOES

Alsacienne—Boil small, new potatoes. Toss potatoes in butter with finely diced, fried bacon and glazed onions.
    2¼ lb. (1 kg) potatoes
    4 oz. (115 g) butter
    6 oz. (170 g) bacon
    18 onions

Anna—Cut potatoes into cylindrical shapes; then slice into rounds. Wash and dry. Set in circles at bottom of Anna mold (or thick saucepan), overlapping the slices. Season; spread a light coating of butter on each layer. Proceed until mold is filled. Cover, and cook in a hot oven for 30 minutes. When half-cooked, turn mold over to color both sides evenly. Drain butter; arrange potatoes on dish.
    1½ lb. (675 g) potatoes
    salt and pepper to taste
    6 oz. (170 g) butter

Berny—Add chopped truffle pieces to croquette mixture. Divide preparation into 2-oz. (60 g) croquettes; shape like plums. Dip in beaten egg, then roll in very fine splinters of almonds; deep-fry.
    2 oz. (60 g) truffle peelings
    1 lb. (450 g) croquette mixture
    beaten egg as needed
    4 oz. (115 g) almonds

Biarritz—Mash potatoes; mix with minced, lean ham. Enrich with butter and cream; add diced, blanched green peppers and chopped parsley.
    2¼ lb. (1 kg) potatoes
    6 oz. (170 g) ham
    2 oz. (30 g) butter
    2 fl. oz. (½ dcL) cream
    6 oz. (170 g) green peppers
    parsley to taste

Bignon—Peel potatoes; cut into large cubes. Remove center; fill with sausage meat. Sprinkle with buttered breadcrumbs; bake in oven. Pour a thread of Madeira sauce over each when serving.

Boulangère—Slice potatoes and onions, using twice as many potatoes as onions. Place in alternate layers in a casserole. Season each layer; cover with good chicken stock or white veal stock. Bake in oven.

Colbert—Peel potatoes; cut into large dice. Toss in butter; bake in oven. When cooked, add liquid meat glaze and chopped chives.

2¼ lb. (1 kg) potatoes
5 oz. (140 g) butter
3 fl. oz. (¾ dcL) meat glaze
chives to taste

Colombine—Peel and slice potatoes; sauté in butter. Add julienne of blanched red and green peppers.

Crêpes—Peel, wash, and dry potatoes. Put through a fine mincer; dry raw pulp in a towel. Season; add nutmeg, beaten eggs, milk, and noisette butter. Mix well; let mixture rest for 20 minutes. Shape into pancakes about ½ inch (1 cm) thick; pan-fry.

2¼ lb. (1 kg) potatoes
salt and pepper to taste
nutmeg to taste
4 eggs
6 fl. oz. (1¾ dcL) milk
2 oz. (60 g) noisette butter

Croquettes—Cook potatoes in salted water; drain and dry. Press through a sieve; place purée in a saucepan. Season; add butter and nutmeg. Mix until the purée resembles a dry paste; add egg yolks.

Cool and shape. Dip in beaten egg and breadcrumbs; deep-fry.

2¼ lb. (1 kg) peeled potatoes
salt and pepper to taste
2 oz. (60 g) butter
pinch of nutmeg
3 egg yolks
beaten eggs and breadcrumbs as
    needed

Croquettes with Chervil—Proceed as for croquettes above, adding 4 oz. (115 g) minced, sautéed chervil to the mixture.

Croquettes à la Lyonnaise—Proceed as for croquettes above, adding 4 oz. (115 g) minced, sautéed onion to the mixture.

Croquettes à la Parmesane—Proceed as for croquettes above, adding 3 oz. (90 g) grated Parmesan to the mixture.

Dauphine—Prepare croquette mixture, and mix thoroughly with pâte à chou made without sugar. Shape into small cylinders. Dip in beaten eggs and breadcrumbs; deep-fry.

2¼ lb. croquette mixture
12 oz. (340 g) pâte à chou

Dauphinoise—Slice potatoes fine; moisten with boiled milk and beaten eggs. Season, and add nutmeg and the first 4 oz. grated Gruyère cheese; mix. Put in a buttered dish rubbed with garlic. Sprinkle with the second 4 oz. of Gruyère cheese; dot with butter. Bake in slow oven.

2¼ lb. (1 kg) potatoes
20 fl. oz. (6 dcL) milk
2 eggs
salt and pepper to taste
nutmeg to taste

4 oz. (115 g) Gruyère cheese
garlic as needed
4 oz. (115 g) Gruyère cheese for
  top
2 oz. (60 g) butter

Dijonnaise—Boil and slice potatoes; mix with chopped, lean ham. Bind with a thin white sauce flavored with Dijon mustard.
  2¼ lb. (1 kg) potatoes
  6 oz. (170 g) ham
  10 fl. oz. (3 dcL) white sauce
  mustard to taste

Duchesse—Proceed as for croquettes, but make a softer mix. Pipe into the shape of madeleines, and gild with beaten egg. Or pipe as a border, and gild.

Duchesse with Cheese—Make duchesse mixture; allow to cool. Roll out mixture on slab, and cut with small circular cutter into galettes. Set on buttered tray; brush with beaten egg. Cover with thin slice of cheese cut with same cutter. Set in hot oven just before serving.

Farcies—Bake long, large potatoes in oven. Scoop out two-thirds of the pulp. Rub pulp through a sieve, and mix with such ingredients as duxelles; grated cheese; chopped ham; sautéed onions; mirepoix; sausage meat; chicken liver purée, etc. Season well, and enrich mixture with a little butter if necessary. Stuff shells. Sprinkle with grated cheese or buttered breadcrumbs; brown in oven. Use equal quantities of pulp and second ingredient.

Fourrées—Bake medium-size potatoes. Cut a circular piece from the side, and keep as a lid. Scoop out three-quarters of the pulp, and stuff shells with selected fillings (as above) mixed with pulp. Replace lids, and heat.

Fourrées à la Cancalaise—Fill potatoes with one-quarter potato pulp and three-quarters chopped oysters and mushrooms moistened with white wine.

Fourrées à la Catalane—Fill potatoes with equal quantities of braised, chopped cabbage and potato pulp.

Fourrées à la Chasseur—Fill potatoes with one-quarter potato pulp and three-quarters sautéed, mashed chicken livers and minced mushrooms.

Fourrées à la Princesse—Fill potatotes with asparagus tips gently mixed with all of the pulp.

Fourrées à la Soubise—Fill potatoes with equal quantities of pulp and onion purée and cream.

Gaufrette—Peel potatoes. Cut with gaufrette cutter; deep-fry.

Hungarian—Sauté chopped onion in butter; season with paprika. Add peeled, seeded, chopped tomatoes and potatoes cut into thick, round slices. Add seasoning; moisten with chicken or veal stock; bake in oven.
  6 oz. (170 g) onions
  1 oz. (30 g) butter
  paprika to taste
  6 tomatoes
  2¼ lb. (1 kg) potatoes
  salt and pepper to taste
  chicken or veal stock as needed

Macaire—Bake large potatoes in their skins. Scoop out pulp, and mash with butter, salt, and pepper.

Form the mixture into a flat cake in a buttered sauté pan; fry on both sides.

2¼ lb. (1 kg) potato pulp
4 oz. (115 g) butter
salt and pepper to taste

Maître d'Hôtel—Boil unpeeled potatoes in lightly salted water until three-quarters cooked; peel, and slice evenly. Put in dish, and barely cover with boiling milk; add butter. Cook until liquid has boiled down and potatoes are tender.

2¼ lb. (1 kg) potatoes
milk as needed to cover
1 oz. (30 g) butter

Marquise—Mix croquette paste with reduced tomato sauce. Pipe into meringue shapes, and gild with beaten egg.

2¼ lb. (1 kg) croquette paste
12 fl. oz. (3½ dcL) tomato sauce
beaten egg as needed

Mousseline—Bake unpeeled potatoes; remove pulp and rub through a sieve. Heat pulp in pan with butter and yolks; season. Add nutmeg and whipped cream. Pile in buttered dish; sprinkle with melted butter. Brown quickly in hot oven.

2¼ lb. (1 kg) potato pulp
8 oz. (225 g) butter
4 egg yolks
salt and pepper to taste
nutmeg to taste
7 fl. oz. (2 dcL) whipped cream
melted butter as needed

Nests—Finely julienne potatoes; wash and dry well. Heat two empty wire strainers in hot oil. Line the first strainer with the cut potatoes, and press the other strainer on the potatoes to hold them in position. Grip the two handles, and drop the scoops into hot fat to deep-fry.

Noisette—Make potato balls from peeled potatoes, using a parisienne cutter; fry in butter until golden brown.

Normande—Peel potatoes, and cut into very thin slices; wash and dry. Lay slices in buttered dish, alternating with shredded white of leek and a sprinkling of chopped parsley. Season each layer; add bouquet garni. Cover with white stock; dot with butter. Bake in oven.

2¼ lb. (1 kg) potatoes
4 large leeks
parsley to taste
salt and pepper to taste
bouquet garni
white stock to cover
4 oz. (115 g) butter

O'Brien—Cook potatoes in lightly salted water; peel. Chop potatoes, then toss in very hot butter till they are well colored and crisp. Add chopped, stewed red pimentos; mix well.

Parisienne—Proceed as for Noisette potatoes; toss cooked potatoes in concentrated meat jelly.

Pont-Neuf—Peel potatoes, and cut into pieces ½ inch (1 cm) thick and 2½ inches (6½ cm) long; deep-fry. These are simply very thick french fries.

Portuguese—Dice raw potatoes; simmer in stock flavored with tomato purée, garlic, chopped onions, thyme, and bay leaf.

2¼ lb. (1 kg) potatoes
stock to cover
aromatics and herbs to taste

Purée—Peel potatoes, and cook in fast-boiling, salted water. Rub through sieve. Heat the purée, and blend with butter and a little boiling milk. Mix well.
2¼ lb. (1 kg) potatoes
6 oz. (170 g) butter
2 fl. oz. (½ dcL) milk

Quenelles à l'Alsacienne—Add beaten eggs and flour to potato purée to produce a fairly firm paste. Season and add nutmeg. Roll small portions into cork-shapes or mold with a tablespoon. Drop one by one into boiling salted water. Poach for about 8 minutes; drain. Pour melted noisette butter over the potatoes before serving.
4 eggs
6 oz. (170 g) flour
2¼ lb. (1 kg) potato purée
salt and pepper to taste
nutmeg to taste
noisette butter as needed

Robert—Prepare a mixture of Macaire potatoes. Add beaten eggs and chopped chives. Cook in pan as for Macaire recipe.
2¼ lb. Macaire potatoes
6 whole eggs
chives to taste

Saint-Flour—Line bottom of deep casserole with a layer of cabbage braised in lard; cover with a layer of thickly sliced potatoes and a little lean, diced ham. Season; add a little minced garlic. Moisten with stock;

sprinkle with grated cheese. Bake in a slow oven.
8 oz. (225 g) cabbage
2¼ lb. (1 kg) potatoes
6 oz. (170 g) ham
salt and pepper to taste
garlic to taste
stock as needed to cover
cheese as needed

Savoyarde—Proceed as for Dauphinoise recipe, replacing milk with light-colored stock or consommé.
Soufflés—Peel potatoes. Trim into long rectangles, then cut to form squares about ⅛ inch (4 mm) thick. Wash and dry well. Cook in fat at 350° F (180° C) until the squares begin to rise to the surface (about 6 or 7 minutes). Drain in basket. Plunge into second pan of hotter fat, at least 375° F. (190° C). When potatoes puff up, drain them, and spread them on a cloth. Sprinkle lightly with salt, and serve.
Straw—Cut peeled potatoes into very thin julienne; wash and dry. Fry in hot fat; drain. Just before serving, plunge into very hot fat for a few seconds.

SPINACH

All recipes are for 2 lb. (900 g) of spinach.
Basic Preparation: Strip leaves; remove spine. Put spinach in pan with small amount of water; add a little salt and 1 oz. butter. Cover, and cook rapidly; strain dry. Chop or sieve if necessary. Add 2 oz. butter to pan; return spinach, and toss.
3 fl. oz. (1 dcL) water
salt to taste

1 oz. (30 g) butter
2 oz. (60 g) butter

Barquettes—Make oval boats with duchesse potato mixture. Fill with spinach purée, cover with Mornay sauce, and sprinkle with grated cheese. Brown under broiler.

Brown Butter—Proceed as for basic preparation. Brown extra butter in pan, and pour over spinach. Serve.

Comtesse—Proceed as for basic preparation. Chop the spinach, and add 2 chopped, hard-boiled eggs and enough cream to moisten.

Crème—Proceed as for basic preparation. Add one-quarter of its cooked volume of cream, and gently simmer for 5 minutes. Dish into a timbale.

Crêpes—Proceed as for basic preparation. Chop the spinach fine. Add an equal quantity of Yorkshire pudding batter; mix well. Cook in hot oven in buttered molds; use as garnish for roast beef.

Yorkshire pudding batter:
1 lb. (450 g) flour
12 eggs, added one by one
40 fl. oz. (1.2 L) boiled milk
salt, pepper, and nutmeg to taste

Garlic—Proceed as for basic preparation. Chop the spinach, and mix with one-third its volume of mashed potatoes. Season; add powdered garlic.

Italian—Proceed as for basic preparations. Chop the spinach, and mix with very finely chopped anchovy fillets. Flavor with garlic salt and cayenne pepper.

6 anchovy fillets
garlic salt and cayenne pepper to taste

Parmentier—Scoop out flesh from large baked potatoes. Mix with an equal amount of cooked, chopped spinach. Return mixture to potato shell. Sprinkle with cheese and melted butter; brown under broiler.

Soufflé—Make spinach purée. Add béchamel sauce; bind with egg yolks. Season strongly, and mix. Incorporate stiffly beaten egg whites as fast as possible. Spoon into buttered mold; cook in oven.

10 fl. oz. (3 dcL) spinach purée
10 fl. oz. (3 dcL) béchamel sauce
4 egg yolks
salt and pepper to taste
4 egg whites

Subrics—Proceed as for basic preparation. Chop the spinach. Add béchamel sauce, thick cream, the whole eggs, and the well-beaten yolks. Add salt, pepper, and nutmeg to taste. The mixture should be stiff. Heat clarified butter to a depth of ½ inch (2½ cm) in a pan. Drop teaspoonfuls, piece by piece, into hot butter. Turn each subric over to brown other side (they should not touch each other in the pan); drain. Serve with a cream sauce, presented separately.

7 fl. oz. (2 dcL) béchamel sauce
2 fl. oz. (½ dcL) cream
2 whole eggs
6 egg yolks
salt, pepper, and nutmeg to taste
clarified butter for frying

SWEET PEPPERS

Recipes are for 2¼ lb. (1 kg) peppers.

Basic Preparation: Grill peppers to loosen skins; remove skins. Cut off stalks, and clear interior of seeds and membrane.

Boston Style—Peel and seed small peppers. Fill with seasoned crabmeat. Dip in melted butter, then breadcrumbs; grill, turning once.

Fondue—Sweat finely shredded peppers in butter in a covered pan. Season with salt and a pinch of sugar. Cook until pulp, adding drops of water as needed to keep peppers from frying.

Fritot—Seed and peel small pepper. Fill with salpicon of mushrooms and onions softened in butter. Bind with tomato sauce mixed with minced garlic and chopped parsley. Stand in maceration of oil, vinegar, salt, and pepper for 1 hour; then remove. Dip peppers in light batter, and deep-fry.

Au Gratin—Peel and seed the peppers. Cut in half lengthwise; sauté in butter. Line casserole with Mornay sauce and softened onions; lay peppers on this bed. Cover with more Mornay sauce; sprinkle with cheese. Brown in slow oven.

  butter as needed
  3 oz. (90 g) onion
  16 fl. oz. (4½ dcL) Mornay sauce
    in all
  3 oz. (90 g) cheese

Ménagère—Peel and seed the peppers. Stuff with pork sausage meat and seasoned, cooked rice in equal proportions. Simmer in veal stock flavored with tomato purée. Don't overstuff.

Oriental—Peel and seed the peppers. Cut into large dice. Put in a casserole with chopped onion sautéed in butter; add a little chopped garlic. Moisten with stock, and simmer gently for 35 minutes.

  8 oz. (225 g) onions
  garlic to taste
  10 fl. oz. (3 dcL) stock

Stuffed—Seed and peel peppers. Stuff with pilaf, and braise in veal stock.

SWEET POTATOES

All recipes are for 2¼ lb. (1 kg) sweet potatoes.

Algerian—Boil and peel the sweet potatoes. Mash, and mix with chestnut purée; bind with egg yolks, Allow to go cold; form into croquettes. Dip in beaten eggs and breadcrumbs; deep-fry.

  12 oz. (340 g) chestnut purée
  14 egg yolks
  beaten eggs as needed
  breadcrumbs as needed

Creole—Boil, peel, and slice the sweet potatoes. Put in buttered dish; sprinkle with brown sugar and butter. Add zest of orange, salt, and nutmeg. Bake in oven until syrup is formed.

  4 oz. (115 g) brown sugar
  2 oz. (60 g) butter
  zest of 1 orange
  salt to taste
  pinch of nutmeg

Fritters—Boil, peel, and slice the sweet potatoes. Dip in batter; deep-fry.

Honey—Boil sweet potatoes in water. Peel; dry in oven. Serve with warmed honey poured over.

Lavigière—Bake sweet potatoes in oven. Scoop out center. Mix pulp with a little butter and equal parts of chestnut purée. Return mixture to shell, and serve.

SWISS CHARD

Basic Preparation: Cook young leaves in unsalted water like spinach, to prevent them from turning black, and the ribs of the leaves like salsify.

Butter—Cook ribs *à blanc.* Drain, chop, and simmer in pan with a little butter. Add thick cream. Cook gently until sauce thickens.
3 lb. (1.35 kg) Swiss chard
5 oz. (140 g) butter
5 fl. oz. (1½ dcL) cream

Sauced—Cut ribs into 5-inch (12.5 cm) pieces. Cook in salted water; drain. Arrange in a dish. Serve with one of the following sauces: melted butter, cream, hollandaise, Italian sauce, or vinaigrette.

TOMATOES

Fondue—Cook onions in butter and oil. When they begin to color, add peeled, seeded, and chopped tomatoes, grated garlic, salt, and pepper. Cook until pulp. Add chopped parsley.

2 oz. (60 g) onions
12 oz. (340 g) tomatoes
2 cloves garlic
salt and pepper to taste
parsley as needed

Fondue à la Grecque—Sauté chopped onions in oil; add tomato fondue and finely diced, blanched green pepper. Season; add garlic powder.
1 oz. (30 g) onions
1 fl. oz. (¼ dcL) oil
8 fl. oz. (2¼ dcL) tomato fondue
1 small green pepper
salt, pepper, and garlic powder to taste

Fondue à la Niçoise—Proceed as for Fondue à la Grecque, but flavor with chopped tarragon.

Glazed—Rub whole tomatoes through a sieve. Reduce by half. Strain again through a fine sieve. Reduce once more by half until a sticky consistency has been reached. Use to heighten flavor of soups and sauces. Keep in jars in refrigerator.

Gratin of Tomatoes and Eggplant —Fry equal quantities of tomatoes and eggplant in oil. Arrange in alternate layers in casserole. Sprinkle with breadcrumbs, drizzle with oil; brown in moderate oven.

Mousse—Skin, seed, and chop tomatoes. Sauté gently in butter. Add velouté that has been thickened with gelatin softened in cold water. Rub mixture through sieve. Allow to go cold, then add partially whipped cream. Add a little lemon juice. This mousse is served cold as a luncheon dish.

1 lb. (450 g) tomatoes
2 oz. (60 g) butter
2 fl. oz. (½ dcL) velouté
1 Tbs. (15 mL) gelatin
5 fl. oz. (2½ dcL) cream
lemon juice to taste

Provençale—Cut tomatoes in half; season. Sprinkle with breadcrumbs, parsley, and minced garlic mixed together; drizzle a little oil over each half. Bake in oven.

Soufflé—Add béchamel sauce to very thick tomato purée. Mix in egg yolks; blend thoroughly. Fold in stiffly beaten egg whites. Turn into buttered soufflé dish; bake.

20 fl. oz. (6 dcL) tomato purée
4 fl. oz. (1½ dcL) béchamel sauce
6 eggs, separated

Soufflé Tomatoes—Scoop out pulp from firm but ripe tomatoes. Sprinkle with oil, and bake in oven for 5 minutes; allow to cool. Fill with soufflé mixture above. Sprinkle with a little grated cheese. Cook in a slow oven for 10 minutes.

Stuffed Tomatoes—Choose medium-size tomatoes. Cut a slice from stem end; remove core and seeds. Season shell inside; pour a few drops of oil into each shell. Bake in hot oven for 5 minutes.

Stuffed Tomatoes à la Bonne Femme—Proceed as for Stuffed Tomatoes, above. Stuff with sausage meat, softened onion, breadcrumbs, parsley, and garlic. Cover with more breadcrumbs; sprinkle with oil. Bake in moderate oven.

16 oz. (450 g) sausage meat
3 oz. (90 g) onions
2 oz. (60 g) breadcrumbs
parsley to taste
1 clove garlic
breadcrumbs to cover
oil as needed

Stuffed Tomatotes à la Niçoise—Proceed as for Stuffed tomatoes, above. Stuff with rice cooked in meat stock, chopped eggplant cooked in oil, breadcrumbs, parsley, and garlic. Cover with more breadcrumbs; sprinkle with oil. Bake.

16 oz. (450 g) cooked rice
6 oz. (170 g) cooked eggplant
2 oz. (60 g) breadcrumbs
parsley to taste
1 clove garlic
breadcrumbs to cover
oil as needed

Stuffed Tomatoes à la Reine—Proceed as for Stuffed Tomatoes, above. Stuff with a salpicon of minced chicken and chopped, sautéed mushrooms, bound with a thick velouté. Cover with breadcrumbs, sprinkle with butter, and bake.

16 oz. (450 g) chicken
5 oz. (140 g) cooked mushrooms
1½ fl. oz. (¾ dcL) velouté sauce
breadcrumbs to cover
butter as needed

TURNIPS

All recipes are for 2¼ lb. (1 kg) of turnips.

Czech—Cut turnips in thick julienne; cook in lager beer. Season with salt, pepper, and a little sugar.

Hungarian—Peel and quarter turnips; cover with boiling salted water seasoned with caraway. Cook until tender; drain. Turn into buttered casserole; pour scalded cream, seasoned with a little salt, cayenne, and powdered sweet bail, over turnip pieces. Add the zest of a lemon, sprinkle lightly with breadcrumbs, and bake for 15 minutes in hot oven. Serve with pork or duck.

¼ tsp. (⅘ mL) caraway seeds
5 fl. oz. (1½ dcL) cream
salt, cayenne pepper, and pow-
    dered sweet basil to taste
zest of 1 lemon
breadcrumbs as needed

Purée—Slice turnips, cook in salted water, and chop. Sauté in butter; rub through a sieve. Thicken purée with approximately the same quantity of mashed potatoes to obtain a satisfactory consistency.

ZUCCHINI

Anglaise—Peel zucchini; cut in pieces. Cook in salted water; drain. Serve with melted butter or hollandaise sauce.

Beignets—Peel zucchini; cut into ½-inch-thick (2½ cm) slices. Sprinkle with salt. Let stand for ½ hour. Drain and dry. Dip in batter; deep-fry.

Clermont—Peel zucchini; remove seeds, and dice. Simmer in butter with sliced artichoke hearts; finish with chopped parsley. Use twice as much zucchini as artichoke hearts.

Crème—Peel zucchini; cut in pieces. Cook in salted water; drain. Toss in melted butter, then lightly coat with cream.

Czarina—Peel zucchini; cut into olive shapes. Simmer in stock; drain. Arrange in a dish; moisten with light cream. Garnish with fresh chopped fennel and parsley.

Etuvés—Peel and seed zucchini. Cut flesh in thick julienne; toss in butter for 2 minutes. Cook in white stock; drain. Moisten with bâtarde sauce mixed with lemon juice.

Glazed—Peel zucchini; cut into the shape of large olives. Cook in salted water, with a little butter and a dash of sugar, until tender. Remove zucchini. Reduce cooking liquid to a glaze consistency. Return vegetables; toss in glaze. Use as a garnish.

Stuffed—Cut zucchini in half lengthwise; parboil. Stuff with duxelles or chicken forcemeat. Sprinkle with buttered breadcrumbs; brown under broiler.

Starches

GNOCCHI

Basic Preparation no. 1: Make unsweetened pâte à chou with milk; mix with grated cheese. Put in piping bag; extrude in short lengths, and let dop into boiling water. Poach; strain. Arrange on a dish, cover with Mornay sauce, and brown in hot oven.

    16 oz. (450 g) pâte à chou
    milk as needed
    2 oz. (60 g) cheese
    Mornay sauce as needed

Basic Preparation no. 2: Boil milk with butter; add salt and nutmeg. Add semolina; cook for 20 minutes. Add egg yolks; beat. Cool on buttered tray; cut into round shapes.

    40 fl. oz. (1.15 L) milk
    3 oz. (90 g) butter
    salt and nutmeg to taste
    8 oz. (225 g) semolina
    2 egg yolks

Basic Preparation no. 3: Mix potato purée with an equal quantity of chicken forcemeat. Form into small balls, and poach in salted water.

MACARONI AND SPAGHETTI

All recipes are for 16 oz. (450 g) of uncooked pasta. All recipes are also suitable for noodles.

Anchovies—Proceed as for Italian recipe. Mix with chopped anchovy fillets.

    3 oz. (90 g) anchovy fillets

Béchamel—Add béchamel sauce to cooked pasta; season. Enrich with butter just before serving.

    4 fl. oz. (1 dcL) béchamel sauce
    3 oz. (115 g) butter

Creole—Add grated cheese to cooked pasta; mix with coarsely chopped red and green peppers, zucchini, and tomatoes sautéed in oil with a touch of garlic. Mix with pasta, and serve.

    2 oz. (60 g) cheese
    2 each red and green peppers
    2 zucchini, sliced
    8 oz. (225 g) tomatoes
    oil as needed
    1 clove garlic

Italian—Add grated Parmesan and Gruyère cheeses to cooked pasta; season with nutmeg. Enrich with butter; toss to mix thoroughly.

3 oz. (90 g) each Gruyère and
    Parmesan cheese
nutmeg to taste
4 oz. (115 g) butter

Milanaise—Proceed as for Italian
recipe. Add demi-glace flavored
with tomato and diced lean cooked
ham. Garnish *à la milanaise.*
    4 fl. oz. (1 dcL) demi-glace
    6 Tbs. (90 mL) ham

Nantua—Proceed as for Italian
recipe. Serve in a prebaked, deep
pie crust with alternate layers of
shellfish bound with Nantua sauce.
    prebaked pie crust
    16 oz. (450 g) ragoût of shellfish
    7 fl. oz. (2 dcL) Nantua sauce

Napolitaine—Proceed as for Italian recipe. Add tomato sauce to
pasta; mix. Serve in deep dish;
sprinkle with grated cheese.
    4 fl. oz. (1 dcL) tomato sauce
    cheese as needed

Sicilian—Proceed as for Italian
recipe. Add purée of chicken livers
mixed with velouté sauce.
    5 fl. oz. (1½ dcL) liver purée
    2 fl. oz. (½ dcL) velouté sauce

NOODLES

Basic Preparation: Mix flour, eggs,
yolks, and salt. Let stand for 2
hours. Roll out thinly; let rest for 1
hour. Cut into strips.
    16 oz. (450 g) flour
    5 eggs
    2 yolks
    salt to taste

Alternatively, poach commercial
noodles in boiling salted water.
    16 oz. (450 g) noodles
    8 pt. (3½ L) water
    1 Tbs. (15 mL) salt

Grand-Mère—Mix cooked pasta
with diced, fried bacon, fried croûtons, and chopped chives.
    16 oz. (450 g) pasta
    6 oz. (170 g) bacon
    croûtons as needed
    chives to taste

Au Gratin—Cook noodles as for
basic preparation. Mix with 4 oz.
grated cheese, the first 2 oz. butter,
salt, and nutmeg. Sprinkle with 2
oz. grated cheese, and dot with the
second 2 oz. butter. Brown in oven.
    16 oz. (450 g) pasta
    4 oz. (115 g) cheese
    2 oz. (60 g) butter
    salt and nutmeg to taste
    2 oz. (60 g) cheese
    2 oz. (60 g) butter

RAVIOLI

Basic Preparation: Mix flour, eggs,
salt, and butter into paste; let stand
for 1 hour. Roll out thinly; stamp
out with cutter. Fill center with little balls of stuffing; moisten edges
of paste. Fold; poach in water.
    16 oz. (450 g) flour
    2 eggs
    salt to taste
    1 oz. (30 g) butter

Beef Stuffing—Mix minced,
cooked beef, blanched and drained
spinach, chopped shallots, whole
egg, salt, pepper, and nutmeg.

10 oz. (280 g) beef
10 (280 g) spinach
1 oz. (30 g) shallots
2 eggs
salt, pepper, and nutmeg to taste

RICE

Basic Preparation: Cook long-grained rice for 15 minutes in plenty of boiling salted water; drain. Put in sauté pan with butter, mix with fork. Place in moderate oven for 15 minutes.
16 oz. (450 g) rice
5 oz. (140 g) butter

Pilaf—Sweat chopped onion in butter; add rice, and stir to coat. Moisten with white consommé; season. Cover, and cook for 17 minutes in oven. Transfer to another dish when cooked; enrich with butter.
3 oz. (90 g) onion
4 oz. (115 g) butter
16 oz. (450 g) rice
40 fl. oz. (1.15 dcL) white consommé
salt and pepper to taste

Risotto—Cook chopped onions in butter until soft. Add rice, and cook until rice has absorbed butter. Add consommé in six installments as fast as rice will absorb it. Stir rice with wooden spoon; rice will be creamy when finished. Total cooking time will be about 20 minutes.
3 oz. (90 g) onion
4 oz. (115 g) butter
16 oz. (450 g) rice
40 fl. oz. (1.15 L) consommé

The risotto can be finished with various additions as follows:

Certosina—Proceed as for basic risotto. Serve with a mixture of seafood, mushrooms, and green peas bound with a wine sauce.

Egyptian—Proceed as for basic risotto. Add salpicon of sautéed chicken livers, diced ham, and sautéed mushrooms.

Gourmet—Proceed as for basic risotto; mix with diced, sautéed chicken livers; set in a border mold; fill center with asparagus tips bound with Cream sauce.

Parisienne—Proceed as for basic risotto. Mix with sliced, sautéed mushrooms and grated Parmesan; bind with tomato sauce.

Piémontaise—Proceed as for basic risotto. Add pinch of saffron to the rice while cooking; mix with diced, sautéed mushrooms, Parmesan, and butter.

Saint-Denis—Proceed as for Risotto à la Parisienne, using meat glaze instead of tomato sauce.

Turque—Proceed as for basic risotto. Use saffron rice, and mix with chopped, stewed tomatoes.

Desserts

BAVAROIS

Bavarois Clermont—Proceed as for Bavarois à la Crème. Add candied chestnut purée and candied chestnuts (marrons glacés) broken into tiny pieces.

> 3 oz. (90 g) each candied chestnut purée and candied chestnuts for each 16 fl. oz. (4½ dcL) preparation

Bavarois à la Crème—Work superfine sugar with egg yolks. Dilute the mixture with boiled milk and gelatin moistened in cold water. Put mixture on low heat until it coats a spoon. Strain into bowl; let cool. When mixture begins to thicken, stir in whipped cream, powdered sugar, and vanilla sugar.

> 16 oz. (450 g) superfine sugar
> 14 egg yolks
> 30 fl. oz. (8½ dcL) milk
> 1 oz. (30 g) gelatin
> 30 fl. oz. (8½ dcL) cream
> 2 oz. (60 g) powdered sugar
> 1½ oz. (45 g) vanilla sugar

Bavarois with Fruit—Dilute fruit purée with 30 degrees (Baumé) density syrup. Add lemon juice and dis-

solved gelatin. Strain; let cool. When mixture begins to thicken, stir in the whipped cream. Use the same sort of fruit to finish the dish as you use for the purée. If strawberry, raspberry, or similar soft fruit is used, it may be added raw. If fruit with a pulpy purée, such as peaches or pears, is used, the fruit should first be poached.

> 20 fl. oz. (6 dcL) fruit purée
> 20 fl. oz. (6 dcL) syrup
> juice of 3 lemons
> 1 oz. (30 g) gelatin
> 20 fl. oz. (6 dcL) whipped cream
> fruit as needed

Diplomate—Line timbale mold with a layer of Bavarois à la Crème. Let it set. Then cover this with a layer of chocolate-flavored Bavarois à la Crème. Let it set. Fill mold with strawberry-flavored Bavarois with Fruit.

Diplomate aux Fruits—Prepare Bavarois with Fruit mixture. Unmold onto a génoise base. Garnish with the same fruit as used in preparation.

Reine—Line mold with Bavarois à la Crème mixture. Fill interior with strawberry-flavored Bavarois with Fruit mixture. Unmold, and garnish with strawberries macerated in Kirsch.

Religieuse—Line mold with Bavarois à la Crème preparation. Fill interior with same mixture flavored with chocolate.

Rubanés—Fill mold with assorted layers of different flavors and colors to taste. Almond, walnut, coffee, chocolate, and other flavors may be prepared by adding flavored pastes or extracts to the Bavarois à la Crème recipe.

BEIGNETS

Fruit Beignets no. 1—For firm fruits such as apricots, apples, pears, or peaches. Select fruit that is not overripe. Cut in half; remove the core and pit. Macerate for 1 hour in liqueur of choice; dry. Dip in beignet batter. Fry in hot fat; drain. Sprinkle with icing sugar; glaze under grill or salamander.

Fruit Beignets no. 2—For soft fruits such as oranges and strawberries. Sugar fruits very thoroughly, as frying tends to make them tart. Proceed as for Fruit Beignets no. 1.

Soufflés—Cook pâte à chou in deep fat. May be filled with jelly, marmalade, or cream.

BOMBES

These ice desserts are formed in conical molds. The lining is more satisfactory when a plain or single-flavored ice cream mixture is used. The filling is completed with a bombe or mousse mixture flavored according to the recipe. Any fruit

used should be macerated in liqueur and sugar before being added.

Basic Bombe Mixture: Whisk syrup with egg yolks over high flame to obtain a thick, creamy consistency. Rub through a sieve. Whisk again until quite cold. Add whipped cream flavored to taste.

> 36 fl. oz. (1 L) sugar/water syrup at 28 degrees density
> 32 egg yolks
> 60 fl. oz. (1.7 L) cream
> 60 fl. oz. (1.7 L) fruit purée

Basic Syrup for Bombes: Heat sugar and water until temperature reaches 220°F (140°C).

> 3½ lb. (1.575 kg) sugar
> 36 fl. oz. (1 L) hot water

Basic Cream Mixture: Work sugar and egg yolks to ribbon stage. Blend mixture into boiling milk flavored to taste. Cook on stove until mixture thickens enough to coat a spoon. Do not boil. Strain, and stir from time to time until cold.

> 10 oz. (280 g) sugar
> 10 egg yolks
> 40 fl. oz. (1.15 L) milk

The list below indicates the correct lining and filling for each variation.

African—Line mold with chocolate. Fill interior of bombe with vanilla filling.

Aïda—Line mold with strawberry ice cream. Fill interior of bombe with vanilla mixture.

Aiglon—Line mold with strawberry ice cream. Fill interior of bombe with Chartreuse.

Almara—Line mold with vanilla ice cream. Fill interior of bombe with strawberry mixture. Surround base with strawberries soaked in Kirsch.

Almería—Line mold with anisette ice cream. Fill interior of bombe with grenadine-flavored mixture.

Américaine—Line mold with strawberry ice cream. Fill interior of bombe with tangerine mixture. Decorate with pistachios.

Apricot—Line mold with apricot ice cream. Fill interior of bombe with Kirsch and layers of apricot jam.

Batavia—Line mold with pineapple ice cream. Fill interior of bombe with strawberry mixture and diced ginger.

Bourdaloue—Line mold with vanilla ice cream. Fill interior of bombe with anisette mixture. Decorate with candied violets.

Camargo—Line mold with coffee ice cream. Fill interior of bombe with vanilla mixture.

Ceylon—Line mold with coffee ice cream. Fill interior of bombe with rum mixture.

Coppelia—Line mold with coffee ice cream. Fill interior of bombe with praline mixture.

Czarina—Line mold with vanilla ice cream. Fill interior of bombe with kümmel mixture.

Diable Rose—Line mold with strawberry ice cream. Fill interior of bombe with Kirsch mixture. Decorate with candied cherries.

Espagnole—Line mold with coffee ice cream. Fill interior of bombe with vanilla praline mixture.

Fedora—Line mold with orange ice cream. Fill interior of bombe with praline mixture.

Frou-Frou—Line mold with vanilla ice cream. Fill interior of bombe with rum and candied fruit mixture.

Grand-Duc—Line mold with orange ice cream. Fill interior of bombe with Bénédictine mixture.

Jaffa—Line mold with praline ice cream. Fill interior of bombe with Curaçao mixture.

Javanaise—Line mold with coffee ice cream. Fill interior of bombe wth vanilla mixture.

CHARLOTTES, COLD

Chantilly—Line mold with finger biscuits or génoise cut in batons. Fill with flavored or plain whipped cream.

Colinette—Line mold with ladyfingers. Fill with whipped cream flavored with vanilla.

Montreuil—Line mold with ladyfingers. Fill with a fruit bavarois made with peach purée, crème anglaise, and the necessary quantity of whipped cream.
> 20 fl. oz. (6 dcL) peach purée to each 40 fl. oz. (1.15 dcL) crème anglaise
> whipped cream as needed

Napolitaine—Bake génoise in buttered mold. Scoop out the center; fill with whipped cream mixed with chestnut purée. Decorate with cream and fresh fruits.
> 20 fl. oz. (6 dcL) cream to 8 fl. oz. (2¼ dcL) chestnut purée

Opéra—Line mold with wafers. Fill with Bavarois à la Crème mixed with chestnut purée and diced, candied fruits macerated in maraschino liqueur.

> bavarois mixture as needed
> one-fourth the above volume of chestnut purée
> 2 oz. (60 g) candied fruits per 16 fl. oz. (4½ dcL) finished mixture

Russe—Line mold with finger biscuits. Fill with bavarois mixture of choice. The flavor chosen decides the name of the dish, such as Charlotte Russe au Chocolat, Charlotte Russe à l'Orange, etc.

CHARLOTTES, HOT

Apple—Line a well-buttered mold with thin, oblong slices of trimmed bread that have been dipped in butter and cut to the height of the mold. Fill interior with quartered apples partially cooked in butter. Cover, and bake in oven. Serve with apricot sauce poured over the charlotte. Other fruits may be used with the above recipe, but they must be firm, or they will soften the bread lining too much and cause the charlotte to collapse.

CREAMS, FILLINGS, AND ICINGS

Butter Cream—Beat egg yolks and sugar together. Cook in a bain-marie. Let cool, then add butter and flavoring.

> 16 egg yolks
> 16 oz. (450 g) sugar
> 16 oz. (450 g) butter
> flavoring as required

Chantilly—Whip cream over ice to froth stage; add sugar.

> 36 fl. oz. (1 L) cream
> 4 oz. (115 g) superfine sugar

Crème Anglaise (Vanilla Cream)—Beat the egg yolks and sugar. Add to boiling milk flavored with vanilla. Whip in a bain-marie until thick.

> 16 egg yolks
> 16 oz. (450 g) sugar
> 40 fl. oz. (1.15 L) milk
> vanilla to taste

Crème Caramel—Cover a mold with sugar cooked to a golden caramel. Fill with vanilla-flavored custard.

Custard—Boil milk and sugar. Add a stick of vanilla. Infuse for 20 minutes; remove vanilla. Pour infusion little by little over whisked eggs and egg yolks. Pass through a sieve; let rest for 5 minutes. Remove *all* froth. Pour mixture into coated molds. Cover, and poach in bain-marie or in cool oven. Unmold to serve.

Fondant—Cook sugar, water, and white corn syrup over high flame until temperature reaches exactly 230°F (112°C). Pour mixture onto lightly oiled marble slab. Allow to cool slightly, then work with spatula, folding from edges to center to produce a smooth, white fondant. Cover with damp cloth. Keep in cool place.

> 5½ lb. (2½ kg) lump sugar
> 45 fl. oz. (1.30 L) water
> 4 oz. (115 g) white corn syrup

Fondant Icing—Soften required quantity with a little syrup cooked to 214°F (101°C), stirring constantly. Flavor as required.

Frangipane—Work the whole eggs and the egg yolks gradually into the sugar; then add flour, milk, and crushed macaroons. Boil for a few minutes until cooked.

16 oz. (450 g) sugar
8 eggs
16 egg yolks
10 oz. (280 g) flour
6¼ pints (3 L) milk
4 oz. (115 g) macaroons

Meringue—Whisk whites until foamy; beat in superfine sugar slowly until whites are very stiff.

8 whites
16 oz. (450 g) superfine sugar

Meringue à l'Italienne—Cook sugar to large ball stage and 39° Baumé density (250°F, 121°C). Whip egg whites to maximum peak to be ready simultaneously with sugar. Pour cooked sugar into whites, slowly but without pause. Beat briskly with whisk.

16 oz. (450 g) sugar
8 egg whites
water as needed to dissolve
1 Tbs. (15 mL) glucose

Praline—Mix equal weights of sugar and peeled almonds or hazelnuts that have been dried, browned in the oven, and pounded. Melt the sugar with a little water until it becomes golden. Add the nuts; mix well. Pour onto a buttered baking tray; cool. Pound in a mortar as finely as possible.

Pâtissière—Beat yolks with sugar to a foam. Add flour, then mix with milk. Add vanilla bean. Bring slowly to boil; cook until thick. Remove vanilla bean.

12 egg yolks
16 oz. (450 g) sugar
4 oz. (115 g) flour
40 fl. oz. (1.15 L) milk
1 vanilla bean

Royal Icing—Beat egg whites; add icing sugar to make a fairly stiff but spreadable paste.

8 egg whites
icing sugar as needed

CRÊPES

Use the basic recipe given under Pastes and Pastry. Crêpes should not be larger than 5 inches (12.5 cm) in diameter. Recipe will produce approximately 40 crêpes.

Du Couvent—Cook crêpe on one side; turn. Sprinkle the uncooked side with diced, fresh, ripe pears. Cover with another layer of batter; cook in oven. Serve very hot.

Gelée de Groseilles—Cook crêpes. Spread with red currant jelly. Roll up and serve.

Georgette—Proceed as for Crêpes du Couvent. Use chopped pineapple soaked in Kirsch instead of pears.

Gil-Blas—Allow sugar to absorb brandy and a few drops of lemon juice. Beat together with butter to make a paste. Spread on crêpe. Roll up and serve.

3 oz. (90 g) sugar
1 Tbs. (15 mL) brandy

lemon juice to taste
8 oz. (225 g) butter

Jeanette—Proceed as for Crêpes Gil-Blas, substituting maraschino for brandy.

Normande—Proceed as for Crêpes du Couvent, substituting sliced apples sautéed in butter for the pears.

Parisienne—Add cream and chopped meringue to the batter.

Paysanne—Flavor the batter with essence of orange blossom.

Russe—Proceed as for Crêpes à la Parisienne. Flavor with kümmel.

Suzette—Proceeed as for Crêpes Gil-Blas. Flavor with Curaçao and tangerine.

CROQUETTES

Chestnut—Peel chestnuts, and cook them in light syrup flavored with vanilla. Reserve one small chestnut for each croquette. Rub remainder through a sieve. Dry purée over fire; thicken with egg yolks and butter. Divide preparation into portions; roll small chestnut into center of each. Dip in beaten egg and breadcrumbs, and deep-fry; serve apricot sauce separately.

    10 egg yolks and 1 oz. (30 g) butter per 2¼ lb. (1 kg) chestnut purée

Fruits—Make a macédoine of fruits. Bind with frangipane mixture. Dip in beaten eggs and breadcrumbs; deep-fry.

Rice—Cook rice in sweetened milk. Mix gently with fork; do not break rice grains. Thicken with egg yolks. Let cool, and shape. Dip in beaten eggs and breadcrumbs; deep-fry. Serve with a sauce such as red currant, raspberry, or apricot. Serve immediately from pan.

    16 oz. (450 g) rice
    40 fl. oz. (1.15 L) milk
    10 oz. (280 g) sugar
    16 egg yolks
    beaten eggs as needed
    breadcrumbs as needed

FRUIT DESSERTS, COLD
Apricots

Aiglon—Poach apricots in syrup. Arrange on vanilla ice cream. Sprinkle with crystallized violets; veil with spun sugar. Peaches and nectarines may be substituted for apricots.

Aurore—Peel and poach apricots. When cold, arrange on strawberry mousse. Nectarines and peaches may be substituted for apricots.

Duchesse—Poach apricots; cool and drain. Place in almond paste tartlet lined with vanilla custard. Cover with apricot purée. Decorate around tartlet with Chantilly cream. Garnish with diamonds of angelica.

Negus—Peel and poach apricots. Arrange on chocolate ice cream. Cover with apricot purée. Decorate with Chantilly cream.

Parisienne—Poach apricot halves in syrup; cool and drain. Place vanilla ice cream in each depression. Join two halves, and set on macaroon. Cover with vanilla-flavored Chantilly cream. Sprinkle with slivered almonds.

Blackberries

Anglaise—Fill prebaked tartlets with fruit macerated in sweetened maraschino. Coat with red currant jelly. Garnish with chopped nuts.

Cherries

Claret—Stone the cherries, and poach in enough red wine to cover. Add sugar and a pinch of cinnamon to poaching liquid. Allow fruit to cool in syrup; drain. Reduce liquid by one-third. Add red-currant jelly, and allow syrup to cool. Pour over cherries. Serve cold.

Danoise—Fill a flan case with stoned, macerated cherries. Cover with danoise mixture, and bake in moderate oven. Cool. Cover with slightly melted gooseberry jelly mixed with a little white rum.

1 9-inch flan case
1 lb. (450 g) cherries
Danoise:
4 oz. (115 g) softened butter
4 oz. (115 g) sugar
4 oz. (115 g) ground almonds
2 eggs
4 fl. oz. (1 dcL) gooseberry jelly
white rum to taste

Figs

Carlton—Remove stalks from ripe figs, and cut in quarters. Cover with whipped cream flavored with raspberry purée. Chill and serve.

Chantilly—Remove stalks from figs; cut in half. Macerate in Kirsch and sugar; drain. Arrange on a dish, and cover with Chantilly cream. Chill and serve.

Grecque—Poach figs in white wine, sugar, and lemon juice; serve cold in poaching liquid.

1 lb. (450 g) fresh figs
7 fl. oz. (2 dcL) white wine
1 oz. (30 g) sugar
1 fl. oz. (¼ dcL) lemon juice

Port—Cut figs into halves. Poach in port syrup for 6 minutes only. Serve cold in syrup.

equal quantities of syrup and
    port wine

Peaches and Nectarines

All recipes are suitable for nectarines as well as peaches.

Carigan—Poach and cool peaches. Split, and fill with chocolate ice cream. Set on génoise covered with chocolate sauce. Pears and apples may also be used.

Château Lafite—Poach peaches in red wine and sugar; cool. Reduce syrup by three-quarters. Add raspberry and red currant jelly to syrup. Cover fruit.

2¼ lb. (1 kg) peaches
10 oz. (280 g) sugar to 26 fl. oz.
    (7½ dcL) red wine
5 fl. oz. (1½ dcL) each raspberry
    and red currant jellies

Dame Blanche—Poach and cool peaches. Set on a base of vanilla ice cream. Cover with diced pineapple macerated in Kirsch. Decorate with Chantilly cream.

Jeanne d'Arc—Arrange peaches on a white mousse or blancmange flavored with maraschino; cover with the same mixture. Veil with spun sugar. Pears, strawberries, and apples may also be treated in this manner.

Louise—Stone and poach peaches, but allow to remain firm. Halve fruit. Fill with ice cream to taste. Join halves together. Serve on a bed of Chantilly cream.

Mistral—Halve peaches. Sprinkle with superfine sugar. Cover with strawberry purée. Sprinkle with chopped almonds, and cover with Chantilly cream. Apricots may also be used in this way.

Rose-Chéri—Poach and cool peaches. Arrange on pineapple ice cream. Cover with custard. Decorate with crystallized violets and angelica.

Sarah Bernhardt—Poach and cool peaches. Arrange on pineapple ice cream. Cover with a strawberry mousse flavored with Curaçao.

Pears

Alma—Poach pears in a mixture of port wine and water. Drain and cool. Cover with whipped cream. Garnish with toasted almonds.

    2¼ lb. (1 kg) pears
    17 fl. oz. (2 dcL) port wine
    40 fl. oz. (1.15 L) water
    8 oz. (225 g) sugar
    1 fl. oz. (½ dcL) concentrated orange juice
    whipped cream and toasted almonds as needed

Bar-le-Duc—Poach pear halves. Arrange on raspberry ice cream. Cover with fresh red currants lightly bound with honey. Heat honey slightly, add currants, and pour while slightly warm; then allow to cool.

Casanova—Poach pear halves. Arrange on raspberry ice cream. Cover with whipped cream flavored with Bénédictine. Sprinkle with grated chocolate.

Hélène—Poach and cool pears. Arrange on vanilla ice cream. Garnish with crystallized violets. Serve with chocolate sauce.

Mariette—Poach and cool pears. Arrange on chestnut purée. Cover with apricot sauce lightly flavored with white rum. Apples may also be served in this style.

Mary Garden—Poach pear halves. Arrange on thick raspberry purée mixed with chopped, glazed cherries. Decorate with chantilly cream.

Pineapple

Creole—Poach pineapple slices. Arrange on rice mixed with diced, crystallized fruits. Cover with apricot purée flavored with white rum.

Edouard VII—Cut lid off whole pineapple. Scoop out flesh, and dice; drain. Mix with vanilla ice cream and stoned, macerated cherries. Refill shell; replace lid.

Geisha—Fill a prebaked tartlet with orange ice cream. Cover with finely diced pineapple macerated in sugar and Kirsch. Coat with a thick pineapple syrup.

Mascotte—Cut thin génoise to size of macerated pineapple slices. Spread with apricot jam. Put pineapple slice between two slices of génoise. Cover with meringue, and sprinkle chopped walnuts on top. Bake to set; serve cold.

Savoyarde—Arrange pineapple slices on a bed of rice. Place a poached peach half on top. Cover with strawberry purée. Decorate with Chantilly cream.

Strawberries

Cardinal—Set ripe strawberries in timbale or dish. Cover with purée of raspberries. Sprinkle with slivered almonds. Peaches and pears may also be served in this manner.

Creole—Macerate ripe strawberries and an equal quantity of diced pineapple in sugar and Kirsch. Arrange on slices of pineapple to form a pyramid. Sprinkle with Kirsch-flavored syrup.

Femina—Mix ripe strawberries with sugar and Curaçao. Leave to macerate for 1 hour. Arrange on a dish lined with orange-flavored ice cream mixed with a little of the macerating liquid. Most fruits may be treated in this style.

Marquise—Macerate strawberries in Kirsch; drain. Roll in super-fine sugar. Arrange on a base of Chantilly cream mixed with strawberry purée.

Melba—Line a coupe with vanilla ice cream. Arrange ripe strawberries on top. Cover with raspberry purée. Peaches, nectarines, and pears may also be treated in this manner.

Ritz—Sprinkle ripe strawberries with sugar, and let stand for 1 hour. Arrange in a timbale or coupe, and cover with a purée of strawberries combined with a purée of raspberries and Chantilly cream mixed together.

1 pt. (450 g) strawberries
sugar as needed
4 oz. (115 g) each purée
8 oz. (225 g) Chantilly cream

Romanoff—Macerate strawberries in orange juice flavored with Curaçao; drain. Arrange on a dish, and cover with Chantilly cream.

Zelma Kuntz—Place ripe strawberries in a coupe or timbale. Cover with fresh raspberry purée combined with an equal volume quantity of Chantilly cream. Decorate with more Chantilly cream, and sprinkle with chopped hazelnuts.

Tangerines

Almina—Scoop out center of tangerine. Fill with bavarois flavored with Kirsch. Add a few crystallized violets. Close with lid of tangerine.

Crème—Scoop out center of tangerine. Fill shells with a thick, tangerine-flavored bavarois combined with fresh cream. Close with lid.

2 parts bavarois
1 part cream

FRUIT DESSERTS, HOT
Apples

Anglaise—Peel and core apples. Fill center with butter, sugar, and currants. Wrap in short pastry, brush with egg wash, and bake.

Astor—Peel apple; scoop out center to make a shell. Poach very carefully. Fill with poached black currants bound with apricot sauce. Cover with meringue; scatter slivered almonds on top. Bake to set meringue.

Au Four—Core unpeeled apples. Cut skin all around top. Fill with butter and powdered sugar mixture. Cook gently in oven.

Beignets—Peel and core apples. Cut into rounds ⅓ inch (1 cm) thick. Macerate for 20 minutes in sweetened brandy or rum; drain and dry. Dip in light batter; deep-fry. Sprinkle with powdered sugar, and glaze.

Cardinal—Peel, core, and cut apples into quarters. Poach in syrup; remove and drain. Reduce syrup; add crème de cassis liqueur. Cover apples with sauce; sprinkle with chopped walnuts. Pears may also be served in this style.

Châtelaine—Peel and core apples. Bake in oven in butter and syrup mixture, but keep firm. Fill center with diced, glacé cherries bound with apricot purée. Cover apple with thin frangipane cream; sprinkle with crushed macaroons.

Condé—Peel, and poach apples in light syrup; keep firm. Arrange on a bed of rice.

Diable—Peel, core and poach apples, but allow to remain firm. Cover with Chantilly cream. Heat Kirsch in ladle; ignite. Pour over apples when serving. Peaches, apricots, and pears may also be served in this style.

Favorite—Peel, core and poach apples, but allow to remain firm; cool. Cover with frangipane. Dip in beaten egg and breadcrumbs; deep-fry. Peaches, apricots, and pears may also be served in this style.

Feu d'Enfer—Peel and poach apples. Add liqueur to taste, and ignite. Peaches, pears, apricots, and nectarines may be substituted for apples.

Gratinées—Peel, core, and quarter apples. Poach in syrup or stew in butter; keep firm. Lay in ovenproof dish. Cover with crushed macaroons; sprinkle with melted butter. Brown in slow oven.

Marie—Peel and core apples. Poach, but keep firm. Fill with apricot pulp. Arrange on a tartlet lined with chestnut purée. Cover with rum-flavored apricot sauce.

Marie Stuart—Proceed as for Anglaise recipe. Fill cavity with crème pâtissière. Wrap in puff pastry, and bake.

Muscovite—Peel and poach apples carefully. Scoop out interior, and fill with a soufflé made with a fruit purée. Flavor with kümmel.

Rissoles—Roll puff pastry; cut in circles 3 to 4 inches (7½ to 10 cm) in diameter. Drop 1 Tbs. (15 mL) concentrated apple purée in the center of each circle. Fold pastry to enclose; seal edges with water. Fry in deep-fat; drain. Serve with Kirsch-flavored apricot sauce. Peaches, tangerines, pears, and oranges may also be used.

Apricots

Beignets—Peel raw apricot halves. Macerate in Kirsch and syrup; drain. Dip in frying batter; deep-fry. Dust with icing sugar.

Serve Kirsch-flavored apricot sauce separately.

Bourdaloue—Bake a *brisée fine* crust without coloring. Spread this base with frangipane cream, and sprinkle with finely chopped macaroons. Lay apricot halves poached in syrup on top, and cover with another layer of frangipane. Sprinkle surface with more chopped macaroons, and drizzle with melted butter. Glaze quickly under salamander. Other fruits such as bananas, apples, nectarines, and peaches may be used.

En Chemise—Dust peeled, raw apricot halves with sugar. Wrap in puff pastry. Brush with egg yolk, and bake. Arrange on dish; sprinkle with icing sugar.

Colbert—Poach halved apricots in syrup, but keep them firm. Fill cavities with cooked rice; join the halves together. Dip in egg and fine white crumbs; deep-fry. Stick a small piece of angelica into each to represent the stalk. Serve with Kirsch-flavored apricot sauce.

Condé—Into nests of cooked rice, place chopped apricots poached in syrup and mixed with a little crystallized or candied fruit. Coat with Kirsch-flavored apricot syrup. Other fruit sauces, such as pineapple, banana, or pear, can accompany this dessert.

Cussy—Coat the flat side of some macaroons with apricot purée. Set a poached apricot half in each. Cover with Italian meringue. Arrange in the form of a crown. Bake in a cool oven to dry out, but not to color, the meringue. Serve a Kirsch-flavored sauce such as apricot, nectarine, or peach.

Flambés—Cook apricots in syrup; drain. Put 2 or 3 into individual, ovenproof dishes. Add a little syrup, slightly thickened with cornstarch, to each, and heat to boiling. When ready to serve, pour 1 tsp. (5 mL) Kirsch into each container, and ignite.

Au Gratin—Make short-pastry tartlets; bake blind. Spread with crème pâtissière. Set a poached apricot half on top. Cover with more pastry cream and crushed macaroons. Sprinkle sugar on top; set to glaze.

Meringues—Proceed as for Apricots au Gratin, but spread meringue on top instead of crème pâtissière. Decorate with similar meringue. Sprinkle with sugar, and bake to set. Either individual tartlets or one large tartlet may be used.

Bananas

Beauharnais—Peel bananas, and lay in dish. Dust with sugar, and sprinkle with white rum. Bake for 5 minutes. Pour thick cream over bananas. Sprinkle with crushed macaroons and melted butter. Glaze in very hot oven. Serve from dish.

Beignets—Proceed as for Apricot Beignets, substituting bananas for apricots.

Creole—Peel bananas, cut in half lengthwise. Cook lightly in butter flavored with rum. Set on bed of warm rice. Cover with crushed macaroons. Dust with sugar, and brown in oven. Serve with apricot sauce.

Flambés—Proceed as for Apricots Flambés, substituting bananas for apricots.

Au Four—Bake unpeeled bananas in oven. Remove one piece of skin when serving. Pour melted butter over bananas. Serve with tartlet containing red currant jelly.

Meringue au Chocolat—Mask bottom of dish with thick chocolate cream. Place banana slices over this base. Cover with meringue, and decorate with either piped meringue, glacé cherries, walnut halves, pecans, strips of angelica, or as desired. Dust with sugar, and brown in oven.

Niçoise—Remove one segment of banana skin. Remove flesh without breaking the skin. Mash flesh, and flavor with maraschino. Refill shells. Sprinkle with sugar and a little melted butter; glaze under salamander or grill.

Cherries

Beignets—Pit the cherries. Soak in Kirsch; drain. Dip in light batter; deep-fry.

Eldorado—Poach cherries in syrup; drain. Mix with brandy-flavored sabayon. Serve hot.

Henri IV—Line puff pastry tartlets with red currant jelly. Cover with vanilla ice cream. Top with poached cherries. Mask and decorate with meringue. Bake in oven.

Jubilee—Pit the cherries. Poach in syrup flavored with red currant jelly. Put cherries in timbales. Reduce syrup; slightly thicken with cornstarch. Cover cherries with syrup. Pour Kirsch over each timbale, and ignite.

1¼ lb. (675 g) cherries
1 Tbs. (15 mL) cornstarch per 10 fl. oz. (3½ dcL) syrup
1 tsp. (5 mL) Kirsh per portion

Oranges

Javanaise—Hollow out oranges. Fill with orange ice cream mixed with diced crystallized ginger. Sprinkle with a little Curaçao. Coat with meringue; brown in oven.

Surprise—Scoop out flesh from oranges. Fill with fruit soufflé. Bake in oven.

Peaches and Nectarines

Beauséjour—Halve and pit ripe peaches. Stuff with marzipan flavored with white rum. Join halves, and wrap in puff pastry. Coat with egg wash, and bake. Serve peach sauce separately.

Flambés—Poach peaches in syrup, and halve. Set on purée of fresh strawberries. Sprinkle with Kirsch, and ignite. Serve at once.

Forbes—Halve peaches. Place in tartlets lined with raspberry purée. Sprinkle with Kirsch. Cover, and decorate with meringue mixed with chopped almonds. Brown in oven. Sprinkle Kirsch on top; ignite when serving.

Montréal—Poach peach halves in syrup. Place on large macaroons soaked in Bénédictine. Dust with powdered sugar. Sprinkle warm Kirsch on top; ignite, and serve at once.

Pears

Au Gratin—Line tartlets with crême pâtissière. Place poached, diced pears on top. Cover with additional crème pâtissière. Sprinkle with crushed macaroons, dust with sugar, and glaze.

Saint-George—Place a poached pear on a cooked brioche base. Cover and decorate with meringue; brown in oven. Serve Kirsch syrup separately.

En Vogue—Poach pears in syrup. Place on vanilla ice cream. Cover with a sweetened red wine sauce; scatter toasted, slivered almonds on top. Surround with a warmed macédoine of fruits.

Pineapple

Andalouse—Form a bed of cooked, vanilla-flavored rice. Cover with slices of poached pineapple. Coat with rose-colored meringue; decorate and bake. Serve pineapple syrup separately.

Meringue—Set slices of pineapple on a bed of rice. Cover with meringue. Dot meringue with red currant jelly; bake to set.

FRUIT ICES

All recipes are for ices with a syrup base. All degree measurements refer to the *Baumé* degree scale.

Apricot—Add juice of 2 lemons per 36 fl. oz. (1 L) of apricot purée. Heat syrup to 18–19 degrees density.

Bananas—Macerate 20 fl. oz. (6 dcL) crushed bananas in an equal quantity of maraschino-flavored syrup. Add juice of 3 lemons. Heat syrup to density of 21–22 degrees.

Cherry—Use 20 fl. oz. (6 dcL) pitted cherries. Pound their stones. Macerate cherries and stones in equal quantity of Kirsch-flavored syrup. Add juice of a half a lemon. Pass through a sieve. Heat syrup to density of 21 degrees.

Lemon—Infuse the zest of 3 lemons in 20 fl. oz. (6 dcL) of syrup for 3 hours. Add juice of 4 lemons and 2 oranges; strain. Heat syrup to density of 22 degrees.

Pineapple—Macerate 20 fl. oz. (6 dcL) crushed pineapple in an equal quantity of syrup for 2 hours. Add juice of 3 lemons and a few drops of Kirsch. Heat syrup to density of 20 degrees.

Punch—With syrup at 22 degrees, thin to 17 degrees with white wine or champagne. Add orange and lemon peel. Infuse for 1 hour; strain. Bring density to 18 degrees. When chilled, add one-quarter the syrup volume of Italian meringue. Just before serving, add rum or chosen liqueur. Serve like a sherbet.

Sorbets—Proceed as for Punch Ice, but thin to 15 degrees with wine, liqueur, or fruit juices. Add Italian meringue as for Punch Ice.

Strawberry—Mix 20 fl. oz. (6 dcL) crushed strawberries and the juice of 2 lemons and 2 oranges with an equal volume of syrup. Infuse for 3 hours. Pass through a strainer. Heat syrup to density of 22 degrees.

ICE CREAM PREPARATIONS

For each of the following variations, prepare cream as directed and then proceed as for Bombe Basic Cream Mixture.

Almond Cream—Blanch and pound 4 oz. (115 g) almonds in a little water. Add to boiled milk. Infuse for 20 minutes.

Chocolate Cream—Dissolve 8 oz. (225 g) dark chocolate in 10 fl. oz. (3½ dcL) warm water. Add to boiling milk.

Coffee Cream—Infuse 2 oz. (60 g) of fully roasted and ground coffee in the boiled milk for 25 minutes. Strain.

Hazelnut Cream—Pound 4 oz. (115 g) hazelnuts in mortar with a little milk. Add to boiling milk.

Marquises—Heat Kirsch-flavored syrup at 17 degrees. Mix, when almost frozen, with stiffly beaten Chantilly cream mixed with strawberry purée.

   36 fl. oz. (1 L) syrup
   16 fl. oz. (4½ dcL) Chantilly
      cream
   2 fl. oz. (½ dcL) strawberry purée

Mousse—With syrup at 35 degrees of density, add an equal volume of fruit purée. When cold, mix in double volume of whipped cream.

   36 fl. oz. (1 L) syrup
   36 fl. oz. (1 L) fruit purée
   72 fl. oz. (2 L) whipped cream

Walnut Cream—Finely pound 4 oz. (115 g) peeled walnuts in a little water. Add to boiling milk. Let walnuts infuse for 20 minutes.

OMELETTES, SWEET

Célestine—Make omelette with 2 eggs in a 7-inch (18 cm) pan. Spread it with raspberry jam. Make a second omelette with another 2 eggs in a 6-inch (15 cm) pan. Spread with marmalade. Put the smaller omelette on top of the larger one, and roll up together. Sprinkle with sugar, and glaze under grill.

Confitures—Make an omelette with 2 eggs, and fill with any type of jam inside. Glaze top under salamander.

Noël—Flavor omelette with a pinch of lemon rind and a dash of rum. Spread inside with mincemeat. Roll up, and drizzle more rum over. Ignite when serving.

Soufflé—Work sugar with egg yolks. Add flavoring to taste. Fold in stiffly beaten egg whites. Shape as desired, decorate, and glaze in oven.

   8 oz. (225 g) sugar
   6 egg yolks
   6 egg whites

PASTES AND PASTRY

Almond—Mix all ingredients, and work on a board until a smooth paste (marzipan) is formed.

   16 oz. (450 g) ground almonds
   16 oz. (450 g) superfine sugar
   4 egg whites

Almond Pastry—Proceed as for Brisée Fine.

10 oz. (280 g) flour
6 oz. (170 g) ground almonds
5 oz. (140 g) sugar
10 oz. (280 g) butter
1 whole egg
1 egg yolk

Baba—Sift flour; add yeast dissolved in tepid milk. Add eggs, and mix. Distribute butter over paste. Allow to double in bulk. Add salt. Knead to absorb butter. Add sugar, currants, and sultanas; mix.

16 oz. (450 g) flour
1 oz. (30 g) yeast
4 fl. oz. (1 dcL) milk
7 eggs
8 oz. (225 g) butter
½ oz. (15 g) salt
1 oz. (30 g) sugar
2 oz. (60 g) each currants and sultanas

Beignets—Proceed as for frying batter, adding sugar and brandy to the recipe.

1 fl. oz. (¼ dcL) brandy
1 oz. (30 g) sugar

Biscuit de Savoie—Stir sugar and egg yolks to ribbon stage. Flavor with vanilla sugar. Mix flour and potato flour; add to sugar mixture. Fold in stiffly beaten egg whites. Fill buttered molds. Bake in moderate oven.

16 oz. (450 g) sugar
14 egg yolks
vanilla sugar to taste
6 oz. (170 g) each flour and potato
    flour
14 egg whites

Brioche—Take 6 oz. of the flour; stir in yeast dissolved in a little

water. Allow to rise. Mix other ingredients with melted butter, and blend with yeast dough. Dust with remaining flour, and cover. Allow to rise overnight.

16 oz. (450 g) flour
½ oz. (15 g) yeast
1 oz. (30 g) sugar
7 eggs
12 oz. (340 g) butter

Brisée Fine—Put egg, butter, sugar, salt, and water in a well made in the flour. Mix, incorporating flour by degrees; knead twice. Wrap in cloth, and keep cool for several hours. Use for fruit tarts.

1 egg
10 oz. (280 g) butter
2 oz. (60 g) sugar
1 tsp. (5 mL) salt
5 fl. oz. (1½ dcL) water
16 oz. (450 g) flour

Brisée Ordinaire—Proceed as for Brisée Fine. Use as lining paste.

8 oz. (225 g) butter
1 oz. (30 g) sugar
1 tsp. (5 mL) salt
7 fl. oz. (2 dcL) water
16 oz. (450 g) flour

Crêpes—Mix flour, sugar, and salt. Add eggs one by one. Mix batter with wooden spoon. Add milk and brandy, then melted butter and vanilla essence. Allow to rest for 4 hours.

16 oz. (450 g) flour
6 oz. (170 g) sugar
pinch of salt
10 eggs
28 fl. oz. (8 dcL) milk
1½ fl. oz. (½ dcL) brandy

1 oz. (30 g) butter
vanilla essence to taste

Frying Batter—Mix ingredients to
a smooth batter. Fold in stiffly
beaten whites.

16 oz. (450 g) flour
¼ oz. (7 g) salt
1 Tbs. (15 mL) oil
1 whole egg
8 fl. oz. (2¼ dcL) light beer
20 fl. oz. (6 dcL) water
4 egg whites

Galette—Proceed as for Puff Pastry, using 12 oz. (340 g) butter and
giving the dough only 5 turns.

Génoise Fine—Mix sugar and
eggs to ribbon stage. Add liqueur of
choice, then the flour. Work into a
paste. Pour in melted butter, and
gradually amalgamate to obtain
even texture.

16 oz. (450 g) sugar
16 whole eggs
2 fl. oz. (½ dcL) liqueur of choice
12 oz. (340 g) flour
8 oz. (225 g) butter

Génoise Ordinaire—Proceed as
for Génoise Fine. Use for cutting up
or as cake base.

16 oz. (450 g) sugar
12 whole eggs
12 oz. (340 g) flour
8 oz. (225 g) butter
flavoring

Ladyfingers—Mix egg yolks and
sugar to ribbon stage. Add orange
blossom water, then flour. Fold in
stiffly beaten whites. Pipe mixture
onto paper. Sprinkle with sugar,
and bake.

16 eggs, separated
16 oz. (450 g) fine sugar
1 fl. oz. (¼ dcL) orange blossom
    water
12 oz. (340 g) flour
sugar as needed

Pâte à Chou—Boil water and butter with salt and sugar. Add flour,
and stir until mixture comes free
from sides of pan. Remove from
heat. Beat in eggs 2 at a time.

36 fl. oz. (1 L) water
8 oz. (225 g) butter
½ oz. (15 g) salt
1 oz. (30 g) sugar
22 oz. (625 g) flour
12 eggs

Profiteroles—Proceed as for Pâte
à Chou without sugar.

Puff Pastry—Make a flour-and-
water paste, and add salt. Mix to
the same consistency as the butter
you will use. Roll flat. Divide butter
into knobs and spread over area.
Give six turns, two at a time. Set to
rest for 2 hours between each two
turns.

16 oz. (450 g) flour
water to give the correct consistency
½ oz. (15 g) salt
16 oz. (450 g) butter

Savarin—Proceed as for Baba
pastry, using no fruit.

16 oz. (450 g) flour
½ oz. (15 g) yeast
6 fl. oz. (1½ dcL) milk
8 eggs
12 oz. (340 g) butter
½ oz. (15 g) salt
1 oz. (30 g) sugar

Suet Pastry—Put finely chopped beef suet, salt, and water into well made in the flour. Incorporate flour gradually. Mix together; do not knead.

10 oz. (280 g) beef suet
½ oz. (15 g) salt
7 fl. oz. (2 dcL) water
16 oz. (450 g) flour

PUDDINGS, BREAD

English—Butter thin slices of crustless white bread. Lay them at the bottom of a buttered baking dish. Sprinkle with currants and sultanas that have been soaked in warm water and drained. Pour custard over these, and bake in bain-marie in a moderate oven.

French—Soak white breadcrumbs in boiled, sweetened milk flavored with vanilla; rub through a sieve. Add 2 whole eggs and 2 egg yolks; mix well. Add 2 stiffly beaten egg whites. Bake in bain-marie in oven.

10 oz. (280 g) breadcrumbs
36 fl. oz. (1 L) milk
8 oz. (225 g) sugar
vanilla as needed
2 whole eggs
2 egg yolks
2 whites

German—Soak brown breadcrumbs in Rhine wine and beer with sugar and a dash of cinnamon; rub through a sieve. Add 2 whole eggs and butter, then 2 yolks. Finally add 2 stiffly beaten egg whites. Bake as for French Pudding.

Scotch—Proceed as for French Pudding, but add 5 oz. (140 g) sliced seasonal fruit. Serve with a red currant sauce.

PUDDINGS, FRUIT AND JAM

Apple—Prepare suet pastry as described; roll to ⅓-inch (1 cm) thickness, and line a buttered mold or basin. Fill with sliced, raw apples sprinkled with sugar, the zest of 1 lemon, and 1 whole clove. Close the mold with paste, and wrap it in cloth. Tie mold with string, and put it in a saucepan of boiling water. Cook for 3 hours for a 2-pint (1 L) basin. This type of pudding may be made with pears, plums, and other fleshy fruits.

Plum Pudding—Thoroughly mix the ingredients. Pour preparation into pudding basin. Wrap basin in buttered cloth, and tie up. Cook in boiling water for 4 hours.

8 oz. (225 g) raisins
12 oz. (340 g) currants
12 oz. (340 g) sultanas
4 oz. (115 g) mixed peel
4 oz. (115 g) chopped apple
1 oz. (30 g) mixed spice
8 oz. (225 g) white breadcrumbs
9 oz. (250 g) sugar
8 oz. (225 g) flour
12 oz. (340 g) suet
6 whole eggs
4 egg yolks
5 fl. oz. (1½ dcL) brandy
8 fl. oz. (2¼ dcL) dark ale

Roly-Poly—Roll out suet pastry into a square. Spread with jam. Wrap in waxed paper, tie in cloth, and cook in boiling water for 3 hours or steam in a long pudding mold.

PUDDINGS, GRAIN AND CEREAL

Brazilian—Cook tapioca pudding in a mold lined with carmelized sugar.

Chévreuse—Add crystallized, mixed peel and fresh fruits macerated in Kirsch to semolina pudding.

Condé—Cook rice in boiling sweetened milk. Add flavoring of orange, lemon, or vanilla, butter, and salt. Cook in oven for 30 minutes; remove. Add egg yolks; mix. Return to oven for egg yolks to set. Serve cold, garnished with choice of poached fruit such as pears, peaches, and apples.
  16 oz. (450 g) rice
  8 oz. (225 g) sugar
  40 fl. oz. (1.15 L) milk
  flavoring to taste
  4 oz. (115 g) butter
  pinch of salt
  12 egg yolks
  poached fruit as needed

English Rice Pudding—Proceed as for Rice Pudding, but add 3 whole, beaten eggs to the mixture. Pour into buttered baking dish. Cook, and sprinkle top with nutmeg. Serve from baking dish.

Federal—Proceed as for Riz à l'Impératrice. Serve in charlotte molds, and decorate with red currant jelly. Serve cold.

Maltaise—Proceed as for Riz à l'Impératrice. Flavor with orange, and decorate with skinned orange

sections macerated in orange syrup. Serve cold.

Rice—Sprinkle rice into sweetened milk to which a little salt, vanilla flavor, and butter have been added. Cook on stove. When boiling, cover pan, transfer to oven, and cook for 30 minutes. Do not stir. Remove from oven. Add egg yolks, then stiffly beaten egg whites. Fill molds, and allow to set in a bain-marie in moderate oven.
  8 oz. (225 g) rice
  5 oz. (140 g) sugar
  36 fl. oz. (1 L) milk
  pinch of salt
  vanilla to taste
  2 oz. (60 g) butter
  8 eggs, separated

Riz à la Crème—Cook rice; flavor to taste, Mix with whipped cream at the end.

Riz à l'Impératrice—Prepare the rice as for Condé recipe, but without the egg yolks. Add salpicon of mixed fruits macerated in Kirsch. Mix with bavarois preparation and whipped cream. Set decorative jelly in bottom of mold, and fill with mixture. Serve cold.
  16 oz. (450 g) rice
  8 oz. (225 g) mixed fruits
  equal quantities of rice and
      bavarois
  20 fl. oz. (6 dcL) cream
  jelly as needed

Sago—Proceed as for Tapioca. Sprinkle mold with sago, semolina, or vermicelli.

Sicilian—Fill a border mold with Riz à l'Impératrice. Garnish with candied fruits. Fill center with strawberry ice cream.

Tapioca—Sprinkle tapioca into boiling, sweetened milk; enrich with 3 oz. butter. Cook in oven for 20 minutes, then transfer to another pan. Add yolks and 2 oz. additional butter; fold in the stiffly beaten whites. Dust a well-buttered mold with additional tapioca, and poach in a bain-marie in moderate oven. Serve with a custard or fruit sauce.

    8 oz. (225 g) tapioca
    4 oz. (115 g) sugar
    16 fl. oz. (4½ dcL) milk
    3 oz. (90 g) butter
    4 egg yolks
    2 oz. (60 g) butter
    4 egg whites
    tapioca as needed
    sauce as needed

PUDDINGS, SOUFFLÉ

Basic Preparation: Bring milk, butter, and sugar to boil; flavor to taste. Add flour and cornstarch. Mix to a stiff paste, drying over high heat if necessary; let cool. Add the 5 egg yolks, then the 5 stiffly beaten egg whites. Butter a mold. Sprinkle inside with sugar. Pour mixture into mold. Cook over bain-marie in moderate oven. Serve with English custard or a sabayon flavored as desired.

    10 fl. oz. (3 dcL) milk
    4 oz. (115 g) butter
    4 oz. (115 g) sugar
    flavoring to taste
    2 oz. (60 g) flour
    2 oz. (60 g) cornstarch
    5 eggs, separated

Albemarle—Proceed as for basic preparation. Mix with toasted almond bits.

Arlequin—Proceed as for Figaro recipe, but add two extra layers flavored with vanilla and pistachio.

Batchelors—Proceed as for basic preparation. Mix with diced apples and currants.

Cambacérès—Proceed as for Albemarle. Mix with angelica cut into small diamonds. Serve with hazelnut-flavored custard.

Chestnut—Proceed as for basic preparation, using chestnut purée and pieces of marron glacé. Serve with apricot sauce.

Citron—Proceed as for basic preparation. Flavor with juice and zest of lemon.

Figaro—Flavor layers of the basic preparation alternately with melted chocolate and strawberry purée.

Indienne—Proceed as for basic preparation. Flavor with diced, candied ginger and a dash of powdered ginger. Serve ginger-flavored custard separately.

Javanaise—Proceed as for basic preparation, using tea instead of milk. Mix with chopped nuts. Serve with sabayon flavored with tea.

Liqueur—Proceed as for basic preparation. Flavor with chosen liqueur.

Maltaise—Proceed as for basic preparation. Flavor with juice and zest of oranges.

Montmorency—Proceed as for basic preparation, using cherries soaked in Kirsch.

Orléans—Proceed as for basic preparation. Add crushed macaroons and seedless grapes. Serve with custard flavored with Madeira or sweet sherry.

Pineapple—Proceed as for basic preparation with dice of pineapple soaked in Kirsch.

Reine—Proceed as for basic preparation. Use mold with central tube. Butter the tube, and sprinkle with chopped pistachios and crushed macaroons.

Sans-Soucis—Proceed as for basic preparation, using diced apples cooked in butter.

PUDDINGS, SOUFFLÉ FRUIT

These preparations with fruit purée bases give a more pronounced flavor than do those prepared with cream. Furthermore, they are extremely simple to make.

Basic Preparation: Cook sugar in saucepan to 285°F (142°C). Add fruit pulp or purée. If pulp reduces heat of sugar, reheat to correct stage. Test with saccharometer. Pour sugar over stiffly beaten whites. Mix very gently, and cook in moderate oven.

16 oz. (450 g) sugar
16 oz. (450 g) fruit pulp
10 egg whites

Aïda—Use orange flavoring. Add diced, fresh fruits soaked in Curaçao.

Apricot—Use apricot purée.

Bananas—Use diced bananas flavored with Kirsch.

Cherry—Use pitted cherries flavored with Kirsch and raspberry purée.

Pineapple—Use diced pineapple flavored with Kirsch.

Raspberry—Use raspberry purée.

SAUCES AND SYRUPS

Apricot—Purée fresh apricots. Thin with syrup. Thicken slightly, if necessary, with arrowroot.

Cherry—Use equal quantities of chopped, stewed, ripe cherries and red currant jelly. Flavor with Kirsch.

Chocolate—Dissolve grated chocolate in water. Add vanilla sugar. Cook gently for 30 minutes; remove from heat. Add cream and butter; mix until amalgamated.

8 oz. semisweet chocolate
10 fl. oz. (3 dcL) water
1 oz. (30 g) vanilla sugar
2 fl. oz. (½ dcL) cream
½ oz. (15 g) butter

Orange—Mix equal quantities of orange marmalade and apricot purée flavored with Curaçao. Mix with warm water to correct consistency.

Raspberry—Thin raspberry jam with syrup; add Kirsch.

Sabayon no. 1—Mix superfine sugar with egg yolks. Dilute with dry white wine. Whisk in bain-marie until about four times the original volume.

16 oz. (450 g) superfine sugar
12 egg yolks
40 fl. oz. (1.15 L) wine

Sabayon no. 2—Proceed as for Sabayon no. 1, using milk instead of wine. Flavor with a liqueur.

Strawberry—Thin strawberry jam with syrup; add Kirsch.

Syrup—Cook sugar to a light caramel (15 to 18 degrees on saccharometer). Dissolve with warm water to desired consistency. Strain, and flavor with vanilla, spirits, liqueurs, or fruit pulp. Thicken, if necessary, with cornstarch.

TIMBALES

These preparations may be produced with molds lined with almost any kind of pastry or dough: brioche, baba, génoise, or even short crust. If a dough is used, it is sometimes baked blind, then hollowed out and filled with the chosen preparation. If a paste is used and served hot, both lining and filling are cooked at the same time.

Aremberg—Line mold with firm brioche. Fill with sliced pears cooked in a vanilla-flavored syrup. Add a little slightly diluted apricot jam. Seal mold with same paste. Cut slit in center for steam to escape. Cook in moderate oven for 40 minutes.

Bourdaloue—Line mold with almond short paste. Fill with layers of various stewed fruits alternating with layers of frangipane mixture. Cover mold with almond paste. Bake in moderate oven. Turn out, and cover with apricot syrup.

Chantilly—Hollow out cooked savarin. Sprinkle inside with Kirsch syrup. Fill with Chantilly cream and macédoine of fruits. Chill, unmold, and decorate with the same cream.

Condé—Bake short pastry blind. Fill with layers of vanilla-flavored rice mixed with cream and pitted apricots. Allow to set in refrigerator. Unmold, and serve with apricot sauce.

Maltaise—Proceed as for basic condé, using skinned tangerine sections and lime jelly.

Neeno—Proceed as for condé, replacing apricots with chopped, cooked chestnuts and diced, crystallized fruits.

Sicilian—Hollow out cooked brioche. Brush inside with apricot jam. Fill center with orange segments and almost firm lemon jelly. Chill in refrigerator. Unmold, and decorate with orange slices.

MISCELLANEOUS DESSERTS

Baisers de Vierge—Fill meringues with whipped cream mixed with crystallized violets and rose petals. Veil with spun sugar.

Bordelaise—Purée stewed prunes. Mix with whipped cream.
1 part prune purée
2 parts whipped cream

Caprice—Mix whipped cream with broken pieces of meringue.

Cerises—Proceed as for Norvégienne recipe, using half raspberry ice cream and half cherry. Surround with cherries macerated in brandy. Pour Kirsch over top of meringue, and ignite.

Eaton Mess—Crush fresh strawberries with a fork. Mix with an equal quantity of whipped cream. Garnish as desired.

Edouard VII—Proceed as for Norvégienne recipe on round génoise, using diced peaches and strawberry ice cream. Shape meringue or soufflé into a beehive.

Elizabeth—Proceed as for Norvégienne recipe, using vanilla ice cream sprinkled with candied violets. Veil with spun sugar.

Flamri—Put wine and water in saucepan; boil. Add semolina, and cook for 20 minutes. Add sugar, salt, and eggs; allow to cool slightly. Fold in stiffly beaten whites. Spoon mixture into buttered mold, and bake. Serve with fresh fruit purée of choice.

15 fl. oz. (4 dcL) white wine
20 fl. oz. (6 dcL) water
8 oz. (225 g) semolina
10 oz. (280 g) sugar
pinch of salt
2 eggs
6 egg whites
fruit purée as needed

Irlandaise—Proceed as for Norvégienne recipe, using a round génoise base. Cover with ice cream to taste. Cover with Italian meringue. Place on top some dry meringue tartlets; fill with rum, and ignite when serving.

Junket—Warm milk to 95°F. Add sugar and essence of rennet. Add fruit flavor as desired. Set to cool without disturbing. Serve very cold.

40 fl. oz. (1.15 L) milk
2 oz. (60 g) sugar
2 tsp. (10 mL) rennet

Mandarines—Proceed as for Norvégienne recipe, using tangerines and tangerine ice cream.

Milord—Proceed as for Norvégienne recipe, using pears and vanilla ice cream.

Mont Blanc—Mix whipped cream with chestnut purée, using 1 part purée to 2 parts cream.

Mont Blanc aux Fraises—Mix whipped cream with very small strawberries (wild, if possible). Arrange in a pyramid. Surround base with large strawberries rolled in superfine sugar. Use as many strawberries as the cream will support.

Mousseline Réjane—Pipe meringue in macaroon shape onto white waxed paper. Slip paper into boiling, sweetened milk; remove paper as soon as meringues float free. Finish poaching; drain. Set on dish in pairs with a poached apricot half in between. Cover with vanilla custard.

Mousse Monte Carlo—Flavor whipped cream with tangerine. Mix with pieces of broken, dry meringue.

Napolitaine—Proceed as for Irlandaise recipe, using vanilla and strawberry ice cream. Garnish with marrons glacés; surround with tartlets containing brandied cherries.

Norvégienne—Cut 1-inch-thick (2.5 cm) génoise to fit an oval or round platter. Lay a flat pyramid of ice cream on this base, then top the ice cream with fruit of your choice. Cover the pyramid with ordinary meringue, which has been carefully mixed with icing sugar to an overall thickness of at least ⅔ inch (2 cm), bringing the meringue right down to cover the sides of the génoise. Use a piping bag to decorate with the same type of meringue. Add glacé fruit if desired. Bake in very hot oven until meringue has gained a slight glaze.

    8 egg whites, beaten stiff and
        sprinkled with 16 oz. (450 g)
        icing sugar

Oeufs à la Neige—Mold some meringue with a large spoon to represent eggs. Drop these into a pan containing milk flavored with vanilla sugar (sugar stored with 1 or 2 vanilla beans). Turn meringues over in milk to poach evenly. Strain the milk through muslin; pour over the egg yolks. Whisk together, and make a custard. Chill. Arrange meringues on a dish, and pour chilled custard over them.

    20 fl. oz. (6 dcL) milk
    3 oz. (90 g) vanilla sugar
    6 egg yolks

Régence—Soak génoise or graham crackers in milk; pass through sieve. Add eggs, yolks, sugar, and salt. Cook in charlotte mold. Garnish base with apricot purée. Sprinkle brandy on top; flame.

    8 oz. (225 g) génoise or graham
        crackers
    40 fl. oz. (1.15 L) milk
    8 eggs
    10 egg yolks
    10 oz. (280 g) sugar
    pinch of salt
    apricot purée as needed
    1 Tbs. (15 mL) brandy

des Sylphes—Hollow out a savarin. Liberally sprinkle with maraschino syrup on the outside. Fill the center with strawberry mousse. Set on a shallow base. Cover with meringue; decorate, and glaze in very hot oven.

Index